Namgyal Rinpoche in Ireland, 1995
Photo by Monica Evers

Tales of Awakening:

Travels, Teachings and Transcendence

with Namgyal Rinpoche

(1931 – 2003)

Tales of Awakening:

Travels, Teachings and Transcendence

with Namgyal Rinpoche

(1931 – 2003)

Gathered by Rab Wilkie and David Berry

Fairhaven Lantern Media

Order Tales of Awakening at
https://www.createspace.com/3850183

Tales of Awakening:

Travels, Teachings and Transcendence
with Namgyal Rinpoche
(1931 – 2003)

Gathered by Rab Wilkie and David Berry

Cover design: Sarah Berry

Front cover photo of Namgyal Rinpoche with Turkish coffee in hot springs pool, Pamukkale, Turkey, 1970s: John Vartan

Graphic image on spine: *Rebirth,* by Namgyal Rinpoche, from *Unfolding Through Art*, Edited by Karma Chime Wongmo, Boise, Idaho, The Open Path Publishing, 1982; p.151. Used with permission from Bodhi Publishing

Back cover photo of Namgyal Rinpoche in robes, Toronto, circa 1971: Peter Deutsch

© 2012 Fairhaven Lantern Media, awakening@fairhavenlantern.com

ISBN-13: 978-1475192759   ISBN-10:1475192754

BISAC Body, Mind & Spirit / Meditation

Order Tales of Awakening at
https://www.createspace.com/3850183

✧

Vision means seeing means eyes
letting in the light and men are
the pupils of the universe to
explore her. Man is responsible
for the extension of consciousness,
for the exploration of God. God
can only help us if we help him.
The dharmas are, but they need us
to fulfill them so that we may in
turn be filled full and our cups
run over. We must be as cups for
the universe: open-ended bodies
to contain the flow of the universe
only in order to make manifest that
flow and express its shape — until
it changes shape and flows on.
Containers that do not contain.

The Vision and Other Essays, Bhikkhu Ananda Bodhi, Toronto, 1971; p. 16. Used with permission from Bodhi Publishing.

Acknowledgments

Thank you to everyone who contributed to the creation of this book. Over sixty authors shared stories and recollections. Valuable editorial comments were provided by Trudy Gold, Karma Chime Wongmo, Elizabeth Berry, Matt Wright, Rob McConnell, Jerry Troop, Cheryl Little, Myra Jackson, Rosalie Fedoruk, Don Stauffer and Mariama Thera. Wise counsel and support on layout and design given by Trudy Gold, Oksana Shewchenko and Sarah Berry.

The publisher and editors gratefully acknowledge Bodhi Publishing's permission to quote from many of their publications of Namgyal Rinpoche's discourses, as well as from other publications of his teaching that are now their property. The sources for the quotations are cited in each case.

We also thank several anonymous students for their transcriptions of Namgyal Rinpoche's discourses.

We express gratitude to Namgyal Rinpoche for his contributions to the people who share an experience here and to thousands of others.

Rab Wilkie and David Berry

Note on English Usage

The authors of the stories in this book include native English speaking people from Canada, the United States, the United Kingdom, Australia, New Zealand and people from other countries that learned English in varied places. The spellings and language usage in the book were often left in the original to reflect the diversity of authors' cultures, views and experiences.

Contents

Preface – *David Berry*.. 1

Biography –*Rab Wilkie*... 3

Pointing to the Moon – *Karen Russell* 6

One Voice – *Christine Wihak* 7

The Magician – *Rab Wilkie* 7

"Just a Human Being" – *David Berry*.. 9

Meeting the Teacher 11

"You Are Not Really Here" – *Lama Sonam Gyatso*............... 11

Meeting My Teacher – *Henri van Bentum* 12

First Clue – *Rab Wilkie*... 13

First Lesson in Awakening – *Henri van Bentum* 13

"Follow Me" – *Michael Brine* 14

Meeting the Bhikkhu – *David Berry*....................................... 15

"Cornflakes or Weetabix?" – *Sonia Moriceau* 16

Salvation – *Joanna Estelle (Storoschuk)* 17

First Words from the Teacher – *David Berry* 19

How I Came Into Rinpoche's Orbit – *Linda Rainbird*............ 19

The Nature of Questions – *Rob McConnell* 21

Connecting with the Teacher – *Roslyn Langdon* 23

The Meditation Centre and Its First Caretakers........................ 25

"We Are Going to Redeem This Property" – *Lama Sonam Gyatso*.... 26

In The Beginning – *Daisy Heisler*.. 27

A Walk in the Snow – *Marcel Bauer*....................................... 28

Log Cabin – *Jim Heller*.. 28

Nosis – *Michael Brine* 29

My Cup Runneth Over – *Daisy Heisler* 29

Creatures at Night, Prowlers by Day – *Faye Fraser*.............. 30

Early Teachings and Journeys 33

"Think of Something" – *Lama Sonam Gyatso* 33

The Inner War" – *Cecilie Kwiat* 34

"HELP!" Baptism by Canoe – *Lama Sonam Gyatso* 34

Orphans in the Storm – *Daisy Heisler* 36

The Bhikkhu Makes the News – *Rab Wilkie* 36

"Trust Me" – *Lama Sonam Gyatso* 38

She Wouldn't Bow for Anyone! – *Daisy Heisler* 39

A Warp in the World – *Rab Wilkie* 39

"Tony Will Be in Charge" – *Lama Sonam Gyatso* 40

"I Am Not Your Teacher" – *Daisy Heisler* 40

Voyage to India — five stories – *Henri van Bentum* 43

    The Hunting of the Snark 43

    A Pilgrimage to Ceylon and the Gem Mines of Ratnapura ... 46

    Burma and India 49

    Delhi 51

    Epilogue 52

The Third Blessing – *Lama Sonam Gyatso* 53

Letting Go and Going Forward – *Wesley Knapp* 53

The Dead End Goose – *Rab Wilkie* 55

In The Lion's Den – *Henri van Bentum* 56

Zen Jerusalem – *Rab Wilkie* 58

Galapagos Voyage — four stories – *Henri van Bentum* 59

    Blowing In the Wind 59

    Inca Pirca 60

    A Fistfull Of Fives 61

    The Da Vinci Boat and Sun Train 65

The Journey – *Peter Dederichs* 66

The Hat in Mexico – *Steven Gellman* 66

Telepathy – *Rab Wilkie* 67

Stardust – *Graydon Clipperton* 69

Further Journeys: the Bhikkhu Becomes Rinpoche 71

Boiled Eggs and Mixed Nuts – *Henri van Bentum* 71

The Young Mothers of Invention – *Pamela Hyatt* 72

Slices of Liver – *Henri van Bentum* 74

The Photograph – *Rab Wilkie* 75

The Feeling of Enlightenment – *Byron Stevens* 76

Meant to Be – *Peter Dederichs* 78

The Soccer Game – *Henri van Bentum* 78

The Marrakesh Express – *Rab Wilkie* 79

The Gift – *Peter Dederichs* 83

And My Blind Eyes See It Not – *Henri van Bentum* 84

The Darjeeling Demon – *Russell Rolfe* 85

Avalanche – *Russell Rolfe* 88

My Inner Purity – *Russell Rolfe* 91

Enthronement at Green River – *Rab Wilkie* 93

Memory Test – *Lisa Elander (Adamson)* 94

The Money Tree – *Heather Rigby* 95

A Lesson in Love – *Peter Boag* 97

The Rolling Rinpoche Gathers No Dross – *Melodie Massey* 99

Faith in Empty – *Lisa Elander (Adamson)* 100

The Unexpected Gift – *Karma Chime Wongmo* 101

Motherhood in the Desert – *Lisa Elander (Adamson)* 104

Faith and Light – *Steven Gellman* 105

Slackers – *Lisa Elander (Adamson)* 106

Who are you?" – *Lama Sonam Gyatso* 106

Awareness – *Bryan Upjohn* 107

Star Birthing – *Susan Cowen* 108

The Secret (Crete, June, 1975) – *Rab Wilkie* 109

The Dance of the World Serpent – *Jacques Varian* 111

"Ass Backwards" – *Peter Boag* 114

The Light Goes On – *Lisa Elander (Adamson)* 116

Morning Coffee in the Andes – *Lisa Elander (Adamson)* 117

Hoops of Space – *Susan Cowen* 117

The Master Mariner – *Peter Bergerson* 118

The Black Saint – *Melodie Massey* 119

Motel Vigil – *Byron Stevens* 120

A Rose Garden – *Prue Vosper* 121

Inside Passage – *Michael Brine* 122

Caitlin's Trick – *Lisa Elander (Adamson)* 123

Sitting, Waiting – *Charlene Jones* 123

If Music Be the Food – *Lisa Elander (Adamson)* 124

A Thousand-Year-Old Egg – *Henri van Bentum* 125

Delphic Flan – *Melodie Massey* 126

Self and Others – *Charlene Jones* 127

"Don't Get Wet" – *Henri van Bentum* 129

Motivation – *Achi Tsepal* 130

"Alright, Get On With It!" 133

Good Fortune – *David Pooch* 133

Mobsters – *Rab Wilkie* 134

Green Tara – *Charlene Jones* 135

Mandala Offering I – *Matt Wright* 136

Tea for Two – *Matt Wright* 137

Mandala Offering II – *Terry Hagan* 137

Safari – *Terry Hagan* 138

The Bastard! – *John de Jardin* 140

On Becoming a Student – *Stephen Foster* 142

Let it Shine! – *Anna Woods* 148

The Instructed Teacher – *Matt Wright* 149

Bridgeview – *Carina Bomers* 149

The Book Mudra – *Alan Wilkie* 150

The Wheat Sheaf Tavern – *Derek Rasmussen* 151

Opal – *Alan Wilkie* 153

The Latter Years 1990-2003 155

Incarnations – *Rab Wilkie* 155

The Layered Gift – *Lisa Cowen* 158

Good Morning in Polish – *David Berry* 160

"I Know You" – *Gerry Kopelow* 161

Ikebana – *Elizabeth Berry* 162

The Intuitive Gift – *Sharon Davison* 163

Stones – *Sarah Berry* 164

A Last Meow – *Anna and Stephan Hollnack* 165

"Start A Group" – *Gerry Kopelow (Lama Gyurme Dorje)* 166

Le Gourou Faramineux – *Jangchub Reid* 167

An Englishman's Sword – *Brian McLeod* 169

Dream Yoga – *Gerry Kopelow* 170

Damascus – *Brian McLeod* 171

Vision – *Karen Russell* 171

"Your Potential" – *Gerry Kopelow (Lama Gyurme Dorje)* 172

Knife and Fork Wongkur – *David Pooch* 173

"A Secret Teaching" – *Gerry Kopelow* 173

As If by Magic – *Sally Muir* 175

"Shit Disturber" – *Rosalie Fedoruk* 176

Your Money or Your Life? – *David Berry* 179

Last Encounter with a Great Mind – *Mala Sikka* 180

Summer Seeds of Learning – *Trudy Gold* 181

Poetry – *David Berry* 181

Appearing, Disapearing – *Ailo Gaup* 182

Close Encounter – *Donna Youngdahl* 183

Teachings 185

The Black Shirt Talk – *David Berry* 186

Preparatory Practices for Mahamudra – *Cecilie Kwiat* 191

Question Period – *David Berry* 197

The Monkey and the Elephant – *David Berry* 197

The Sword Blessing – *David Berry* 202

Missing the Tea Blessing – *Rob McConnell* 203

Reflections and Appreciations 205

Demonstrating the Dharma – *Tarchin Hearn* 205

The Virtues of Silence – *Sensei Doug Duncan* 206

Shining the Light – *Christine Wihak* 206

Transcendence – *Mark Arneson* 207

Crystal, Clarity – *Lama Chime Shore* 208

Guru Mind – *Gail Angevine* 208

Interview – *Stuart Hertzog with John de Jardin* 209

In Honour of The Great Lama Namgyal: – *Lama Mark Webber* 212

True Love – *Abrah Arneson* 215

Thinking of My Lama – *Tarchin Hearn* 216

An Appreciation – *Mark Eisenberg* 217

Appendix 1: Namgyal Centres and Teachers 219

Appendix 2: Bibliography 225

Bibliography I – The Teachings Of Namgyal Rinpoche 225

Bibliography II – Publications by Rinpoche's Students 228

Evolution has reached the point where Humanity can participate with evolution. This too, is part of evolution. Evolution may in a sense have gone beyond changes in physical form and we are now at a point of a mental leap, producing new mind organs and faculties rather than new anatomical adaptations to the environment.

Namgyal Rinpoche, Toronto, 1971.

Preface (Virginia, USA, 2012) *David Berry*

These stories are drawn from classes, travels and spontaneous conversations with Namgyal Rinpoche, a teacher of meditation and awareness. They convey a level of interaction rare outside monastic life and reveal something about the students who wrote them, what they learned and just a hint of the compassion and wisdom of their teacher. The insights Rinpoche shared were most relevant to those present at each time, place and set of circumstances. Whatever tradition, vehicle, scientific approach, or religious metaphor Rinpoche used, his declared purpose was to teach "compassionate, non-clinging awareness." He vigorously supported people in breaking free of stagnation and trance to move toward the transcendent birthright of all living beings: awakening and realization.

With that in mind, Rab Wilkie and I invited Rinpoche's students around the world to choose, from among the many interactions they had with him, accounts they thought would be useful for readers familiar with exploration of deeper aspects of their own minds and for those with no experience of meditation or spiritual practice. A phrase common in Dharma tradition is "thus have I heard." acknowledging both subjectivity and non authorship of the teaching. There is great diversity here in viewpoint and reports of transmissions received by students at specific moments in their lives. In the sum of the stories and differences among them, the essence of the teaching begins to emerge through the lines and between the lines — at times direct yet often subtle and intuitive. Sometimes authors share insights realized years after the lesson, perhaps even as they wrote the stories presented here.

Many who recount an interaction here are now teachers, contributing to this living lineage around the world. Centers and teachers are listed in Appendix 1 and books of the teachings of Namgyal Rinpoche are listed in Appendix 2 for readers who wish to delve more deeply. This book invites you to notice — then transcend — trance, habit and conditioning in your own thoughts and behaviors; to shift attention to pathways which beckon you toward awakening. Through the stories authors contributed in these pages, a glimpse of the myriad gems shared by Namgyal Rinpoche may be found. May you be well and happy as you journey the path of life's unfolding. May whatever insights you attain be for the benefit of all.

I am quite certain that living the way I am talking about is the future of humanity.

Namgyal Rinpoche, Dharma Centre of Canada, 1998.

Biography (Peterborough, 2011) *Rab Wilkie*

The Venerable Karma Tenzin Dorje Namgyal Rinpoche,
The Bhikkhu Ananda Bodhi, Leslie George Dawson (1931-2003)

Namgyal Rinpoche (known in his lifetime also as Ananda Bodhi and George Dawson) was a Canadian Buddhist monk and teacher. With thorough knowledge and experience of Western spiritual traditions, he played a leading role in bringing Buddhist philosophy (Dharma) and meditation to the West during the latter part of the 20th century.

Following ordinations in India and Burma, training and studies in Thailand and Ceylon, then teaching in Britain, he returned to Canada in 1965 as Bhikkhu Ananda Bodhi.

Along with a growing number of students, he founded the Dharma Centre of Canada in Toronto in 1966 and two years later he was recognized as a master and teacher in the Tibetan tradition by His Holiness the 16th Gyalwa Karmapa. After 40 years spent travelling around the world as a teacher of Liberation, he died while visiting Switzerland in 2003 at the age of 72.

His life was wholly devoted to the teachings of liberation and travelling. He advised his students to establish their own groups and centres for the study and practice of philosophy, religion and meditation; and to become teachers themselves. Today there are dozens of dharma centres and teachers around the world inspired and guided by his example and through which his teachings continue to develop and thrive.

Born Leslie George Dawson (October 11, 1931) and raised in Toronto, he began the pursuit of a career by enrolling at a Baptist seminary, then went on to study philosophy and psychology at the University of Michigan. Unsatisfied with both routes, and after a brief period of political activism, he met a Zen priest and discovered Buddhism.

Finding this a path that reconciled faith and reason, he continued to study Buddhism in London, England (1954-56) where he met his teacher, a Burmese monk, U Thila Wunta Sayadaw (1912-2011) and at the Sayadaw's invitation, followed him to India.

At Bodhgaya — the place of the Buddha's Enlightenment — Leslie Dawson was ordained in 1956 as a novice monk (samanera) with the name, Ananda and he received higher ordination in Rangoon, Burma as a monk (bhikkhu) at the Shwedagon Pagoda several weeks later

As Ananda Bodhi, he began training at his teacher's monastery nearby. After several years of study and meditation under various teachers in Burma, Thailand and Ceylon, he was invited by the English Sangha Association to direct the activities, as Senior Incumbent, of a centre for Buddhist studies in Camden Town, London.

His sojourn in Britain was brief, but during this period (1964-1965) the Bhikkhu Ananda Bodhi was instrumental in establishing new Dharma (Dhamma) centres increasingly further away from the busy city: Hampstead Buddhist Vihara in London, Biddulph Old Hall in Staffordshire and Johnstone House Contemplative Community in Scotland. Johnstone House later became the first Tibetan monastic centre in the West — Samye-ling when it was transferred to the Tibetan Karma Kagyu order.

Soon after his return to Canada, Ananda Bodhi founded the Dharma Centre of Canada in Toronto and instigated the purchase of rural land near the Kinmount for meditation retreats (1966.)

Over the next several years, other centres were established by his students in the Commonwealth countries of Britain, Canada, New Zealand and Australia, as well as in Switzerland, Germany and Idaho, USA. In Toronto he taught regularly, usually from autumn to spring and spent the summer travelling with students, exploring various parts of the world.

The first group voyage of exploration and pilgrimage took place in late fall and early winter of 1967-68. After visiting his teachers and monasteries in Ceylon and Southeast Asia, a meeting was arranged with His Holiness the 16th Karmapa, at Rumtek Monastery in Sikkim.

This fortunate meeting, during which Ananda Bodhi was received by the Karmapa as a respected colleague and reincarnate lama, led to his enthronement in Canada three years later as Karma Tenzin Dorje Namgyal Rinpoche — in accordance with Tibetan tradition.

From 1968, when Rinpoche was given his lama robes and the transmission of Milarepa (the great Himalayan cave yogi) by the Karmapa, to the last transmission (White Manjusri) he received in the 1990s from the Chogye Rinpoche in Nepal, he received, realised and bestowed many other transmissions from some of the most accomplished lamas from Tibet.

He gave a range of discourses, from elucidations of ancient Theravadin texts and teachings of Gautama Buddha, through Mahayana sutras and Zen practices, to the Vajrayana meditations and yogas of Tibet.

Throughout, the Rinpoche made the Buddhist path of awakening universally relevant to a modern and especially Western audience by apt reference to Christian, Sufi and Judaic traditions, as well as to contemporary psychology, science and art.

Books based on his teachings about healing, mysticism and art have also been published and more publications are being prepared from extensive archived collections. Many books and digital recordings based on his discourses are available through Bodhi Publishing and Sakya Namgyal centre, (contacts and links in the Bibliography in Appendix 2.)

Namgyal Rinpoche in South Georgia, British Overseas Territory, South Atlantic Ocean, 2001. Photo by David Berry

Pointing to the Moon (October, 2008) *Karen Russell*

A post with signs pointing in all directions

Distances shared

1,000 miles to Beaufort

2.5 million light-years to Andromeda

A micrometre to heart cells

A nanometre to the atom

He stands pointing his finger to the moon

Dharmas exclaimed

embracing you as you fall into the net of the universe

Relaxing in the now

Released to the play of clarity

He loosens our holds in seeing hearing smelling tasting

touching and minding

He/she stands pointing his or her finger to the moon

This way that way in speed all dissolves

While resting in the whisper of our heart

Connecting with life

The dying is living

Laying on the hammock of life

We dwell in minds nimble creations

Each moment we re-link

Seeing the moon from a different direction

A multitude of awakenings arise

Spacious and aware

Now you are pointing the finger to the moon.

One Voice (Switzerland, 1980s) *Christine Wihak*

Rinpoche was offering public teachings in Zurich. A woman in the audience had been a student of the guru Osho, who had recently died. With a very worried expression on her face, she asked whether she should be taking teaching from someone other than Osho.

Rinpoche replied simply, "If you know that all the Awakened Ones speak with one voice, you should. If you don't know that, you shouldn't."

Don't look to the Lama to save you. If the Lama could, it would have been done long ago. You must walk the path yourself. Put responsibility on your own true nature.

Namgyal Rinpoche, Dharma Centre of Canada, 1993.

The Magician (Aurora, 1953) *Rab Wilkie*

As legend has it, we first met Leslie George Dawson in 1953. Our family had been in Canada for just over a year after emigrating from Scotland and moved from downtown Toronto to the outskirts, to the village of Richmond Hill. It was almost Christmas when my brother and I were asked if we wanted to go to a children's party. Naturally, yes! Even if we had a moment of suspicion upon learning that it was to be at "a home," which is to say an orphanage: our threatened destination whenever we misbehaved which was often. However, "The Loyal True and Blue Orange Home" did have a nice ring to it and the drive up Yonge Street to Aurora that December evening was exciting.

The main event was a magic show. After supper and cake, we went to a basement room with chairs lined up in rows to watch a man doing tricks. Even at the age of seven I was a skeptic, but I liked the flourish of flowers from his hat and an egg from his ear. When he asked for a volunteer many hands went up but I got the nod. My four-year-old brother tagged along behind as I walked with uncertain bravado to the stage. Everyone laughed as the magician smiled and said, "Right — I see we have TWO volunteers!"I was not impressed — especially when he pulled a string of "wieners" from his sleeve and I could see light shining through them. They were long little balloons, made from brown nylons like my mother wore. But it was fun and we returned home in a very good mood.

Fifteen years later I met the Bhikkhu Ananda Bodhi and began attending classed at his house on Harbord Street in Toronto. The neighbourhood seemed vaguely familiar. The smells from a Jewish bakery reminded me of my childhood year in the big city and a few blocks on I noticed 'Central Technical School'. Hadn't that been on my routes to the cinema at age seven? Then, just before reaching the Bhikkhu's house, the sign at the intersection put a lock on it. 'Borden Street'. That's the street our family had lived on! Ananda Bodhi was living and teaching ed just around the corner from my first Canadian home.

Two years later, during a morning class at the Teacher's new residence on Palmerston Boulevard, he introduced us to his visiting sister, Marylin. For many years, he said by way of introduction, she had worked at an orphanage north of Toronto called "The Orange Home." Suddenly I remembered the Christmas party and the legend was born. It all made sense. The Bhikkhu's father had been an 'Irish cop' in Toronto and involved with Protestant Orangemen who, in the previous century, had established the orphanage. So the Bhikkhu's mother could have cajoled him into playing the magician for the kiddies. He was, after all an irrepressible entertainer and if this had been his public debut he would have been 22 — my age when I first met him. Very fortuitous!

Later that year his students had a Halloween party and it was well underway before he made his appearance. After bobbing for apples and dancing, strutting, or prancing in costumes as a prelude to the prize for the best, the celebrants grew silent as all eyes turned to the entrance. And there he stood, The Magician, tarotically attired in a white robe, a red band around his forehead: the Magus among us. He walked slowly around the room in a widdershins circuit, speaking and nodding to revellers as he went. At the completion of his tour, he stood again at the backlit entrance in the Northwest. Facing the rapt crowd, he raised his wand and said, "Carry on . . . ," then vanished. I should have asked him if he'd ever pulled wieners from his sleeve, but you know how it is when greater magic is afoot.

Sometimes a child lying in the grass looks up and orders the clouds to move. They don't. He repeats the experiment and they do move. "Aha," says the child, "I am a magician!" But a true magician is the one who knows which way the clouds are blowing. If you want the clouds in your being to move, you had better learn the motion of clouds.

Namgyal Rinpoche, Dharma Centre of Canada, 1996.

Just a Human Being (Teaching Dharma, Dharma Centre of Canada, 2003) *David Berry*

"A woman in England once challenged me," said Namgyal Rinpoche to the class.

She said 'You are just a human being!'"

The class was quiet as Rinpoche looked around the room slowly without saying anything.

"How did you respond?" I asked.

"I denied it!" he replied with sudden emphasis having waited for the question.

He paused and spoke quietly. "I'm not *just* a human being and neither are you!"

He looked around at the assembled students again, arching his eyebrows and widening his eyes into very large circles.

"I contain lemurs! None of us is JUST a human being!"

"It is the birthright of *all* sentient beings to awaken. Our segmented vertebrae recall the worms from which we evolved hundreds of millions of years ago!"

"Don't trivialize what you are! You will continue to evolve."

Man is the summation of billions of years of different forms of life on this planet. "Man" is an abstraction from this continuum of on-going existence, this continuum of evolution. We can view this continuum as varying degrees of consciousness. Man, as the highest form of consciousness on Earth, has all the previous states of consciousness within him. Each form of life wants to live. Man knows that he wants to live. But unlike the plant that will push aside any obstacle in the soil that prevents its growth to reach the light of the Sun, most of Mankind is not conscious of his deep longing to reach the light.

The Vision and Other Essays, Bhikkhu Ananda Bodhi, Toronto, 1971; p. 1-2. Used with permission from Bodhi Publishing.

Mothers are not responsible for their children. It's the other way around. A child comes to a mother/father relationship whose vibration is the same as its own. That's karma. It is already its own mother/father.

Namgyal Rinpoche, Toronto, 1971

Meeting the Teacher

First encounters with the Teacher can be momentous or the connection can unfold gradually. In either case the first meeting gives a student much to work on for a long time. Here are some stories by students about meeting Ananda Bodhi or Namgyal Rinpoche for the first time.

You Are Not Really Here (England, 1962) *Lama Sonam Gyatso*

When I was a student at Cambridge I was interested in yoga and had joined the Buddhist Society at the University. One day someone told me, "You really should meet this Canadian Buddhist monk, the Bhikkhu, who has just come back from Burma and is now the Incumbent at the Hampstead Vihara in London."

I dutifully wrote a letter, made an appointment and went down to London for the March break. I presented myself at the Vihara and finally the Bhikkhu appeared. Toward the end of the interview he asked me, "Where are you staying?"

I had hitchhiked down from Cambridge without a plan so I replied, "I am not staying anywhere."

To which he replied, "Well, you can stay here. You're not really supposed to because this is a monastery and only for monks, but you're not really here, I can prove it doctrinally."

I ended up staying for the whole weekend. That was my first lesson in anatta, the absence of a permanent or limiting self. I think there was mutual recognition and I never looked back.

For the next three years, I commuted back and forth from Cambridge and received ordination right after graduating. He has been my Teacher ever since.

Meeting My Teacher (Toronto, 1966) *Henri van Bentum*

During one of the darkest moments in my career as an artist, a friend told me about a Canadian Buddhist teacher in Toronto, who seemed to be an understanding and compassionate man. I made a mental note of this and when hit with another setback, I decided to learn more about him.

We met in early spring at a discourse in the basement of a church for seamen and 'down and outers'. His followers and a few curious stray onlookers listened. He sat in a chair at the front, a young man with shaven head, wearing saffron and burgundy robes. I sat at the back. His voice was clear, not loud, but I could understand each word. He touched on coping with city life and then read from and elaborated upon *The Secret of the Golden Flower* - all new to me. Something in his voice, presence and confidence told me I was facing someone who was for real. Measured against all my life experiences and the charlatans I had encountered, the Bhikkhu stood out as being genuine. I was introduced to him at the end of the discourse and we clicked then and there — lifetimes bridged in an instant. I knew little about Buddhism or lamas or Eastern philosophy.

A noticeable change took place in me. I dropped painting activities and attended the Bhikkhu's classes. My weakness was being overly emotional — too much enthusiasm and not enough sober insight. The lucid awareness and direct teaching of Ananda Bodhi made me aware of this imbalance. The Teacher was a master of meditation and insight, teaching compassion and wisdom. He helped me develop a more balanced view of reason and emotion and, by showing me how to strengthen the former, they were brought into harmony and equilibrium. Too often in our society, overly emotional or enthusiastic grown-ups and even children are labelled abnormal. But the Teacher never removed our enthusiasm — only excess of emotions by guiding enthusiasm into mindfulness of expressing and doing, knowing and being. Being a healer, he encouraged his students to be creative. As for myself, I was told "Art is your vehicle to unfolding."

You are not going anywhere unless you constantly have a sense of the transcendental. The notions of 'accumulating merit' and 'strengthening' suggest that it is 'out there' or in the future. It's happening constantly but we don't sense it constantly until we experience 'the thunderbolt that annihilates the rock.' As Kabir said in one of his songs, "The unstruck drum of Eternity is sounded within me but my deaf ears hear it not."

Namgyal Rinpoche, Dharma Centre of Canada, 1993.

First Clue (England, March, 1967) *Rab Wilkie*

The afternoon, before the Chao Khun, Sobhana Dhammasudhi left England for a few weeks to teach in Canada at the invitation of an organisation called the Dharma Centre. He asked me, "Ah, Nai Robin — you come from Toronto? You know Ananda Bodhi, the Canadian Bhikkhu?"

I didn't, but offered the Chao Khun a questioning look as if it were possible. "You might" he went on. "He is like — what do you call it — a 'psychologist?' He makes people angry."

We both chuckled at that and I thought that if I ever returned to Canada I would look him up. This Ananda Bodhi sounded more like a Zen master than a patient Thai monk and maybe I needed more excitement. I'd been studying and meditating at the Thai Vihara near London for only a few weeks, but that was an accident. There had been no Zen Roshi listed in the phonebook.

First Lesson in Awakening (Toronto, 1966) *Henri van Bentum*

Ananda Bodhi had an apartment on Triller Avenue where in the evenings he held classes with six to eight students present. I always arrived early for teachings in the tiny living room. On the windowsill stood a few statues and other small items.

The Bhikkhu said. "Henri, I hear you're an artiste. Do you spot something different in the apartment from last time?"

I looked around, then said, "Not that I can tell."

"Look again!"

I did, and still couldn't see what was different but I had to say something. "Flowers on the table?"

"Yes, yes, good, but anyone can see that, I hope. But do you spot something different other than those colourful flowers?"

I strained my eyes, looked around and tried to focus, but to no avail.

"Give up?" asked the Teacher.

"Yes, Sir." I said hesitantly.

He then went over to the windowsill and pointed at two small Buddha statues. "There, that's how they stood last time," he demonstrated, switching their positions, "and now they're this way."

Follow Me (Toronto, 1967) *Michael Brine*

I was spending a few days in Malta with my greatest friend Peter who had moved there. It was during a difficult time for me. A couple of years earlier I had left my international banking career and gone into a food business near Glastonbury in England. This had not worked out too well so I was trying to get my life back in some kind of order.

We were sitting one quiet sunny evening out on his balcony overlooking the sea and chatting when he stopped talking and went silent. Then suddenly he stood straight up and in a voice which was not his own addressed me, "My son, you will shortly go back to the land of your birth and there you will be given the opportunity to take up your spiritual work again."

He sat down and after a few moments opened his eyes and said, "What the hell just happened?"

I told him. This had never happened to him before.

When I returned to England a few days later I received a message from the Bank of Nova Scotia. They offered me a position on their International Staff for which they had interviewed me earlier in London. First I had to return to Toronto to spend time with them in their head office prior to any posting overseas.

In Toronto I took a room in a house that turned out to be the home of meditators. They told me of a Canadian Buddhist monk, Ananda Bodhi who was giving a talk at the Theosophical Society the following Sunday. I decided to go, and arriving a bit early, browsed through their library. Then, looking at my watch I decided it was time to go in and get a seat.

As I came out from a row of books a gentleman, tallish and wearing glasses, came out from another row and looked at me before turning to go into the hall. As he looked at me I 'heard' in my head the words, "Follow me."

Soon after I was seated, the evening's speaker was introduced and I realised that Ananda Bodhi, who stepped forward to address us, was my guide from the library.

The Buddha is total mindfulness. Awakening is simply a continuum of awareness.

Body, Speech & Mind, a manual for human development, Kinmount, Bodhi Publishing, 2004, p. 13. Used with permission from Bodhi Publishing.

Meeting the Bhikkhu (Toronto, 1971) *David Berry*

I was invited to Toronto by a friend who told me there was a man she thought I would like to meet. Curious, I asked why I would want to meet the man. She said he was a teacher called the Bhikkhu. I did not know what he taught or that a Bhikkhu was a Buddhist monk but it was a chance to get away from my university studies and visit friends for a few days.

We arrived at a large house on Palmerston Boulevard and were ushered upstairs where the Bhikkhu Ananda Bodhi, was giving a class. At the top of the stairs a white scarf was thrust into my hands to present to him. I had no idea what I was stepping into.

We entered a large room where about thirty people were seated on the floor. At the front, one tall man sat in a chair with an altar behind him, crowded with exotic statues and bowls of water. A thangka painting hung on each side. He paused in his talk, turned and looked at me for a maximum of two seconds then his gaze moved on and he continued with his teaching.

"Wow!" I thought, "For just a moment that wide-eyed fellow did not know everyone and everything happening in the room. At the end of the two seconds he knew me and included me in what he was teaching. How did he know? How did he do that?"

I felt or rather I knew that Ananda Bodhi had seen and fully 'gotten' me although neither of us had said a word. I had never encountered such a profound field of intuitive knowing and yet there was something strangely familiar about that level of transference and communication. I immediately wanted to know more about the way of being this kind of knowing came from.

The connection was instant and seeds were planted. But some of us are slow learners and seeds can take a long time to sprout. About twenty-five years later it finally occurred to me to ask myself for the first time, "How did I know he knew?"

Avidya 'not seeing' or 'unwillingness to view' is one of the last fetters to fall. Without that unwillingness, we actually look at the unwholesome and have it be heard and seen. Then it can be dropped. When you see a condition or state you can ask: "How did it get there and what is its purpose?" You might make discoveries.

Namgyal Rinpoche, Dharma Centre of Canada, 1993.

Cornflakes or Weetabix? (England, mid 1960s) *Sonia Moriceau*

Long before I was to meet the Venerable Namgyal Rinpoche I heard of a about a tall Canadian monk from my first teacher, John Garrie Roshi, through a story which impressed me a lot at the time. Little did I know then that decades later I would be at the receiving end of similar exchanges in a mode of communication the Rinpoche used continually.

The story that the Roshi told took place during a retreat in England led by this monk when he was known as the Bhikkhu Ananda Bodhi. The two of them had a conversation in the Roshi's dreams one night. The Bhikkhu was standing at the end of John Garrie's bed and asked him, "What do you want for breakfast, cornflakes or Weetabix?"

Come breakfast time the Bhikkhu turned to him and said, "It was Weetabix, wasn't it?" to which John replied, "No, cornflakes!"

These communications — mind exchanges between Rinpoche and his students — were common. Over the years I worked with Rinpoche, especially during a one-year retreat I undertook in 2001 in Canada. Many times I was in communication with him in this way. There is no doubt that this is how he was able to communicate, individually and simultaneously with a large group of students gathered to listen to his teaching and be in his presence.

Rinpoche could be quite specific and practical, as in the story with Roshi, leaving you in no doubt that some words had been exchanged without needing to voice them aloud or even be in the same room! One simply heard Rinpoche's voice very clearly, for example asking you to pass the water, close a door, or giving you his preference as to what sort of accommodation he'll require when next in England.

I remember when, during one of those wonderful evening events at his home in Kinmount to raise money for the Dharma Centre, he 'asked' me, without needing to move his lips or even look in my direction, to pass a plate of food around. As I clearly heard or sensed the words I stood up and reached for the plate, glancing at him for some reassurance that I had heard correctly. I was met with his very satisfied smile!

His ability to communicate in this way was also how he knew in detail what was going on in one's practice. During an insight retreat I was alone in my cabin practising a particular aspect and having difficulty.

The following day he looked directly at me and told me how to approach this specific point, yet I had not spoken to him. I had merely inquired in the privacy of my own mind — or so I thought! It was a wondrous form of intimacy in communication, so clear, direct and consistent, so unencumbered, yet also scary. In his presence I had to be careful or mindful of what I'd think or wish for. In my experience all wholesome wishes I made in his presence were fulfilled. Similarly, all my shortcomings were vividly exposed.

Do I dare use language to describe this oh-so-fine ability of enlightened Mind? His was the pure state of *Dharmakaya*, a clear, luminous Mind from which there is nothing to hide, nothing to add or take away. Just surrendering and allowing one's mind to fuse with the Teacher's Mind in bliss and emptiness.

This was the biggest teaching I received and still receive from Namgyal Rinpoche. Although his physical presence is no longer here, his voice is still manifesting clearly.

Salvation (Toronto, Spring 1971; Ottawa, 2003)
Joanna Estelle (Storoschuk)

The two months I studied with the Bhikkhu Ananda Bodhi were brief, but dramatic. I was 20 years old and had moved to Toronto for my third year of university. I lived in a flat which, I soon discovered, was two doors down from his house on Palmerston Boulevard. I was intrigued by the frequent comings and goings of young people wearing red strings around their necks from the big house with green trim.

This was a confusing time for me and many other ex-hippies. The heady joy of the 1960s waned and was replaced by the shadow of lives full of drugs, sex and rock 'n roll. Janis Joplin overdosed in the fall of 1970 and Jim Morrison died early the following summer. Shaken by the first realizations of our generation's mortality, many of us started to look for deeper meaning in life. Spirituality beckoned, offering new possibilities of experience to explore.

One spring day I saw a poster in the Fifth Kingdom Bookshop advertising a public talk by Ananda Bodhi on Palmerston. I realized this was the house with the green trim and I knew I had to attend.

It was amazing to see this impressive figure of a man sitting in a large chair on a raised platform and wearing saffron and maroon robes while alternately dispensing profound spiritual truths and telling jokes to a room full of devoted young listeners sitting cross-legged on the floor. Like everyone else present I was immediately transfixed.

I spent most of the next two months attending frequent lectures there on Dharma, participating in empowerments, taking Bodhisattva vows and learning to meditate. Soon, I too was wearing a red string around my neck, much to the chagrin of my Ukrainian Catholic parents. I was so impressed with this teacher that I invited a friend from another university to come to Toronto to hear and meet him. Fortunately for many, David Berry accepted my invitation.

The climactic moment for me came during a particularly intense empowerment. When it was my turn to approach Ananda Bodhi I trembled, white cloth in hand. He peered down at me over his glasses with 'those eyes' and made a brief but clear pronouncement in a booming voice that shook me to the very core of my being: "You will be saved by sound!"

Although I had played the piano as a child, I had no idea what he was talking about and thought, "Right. Sure thing" but I was shaken by his certainty about something in my life that I did not know.

Shortly thereafter (May, 1971), he left Toronto with many of his students to sail around Africa and visit India. During that hot summer in the city, other dramatic events took place in my life and by September I left Toronto, the Dharma Centre and Ananda Bodhi behind. I completely forgot about this incident for almost thirty years. My life had been challenging and I explored many spiritual paths before finding one to which I could commit long-term.

I had studied music as a hobby with many excellent teachers while building a career in management accounting in the federal public service. Not until my mid-forties did I realize musical composition was my true purpose in life. I returned to university to study music part-time at age 51. Music has been the great healer in my life for many years. I share the inner peace that I find in composing through sharing with others the music that I write.

In the fall of 2003, just before Namgyal Rinpoche passed away, I had dinner with David Berry in Ottawa. We reminisced about the 'good old days' and he reminded me that I invited him to the house on Palmerston many years before to meet Ananda Bodhi. I was excited to share that I had just started studying composition with his friend Steven Gellman, another longtime student of Rinpoche, at the University of Ottawa.

Suddenly remembering the long forgotten pronouncement, I gasped. I told David the story and he smiled knowingly as did I. More important, my heart smiled in deep gratitude to Namgyal Rinpoche for shining Light on my life stream at a time when I had not even known that I needed it.

I gave David a note to give to Rinpoche thanking him and a gift of a CD of one of my choral pieces performed by the massed choirs of Canada at the national Canada Day celebrations. A few weeks later, on a visit to the Teacher's house David saw the case open next to the CD player so I know Rinpoche got my note heard my music a few weeks before he died.

First Words from the Teacher (Entryway, Palmerston House, Toronto, 1971) *David Berry*

"You don't have to wait out there!"

How I Came Into Rinpoche's Orbit (Rotoiti Retreat, New Zealand, 1973) *Linda Rainbird*

I left New Zealand in 1972, at the age of 20 to travel around the world. I flew from Sydney to Indonesia to Tel Aviv to London where I began a journey overland aiming for Tibet through the Middle East. I spent six months with a Tibetan family, high in the Himalayas, at the end of which I was allowed to enter Burma for a week, which was rare in those days.

I arrived in Rangoon on a full moon and went straight to a temple, where the following morning I was given a tour by the head monk who allowed me to witness the ordination and entrance into the monastery of two young boys aged four and six. After the ceremony we discussed my travels and what I was hoping to achieve. I took up the offer of visiting a monastery in northern Burma near Mandalay. There I was offered a three-year, three-month, three-day retreat studying Buddhism and meditating.

On my return to Rangoon I thought long and hard and decided this would be too 'Eastern' for me and the discipline too harsh for a novice like myself. I proceeded south after leaving Burma, and after a long haul through the jungles of Sumatra ended my Eastern journey in Bali where I had lived previously. I met, purely by chance, an old friend from New Zealand who was fatally ill with muscular dystrophy and who had received help from a group of Canadians who were headed to New Zealand with their Teacher for a three-month meditation retreat. She gave me an address in Darwin where I could stay before journeying home to New Zealand.

In Darwin I instantly felt very close to people in the house there and was fascinated by one man's 'doodlings' of dakinis, deities and Buddhas which he did constantly, especially after eating. His attention to detail and focus was something I had not seen in a Westerner before. He told me his heart was breaking because he couldn't decide whether to go to Rotorua for the retreat with the Rinpoche or return to Canada.

After I told him wonderful stories of New Zealand he decided to go and I gave him the best possible instructions of how to find Rotorua. Then I kept thinking, "I wish I could go with him and travel overland through the Outback."

The man had arranged a few days before to get a lift in a Land Rover with a stranger who was driving to Brisbane going deep through Aboriginal land. When the Land Rover arrived he threw in his bags, gave everyone a hug goodbye then turned to me and said, "Why don't you come?"

I did the speediest pivot of my life — grabbed my belongings and we were on our way! This proved to be one of the most amazing, incredible, uplifting, liberating, insightful and filled with light, journeys of my life. When we arrived in Brisbane I booked flights to Rotorua as soon as we could because he was 'late.'

It all went like clockwork as if a huge spiritual burgundy carpet had been laid beneath our feet all the way from Darwin to Namgyal Rinpoche. I wondered, "How will we find Rinpoche's retreat when we arrive at Rotorua?" and he said, "Don't worry. It will just happen and we will find our way."

When we got off the bus in Rotorua, I said, "Let's go down this road towards the Post Office," which we did. Half way down the road, we met two of Rinpoche's students, with eyes like spaceships. They hugged my friend, while jumping up and down. I had not experienced such joy in my life before. They ushered us to the Intensive Camp — I was home.

The next morning at the class with Rinpoche we arrived at the same time he did. "Hmmm," he said, "WHO are you?" (Meaning me.) We explained. He was very happy to see my friend and I could see how fond of him he was. From that moment I felt like I was falling in love for the first time, as if I had known Namgyal Rinpoche all my life. At the end of the class he explained the importance of the pivot in the walking meditation and gave further instructions so clearly that I have referred to them ever since.

Rinpoche said my journey had only just begun and he gave me teachings throughout the six weeks of my stay, on how to meditate. I was struggling and kept falling asleep and he was so kind. He said, "You may only do five minutes of meditation a day, but this is not important. This will increase, improve and you won't fall asleep so often. It is important to observe what is happening and the healing that is taking place."

Meditation is the breaking of all bondage. It is the state of freedom but not FROM anything. To be conscious of being free is not freedom.

Namgyal Rinpoche, Dharma Centre of Canada, 1967.

Pose the question, even if non-verbally, but meaningfully. The question is always more important than a technique. With a depth question, a technique is only an aid in the direction of the question.

Namgyal Rinpoche, Toronto, 1971.

The Nature of Questions (Toronto, 1984) *Rob McConnell*

Namgyal Rinpoche welcomed questions after classes and talks. The depth intention of a question reveals characteristics of our current state of mind. The Teacher could mirror that motivation and point us in a more wholesome direction toward our more rapid unfolding. I admit there were times my motivation was less than wholesome, perhaps tied to building up my own ego. Was I saying "Look at me I'm asking a smart question," or even just "Look at me?"

Each time I asked a question from an unwholesome basis the Rinpoche would mock, evade, or cajole. For that I am truly grateful. What is the nature of a wholesome question? I believe it comes from a percolating in our depth of something we can't get a handle on. Through the question something emerges to be resolved. When I recollect my truer questions, the first question I asked Namgyal Rinpoche pops into mind.

In the early 1980's I was in search. I explored meditation and Dharma for a few years and had studied with a number of teachers, most recently some Tibetan lamas. I became disconcerted with the concept of declining kalpa, an epoch of worsening conditions. Randomness or entropy in the universe is increasing, disorganization is increasing and everything will end in total dissolution.

I asked a number of lamas about it and usually got a standard dogmatic answer, "Yes, this is how it is" — with no explanation. I became obsessed with an answer to this process even though my scientific mind accepted the concept of entropy. The question became a symbol of search but I didn't know what I was searching for.

The first time I saw Namgyal Rinpoche, I was sitting in a crowded room filled with people who seemed to know each other. I felt I was crashing a gathering of close friends. Everyone stared at the empty chair at the front of the room as quietness grew. When the Teacher walked in, everyone stood up and began prostrations as he was assisted with his robes. He sat and signalled for us to sit down then asked, "Are there any questions?"

My arm shot up.

His eyes looked straight into me as he said, "Yes."

I felt like the bottom of my soul was falling away. Any description of verbal interactions between a Teacher and student portrays only a small percentage of the occurrence and does not capture the body language, eyes, facial expressions and the certainty that intangible feelings and energy are present. Remarkably, different students have profound differences in their experience of the same interaction. It seems like the classes produced a profound unique experience in each student. Portraying a verbal dialogue, gives only a small taste of the experience but small is better than no taste at all.

I gathered myself up and proceeded to describe the idea of declining kalpa and stated that I was struggling with the concept. I cannot remember the exact details but I remember my impressions of his response.

He outlined the history of consciousness in this epoch and described how the process of awakening is moving in the opposite direction to entropy. As matter and the universe break down and dissolve, mind and awakening are on the increase. Giving the example of humanity on this planet, he said that throughout history, human beings have been becoming more aware. Awakening is on the increase. In his visits to a great many places on Earth, his encounters with people were usually pleasant and positive.

By contrast, the explorers of earlier times often had receptions from other cultures that were much less than cordial. Despite what the news media would have us believe, most people on this planet are kind and have wholesome intentions. Transcendence and a world consciousness are increasing as the awakening of the whole universe increases. It is our function in life to accelerate this process by doing everything possible to awaken and to assist others to awaken. As I drove home after that class, every cell in my body was singing. I had found my Teacher.

You must leave lots of room in your being. The purpose of the teacher is to take your question further, not to answer it.

The Womb, Karma and Transcendence; A Journey towards Liberation, Kinmount, Bodhi Publishing, 1996, p. 123. Used with Permission from Bodhi Publishing.

Connecting with the Teacher (London and Kinmount, 1974)
Roslyn Langdon

"If you want to learn to practise meditation come to Canada in the summer for a three-week meditation course at the Dharma Centre." These were the words of Namgyal Rinpoche at the Kham Tibetan Centre in Saffron Waldron where I had driven from London to meet him. I immediately booked a flight to Toronto at the end of July for myself and my daughter Melanie. Two weeks before we were to leave a group of Rinpoche's students began arriving at my flat in London. "Why are you going to Canada when the Rinpoche is coming to England?" they asked.

As the Teacher had instructed me to go to Canada, I saw no reason to change my plans. Leaving students installed in my flat, Melanie and I arrived at the home of friends in Toronto and waited for news of Rinpoche and the commencement of the course. It came in the form of a phone call from London — the teacher was giving a ten-day teaching there in my flat! Here was I several thousand miles from home, awaiting my first meditation course — which was already taking place in my own home. All I could do was laugh and consider that this must be the loosening-up process I needed before learning to meditate. While waiting for news of the Rinpoche, I visited the Dharma Centre. Young and healthy, I did my share of collecting wood in the forest and painting the temple. After a week, with rumours of Rinpoche's ship arriving soon in Montreal, I returned to Toronto, to be met by the words, "You might as well turn right around as Rinpoche will be at Kinmount tomorrow morning!"

We spent that night informing people and booking a couple of buses to take us to the centre early the next morning. After a short ceremony with a lot of excited and happy students, I met the Teacher on the steps leaving the temple and expressed my pleasure at the use of my flat for his teachings. I was expecting some words of thanks, but he only asked how much longer I was staying. I was due to fly back home in three days.

"Then I'll arrange a blessing for you tomorrow in Toronto so you can go ahead and practise." The following day I joined about a hundred others at a nun's house, (I thought this was to be a blessing just for me!) where we received a Chenrezi Wongkur. Thus commenced a 30-year life-changing relationship with the Teacher.

The next time I visited the retreat centre was October 2003 to receive my yidam empowerment from the Rinpoche — that of Garuda, part of the Healing Triad. Once again he wasn't there as he had passed away a few days before in Switzerland. Instead, I found myself taking part in the great moving memorial to his life. I gratefully later received the empowerment from Lama Sonam Gyatso.

Everybody is playing enlightenment as if it were some kind of Cinderella-Game. They don't want to know what is but what enlightenment could be. 'Oh yes,' they say, 'One day Enlightenment will come.' They are running away from what is and expect Prince Charming to come looking for them with a glass slipper. That view lacks the scientific mind. To activate the scientist within, look at what's there in the microscope directly in front of you. Don't indulge in fantasy. You can't have a concept of what you don't see. People fail because they have preconceived ideas about what they should see. They expect miraculous breathing; they expect to be miraculously lifted. You progress by fulfilling the law, not by breaking the law. Even the miraculous lifting is produced by law.

The Breath of Awakening; A Guide To Liberation Through Anapanasati Mindfulness of Breathing, Kinmount, Bodhi Publishing, 1992, p. 79. Used with permission from Bodhi Publishing.

A Meditation Centre and Its First Caretakers

The Bhikkhu Ananda Bodhi encouraged his small but growing group of city students to buy land in the country for a meditation centre, and they did — 400 acres of meadows and woodland with streams, marsh, ponds, rock outcroppings and a beaver dam. Today, it is a quiet retreat centre but it was not always so. Half a century ago, 'rustic' would be a kind way to describe what the Bhikkhu's pioneers found at the edge of an encroaching wilderness: an abandoned mink farm with derelict log buildings and a cabin that was virtually roofless. Fixing that was the first task of those who came with tents and transformed wasteland into a sanctuary.

The aim, then as now, was to provide a natural, serene environment to support new dimensions of consciousness and creativity for discovery, healing, and liberation. Many different teachings — Eastern, Western, Aboriginal and scientific — have been introduced and explored in depth over the years, and teachers have left their mark, sometimes dedicating a pagoda or statue among hilltop wildflowers, while individuals and groups of various faiths and secular disciplines continue to rent the Centre's facilities or participate in its programs of retreats and courses.

People are supported in calming and awakening, compassion and insight during their stays. Abundant wildlife — deer, fox, and many birds — pass by on their journeys. In spring, dragonflies chase mosquitoes. Night opens vistas of planets traversing a starry sky, the Milky Way stretching to the horizons. Northern Lights and meteor showers enhance a sense of vast space. In summer, those who know where to look, turn off their flashlights to see glow worms on a path next to a wetland.

The following stories give a sense of the early days on the property.

We have pollution because people are not there, not present, not in touch. Humanity should become not only preservers of nature but appreciators. Consider it an honour that every tribe of mosquitoes is here to bite you.

Namgyal Rinpoche, Dharma Centre of Canada, 1996.

"We Are Going to Redeem This Property."
(Kinmount, 1966) *Lama Sonam Gyatso*

The Bhikkhu had been pushing very hard for us to buy land for a meditation centre in the country. I went up to Kinmount with another member of the Dharma Centre and found a property selling for $4,500. I wrote a letter to the Bhikkhu and said we found a property at that price with 400 acres and mentioned that it had a beaver dam, by which I meant a swamp. I wasn't too impressed.

The Bhikkhu almost immediately flew back from Scotland. The first thing he said when he arrived back in Canada was "I want to see this property." So we drove to Kinmount and walked onto the land. Down the trail (past where the temple is now) we crossed the little creek at the bottom of the hill and as we were going up to the field, two deer leapt out of the bushes and ran across the open space.

Returning to the main house, such as it was, the Bhikkhu said to me, "We're going to buy it."

We immediately drove back with the realtor to Bobcaygeon where the Bhikkhu sealed the deal, pulling $500 out of his pocket as a down payment. We never had a mortgage because we formed a Trust and individuals put up $500 or $1000, quickly pooling the $4,500 price. The property was bought in the name of the Dharma Centre and approved at a meeting in Toronto on May 11, 1966.

The Bhikkhu later said he bought the property because Tony had said, "There's a beaver dam." Seeing the dam, he knew that was what he wanted. The main house was a derelict log cabin with no roof, no foundation, no doors or windows, no hydro, no running water, no well and no toilets! No nothing! But hey! The Bhikkhu loved those old logs!

The property, a mink farm abandoned for 30 years, had seen much slaughter of mink. The buildings were in ruins and there were no birds anywhere.

The Bhikkhu said, "We are going to redeem this property. When birds come back we will have redeemed it." The birds did return and are abundant today.

Even birds have a purpose in language; their calls mean "Food!" "Enemy!" "Come here, Baby!"

Namgyal Rinpoche, Dharma Centre of Canada, 1998.

In The Beginning (Kinmount, 1966-67) *Daisy Heisler*

My husband, Jim Bell and I, with four children (aged 9 years to 4 months) were the first caretakers at the Kinmount meditation centre. We arrived in the summer of 1966. We began studying with Ananda Bodhi soon after he arrived in Canada from Britain with two students. A small group met in his tiny apartment. He had a job in a print shop and our group decided he needed to devote his time to teaching instead so a support system was set up. We did not have money but some of the others had more. They provided financial support and we provided manual labor.

We were part of the search group for a meditation centre in the country and when I first sat on the ground we had purchased, I had a revelation that this place would have an impact and change my life completely.

It did. My husband was in the work parties that got the place ready. I became cook, dish-washer and caretaker for hundreds of people while he worked outdoors clearing and building. My sons enjoyed helping him build a log cabin in the woods for the Teacher. We had volunteers but few in the kitchen — they preferred outdoor work.

My life was a rocky road of hard learning while trying to care for my children in the midst of so many types of people. We shared our limited food with many visitors who arrived without notice. There was no system for people to pay their way except on formal meditation weekends. We were not paid or supported so often the cupboard was bare. It was my job to feed people whether they contributed or not.

One Saturday a dozen people arrived and no one brought food. I had only four eggs and two large onions. I usually kept my problems to myself but I confided in Ananda Bodhi as we stood by the stove. He told me to cut up the onions and scramble them with the four eggs. Twelve people besides my family seated themselves around our large table and I watched in amazement as each person took a helping. It was as though the plate would not empty until everyone got breakfast. It was like the fishes and loaves story in the Bible.

We must see God as a very silly being if we think that we have to approach Him in the rituals and formulas of organised religion. And in the sense that the universal flow is continually unfolding through all manner of phenomena, we are continually approaching God.

The Vision and Other Essays, Bhikkhu Ananda Bodhi, Toronto, 1971; p. 5-6. Used with permission from Bodhi Publishing.

A Walk in the Snow (Kinmount, 1966-67) *Marcel Bauer*

During the winter at the meditation centre we kids were getting a little cabin-feverish so the Bhikkhu put us outside — to get a grip on things, so to speak.

We were outside in our bare feet in the snow with no coats. When Mom protested the Bhikkhu assured her we would be fine. Of course he was right. It didn't take more than a few minutes until we were again well adjusted!

We met many interesting people at the centre. I am thankful for the experience and wouldn't change that for anything.

Once, years later, a hummingbird landed on my finger. Like living at the Dharma Centre, that experience caused me to re-evaluate everything I had ever learned.

Log Cabin (Kinmount, 1966-67) *Jim Heller*

I heard the Dhamma first from the Venerable Ananda Bodhi back in the late sixties when he returned to Toronto. He left many guiding imprints in my life back then which have served as pointers along the Path for these many years. One example will serve to illustrate.

I contributed to the Dharma Centre's purchase of property and helped build the Bhikkhu's log cabin which he used for interviews during our first weekend retreat. I had great difficulties with my Vipassana practice which weren't helped by the fact that I missed the breakfast bell the first day and almost missed the lunch bell. (Only two meals a day were allowed.) The mosquitoes and the rustling sounds around my pup tent ensured no sleep that night. By the end of the second day, I was a mess.

I went for my interview in late afternoon and entered the Bhikkhu's cabin to find a chair at the foot of a ladder leading to another chair in the loft where he sat. He looked down on me and I stammered out my inability to continue with the retreat. But I summoned up my remaining resolve to say that this was only Round One! He giggled and replied: "Round One: TKO!"

TKO or Technical Knock-Out is a boxing term for ending a match without a knock-out when a fighter withdraws, is knocked down three times, or is hurt to the extent the referee decides it is not safe for the fight to continue. Rinpoche's humour helped. I decided not to withdraw.

Nosis (Kinmount, 1968) *Michael Brine*

One winter I flew back from working in Trinidad and drove immediately to the meditation centre from Toronto when I heard Ananda Bodhi was there.

I experienced a temperature drop of 140 degrees. After a sweltering 95°F in the Caribbean, the thermometer outside the kitchen window showed minus 45°F!

The Bhikkhu was staying back in the woods in his small log cabin. It was well heated with a wood stove but surrounded by the icy marshes of Union Creek. Even the beaver were hibernating, snuggled in their nearby mud and stick lodge.

Food was prepared in the main house and the morning after my arrival I volunteered to take the Bhikkhu's cooked lunch to him, down the long trail through the woods to his cabin. An instantly cooling vapour trail, my breath and steam from the bundled food, hung in the crystalline air, following me through the perfectly silent woods.

After an equally silent delivery and nods of mutual acknowledgement I returned to the Main Cabin arriving, so it seemed, in no time — almost as if I hadn't left. Except for one unmistakable clue: my nose had frozen! And it has been very sensitive to the cold ever since reminding me of the experience.

I just hope he enjoyed his lunch!

My Cup Runneth Over (Toronto, 1966) *Daisy Heisler*

While caretaking at the meditation centre, I left once to meet with Ananda Bodhi in his Toronto apartment. I had a couple of things on my mind.

I had been meditating on opening chakras. When the energy reached my throat, it got stuck and felt like a finger of flame flicking around, leaving my throat so hot and sore I could barely talk.

Ananda Bodhi went to his kitchen without explaining what he was going to do, leaving me sitting in his living room. A few minutes later he reappeared with a steaming flowered cup in his hand.

He towered over me as he handed me the extremely hot cup and said. "Drink!" with a near smile on his face.

I took the cup of hot creamy soup into my hands and said, in a dismayed wimpy way. "But it's too hot!"

"Drink!"

I sipped and burnt my whole mouth.

"Your karma is in your throat," he said.

As I drank my cup of hot broth we discussed my other concerns. I asked him, "Why are there so many people involved with the teaching, doing so many things that . . ."

"I came to teach the sinners," he said.

Somehow the steam had gone out of my argument about who we all were and why we were all together.

I immediately went back to the meditation centre and found my throat had healed by the time I got back. I was able to pass the energy through my throat chakra successfully.

Creatures at Night, Prowlers by Day (Kinmount, 1969)
Faye Fraser

I met the Bhikkhu in 1967 at a critical time in my life when, as a young woman, I felt I had lost everyone who ever loved me. In particular, my mother had just died tragically. Coincidentally and appropriately for me, the Bhikkhu was embarking on a series of classes on *The Tibetan Book of the Dead (Liberation through Hearing,)* which were a great help. After the first lecture I thought. "Wow, this man is amazing, I hope no one's put off by his strange robes."

For two years, I attended as many of the Bhikkhu's classes as I could, including some about Chinese inner alchemy (*The Secret of the Golden Flower,*) astrology, tarot, art and painting mandalas. I was enraptured. At the new retreat centre, we held our first intensive meditation session – meditating for a minimum of eight hours daily.

I was not from a well-to-do family. I grew up in a Winnipeg slum by the largest railway yard in Canada with scarcely a sprig of grass in sight. I had never been in the deep woods in my life.

Lucky for me, everyone said, I was given the Rinpoche's lovely log cabin to live in for two weeks, a long 20-minute walk from the main house through absolutely primitive forest — full of creatures of all sorts.

"This is amazing," I thought, as I made my way with increasing wonderment and awe to my new home. Such a plethora of new sounds and sights greeted me. Wide-eyed, I sat down to meditate. Night fell and the sounds increased, becoming stranger, curiouser and more terrifying — the screaming of animals, screeching, rustling. "Was that really 'something' rattling my door?" I thought in horror.

The nights and days wore on. To make matters worse, field mice had late night parties chasing each other up and down the logs in the cabin (and over me!) chattering and calling to each other, totally unafraid of me. Did they know I had taken vows not to harm living creatures?

In the mornings in my sleep-deprived state, I would try to do my very slow walking meditation as instructed, knowing full well that sometime, maybe when I did the mindful pivot, a bear would be there, waiting for me face to face. Then beset by hunger and despair I would gear myself up to make it to the main hall for meals, knowing there were bears or other prowlers, around each bend in the narrow pathways, waiting for me, ready to pounce.

As I walked through the forest I tried to sing and made loud noises to scare 'them' away, hoping 'they' wouldn't detect the fearful tremors in my voice and come at me with even greater momentum. It didn't make matters any better to hear that bears HAD indeed ripped meditators' tents!

Finally: confession time. The day of reckoning arrived on the fourth day of the retreat. I would have to confide to the Bhikkhu how I was distracted from my meditation by all those creatures and prowlers.

"Oh but when you are in meditation, you are protected," he said, simply.

'Poof!' The fear was gone. Just like that.

The remaining ten days of the retreat were wonderful. I was lucky to have Rinpoche's log cabin.

A vibration goes forth that can be very beneficial if it is the living word. To say "hello" in a state of love is better than a million mantra said without care. Prayer, when truly practised, helps to strengthen the mind for focus on the work of healing.

Paleochora Discourses, Part I Exploring the Language of Liberation, Part II Healing, Faith and Karma, Kinmount, Bodhi Publishing, 2009, p. 99. Used with permission from Bodhi Publishing.

Throughout history several mystery schools or ancient teachings developed which consciously pursued the path to total awakening. An initiate of a mystery school or teaching would be assigned a series of exercises or tasks designed to lead him or her steadily on that path to complete liberation. This consciously directed training or yoga, frequently embodied in the form of a craft or art, is not for the purpose of becoming an "artist" but for the purpose of becoming a being of art. Thus the exercises given are directed toward the realization "Know thyself." With that in mind, one of the major questions a disciple of this teaching must ask is, Who am I? Your task here is to direct the conscious mind to the depths of your being and to bring that to a conscious knowing.

Unfolding Through Art, Namgyal Rinpoche, Boise, Idaho, The Open Path Publishing, 1982; p. 1. Used with permission from Bodhi Publishing.

Early Teachings and Journeys

In the 1960s Bhikkhu Ananda Bodhi taught in Great Britain then Canada before he began to travel more extensively around the world. Once asked why he traveled so much he answered, "When I travel, people come with me and the experience changes their lives."

"Think of Something" (London, 1964) *Lama Sonam Gyatso*

After graduating I gave everything away, moved down to the Hampstead Buddhist Vihara and went into training for a couple of months, after which I was finally ordained as a novice monk with the name Vanaratana Samanera. Every Wednesday night at the Vihara, the Bhikkhu would give a class on meditation. One night, about ten minutes before the class, he came up to me and said, "Vanaratana, I am going out tonight and I want you to give the meditation class."

"What do you mean give the class? What do I know about meditation?"

"Oh, you'll think of something," he said and walked out. That was the beginning of my teacher training.

"The Inner War" (Toronto, 1965; Balingup, 2002) *Cecilie Kwiat*

I was 25, barely off the streets of San Francisco when I first met the Teacher in 1965. Our last time together was a year before his death. During a three-week meditation course held in Balingup, Australia I had the honour of providing support for his wonderful presence by acting as resident teacher for the group of students gathered there.

Over the years studying and practising with him there are many 'Namgyal stories' in my memory. He showed great kindness in feeding me, travelling with me, teaching me when I was so hungry for spiritual food I could barely digest the blessings he bestowed. But anyone who studied with him knew the bountiful gifts he endlessly showered on us all.

It seems daunting to pick a story. Once we chased each other around the main house at the Dharma Centre until he locked me out.

In the early years, after I'd stopped coming to classes when he announced that all who attended had to meditate, I found my way back one evening. He was speaking about the Vietnam War, and I was so sunken into despair my mind felt like a very dark, very damp hidden basement crawl space.

At one point in the talk, he said, while looking directly into my eyes, "It's the inner war you have to stop."

Take a positive view of everything. Everything is part of the unfolding — even things that we think of as entirely bad such as war. If it weren't for the invention of the spear, we wouldn't be here. We would have been picked up in the jaws of a giant lizard while doing our Mahatma Gandhi number.

Namgyal Rinpoche, Dharma Centre of Canada, 1998.

"HELP!" Baptism by Canoe (Lake Of Bays, Ontario, November 1964) *Lama Sonam Gyatso*

The Bhikkhu found the English to be 'a bit stodgy.' They in turn thought his approach was too advanced for them. So he made a decision to return to Canada, stating, "I am returning to my roots." He and I flew to Gander, Newfoundland on a three-week excursion, (my first trip to Canada,) both of us travelling in business suits. After a long train ride, we arrived in Toronto where he gave classes at the Japanese Buddhist Church on Bathurst Street, thus sowing the seeds for the creation of the Dharma Centre.

Later we went north to stay at Cedar Grove Lodge on Lake of Bays near Minden. One brisk afternoon we went down to the lake, passing a boathouse where we admired a big white motor-boat and wished we could ride in it. We chose a small red canoe and paddled out into the lake. Being from England I had no experience with canoes and apparently neither did the Bhikkhu. We sat up high on the seats, not low with our knees on the bottom of the canoe like you are supposed to do. I was in the bow and the Bhikkhu was in the stern.

We paddled for a while, as far as the Narrows, when a breeze picked up and it was getting choppy so we turned to go back but even with the wind we did not get low in the canoe. We were about halfway back when I was suddenly scooping air with my paddle, lunging forward and spinning around, over and under the canoe. We both ended up hanging on to an upside-down boat suspended in 500 feet of frigid water.

Being a good 'Buddhist' my mind turned to thoughts like, "Oh well, I guess we're going to die now. I wonder where the next rebirth will be."

The Bhikkhu started shouting, "Help! Help!"

Thinking he was drowning, I reached over to grab his arm and got the dirtiest look you could imagine. It hit me. "Oh, that's a smart idea, he's calling for help." I was getting philosophical about my next life and being resigned to die and there he was doing the obvious — calling for help to get us saved. He taught me that when you are in trouble, call for help.

At that time neither of us could swim although I did learn later and Rinpoche took up snorkeling, but the Bhikkhu, being a good Canadian, stayed up to his neck in the water, paddling with his feet to push us closer to shore. Yours truly, typically English, climbed halfway up onto the canoe, which was rolling like a barrel. Someone in the distance seemed to be approaching in a rowboat, flailing his oars. He never reached us, but we passed the time arguing about whether he was coming or going away. Meanwhile the canoe settled further, emitting great gulps of air — glug, glug.

Thankfully, after an hour in the water, we were rescued by the same big white motor launch we had admired earlier. Meanwhile, immersion in the cold water turned the Bhikkhu's body bright red up to his neck, while mine was red only up to the waist. We were instant celebrities at the Lodge and were duly written up in the local Minden paper.

Two weeks later, after we returned to England, three fishermen went out in the same cold lake and drowned. They were not as fortunate as we had been. Their boat overturned and they were found dead with their hands frozen to the ropes.

Can the mind, the known, ever comprehend or contain the unknown? The mind craves to know death but do what it will, it cannot. Therefore it is fearful. How can the unknown cause fear? It is not measurable in terms of pleasure or pain. Fear cannot exist by itself; it comes in relationship to something.

Namgyal Rinpoche, Toronto, 1967.

Orphans in the Storm (Kinmount 1966-67, Vancouver 1992)
Daisy Heisler

I was cooking as usual, at the woodstove with a lion painted on it by a neighbour. Ananda Bodhi was in the Main House kitchen and as he was about to go out the door he turned to me and said, "And yes Daisy, you will look after the orphans."

I was taken by surprise. I already had four small children and was not planning to adopt. Those words stayed with me a while to ponder then were tucked away in the back of my mind and forgotten.

Many years later I went back to school and become a professional videographer. My husband, a physician, insisted we meet a woman who had been living and working with Tibetan orphans in Northern India. We struck up a working relationship to produce a video at my husband's expense using the orphan's artwork. Many of these children had never had a piece of paper to draw on in their lives but had produced beautiful pictures to tell their story. The woman had come back to North America temporarily and had been using a slide show and papers to tell the story they wanted the world to know.

In 1992, I was finishing a hundred hours of editing the video *Tibetan Children's Art* in the small hours of the morning when Ananda Bodhi's words thundered in my head. I was stunned to realize that after all the years since he spoke those words, here I was working and losing sleep with the intent to help and care for Tibetan orphans. The video aired on public television in Northern India and received rave reviews. The woman gave a copy to the Dalai Lama.

The Bhikkhu Makes the News (Toronto, October 1968)
Rab Wilkie

After a year in Britain and a summer job in the bush on a fire lookout tower, I was back in Toronto and reading a newspaper one evening. This was novel. I hadn't read a newspaper for a very long time. As I turned the page, I found myself looking at a photograph of someone I'd met in Scotland the previous summer at Samye-ling, the new Tibetan centre. Evidently, he was now in Toronto and doing yoga. There he was, in the Peacock pose, with a tall figure robed in black standing behind him. The caption below revealed the identity of the robed figure: the Venerable Ananda Bodhi. This was the Teacher of the Dharma Centre, which met at the old headquarters of the Theosophical Society.

The first public talk I attended was boring and, though disappointed, I began to feel at home. It was like a Friday night Dhamma lesson given by the head monk at the Thai Vihara in London, where I'd studied for six months, but longer and more complex. Ananda Bodhi droned on and on quoting from scripture and listing the Four Noble Truths, the Eightfold Path, the Six Perfections and so forth.

Afterwards when most of the over-capacity audience had departed, he apologised for his 'dry discourse' to several of us who had stayed to talk with him. He admitted that the 'laundry lists' had been a ploy. The Globe and Mail had just published an article about him, much to his surprise, hence the unusually large crowd that night. He had intended 'to separate the wheat from the chaff.'

I began attending his classes regularly. The turnout decreased dramatically and in a week the venue changed to an artist's home in the 'old village' on Gerard Street. When teaching a small group his discourses became more interpersonal, focused and brilliant.

I failed to detect any basis for the rumour that this was no ordinary nice Buddhist monk who sometimes used psychological tactics to shock students and wake them up. He certainly plied his profound understanding of modern psychology when teaching but his approach was gentle, almost scholarly. He wove some Zen poetics in for good measure but little to liberate monsters from the Western id until one afternoon following a Dream Study class. Several of us were descending the stairs in his house towards our boots at the front door and, so I thought, all feeling very relaxed and mellow after another exploration of dream psychology with subtle revelations. I was nearing the bottom of the staircase **when suddenly I felt a karate chop to my shoulder.** The Bhikkhu had been right behind me and I'd not noticed.

"Uh thank you, Sir."

"Ahh-hmm," he said and said no more, smiling.

No longer mellow and more alert, I left with the other students, eager.

When most people get bored they try to hypnotize themselves into positive thought. Many are slave to the notion they should have positive thoughts. Most of society's patterns are boring so people shouldn't feel obligated to follow those patterns.

Namgyal Rinpoche, Trance and Transcendence, Dharma Centre of Canada, 1993.

Trust Me (The First Yukon Expedition, 1967)
Lama Sonam Gyatso

The Bhikkhu decided that we had to go to the Yukon and find land up there because catastrophes such as a nuclear disaster might be coming. We looked at establishing refuges in different parts of the world — New Zealand for example, as well as the Yukon — and centres were subsequently founded in both places.

For the trip to the Yukon the Bhikkhu and I each bought a Land Rover. (His red one was bigger than my green one.)

Early one morning I was driving with the Bhikkhu in his Land Rover on the Alaskan Highway (on the unpaved Canadian side.) About half way between Dawson Creek and Whitehorse he said, "You really should see this lovely sunrise behind the car."

"I can't look back at the sunrise while I'm driving." I replied.

"Just let me hold the wheel and then you can turn around and watch the sunrise."

"Yeah, but you don't know how to drive!"

"That's OK," he said. "Trust me. I'll just steer."

He held the wheel and steered the car while I operated the pedals as I turned around and had a wonderful view of the sunrise as we rolled down the highway.

Later on, as we were driving along, he started to take folding money out of his pockets and began to count it. There seemed to be an endless supply of Dana (donations) and I became very interested — fascinated, in fact — as he chuckled away to himself, counting this money.

While watching this out of the corner of my eye I got so absorbed that I did not notice that there was a bend in the road.

The next thing we knew we were off the highway, Rover and Bhikkhu bouncing up and down. He looked quite annoyed and I was frozen in shock. We ended up at the bottom of an embankment, quite far down, in a field of dandelions with the fluff floating off as little white parachutes and we were still moving. I used every ounce of will to lift my right foot, put my foot on the brake and of course stalled the vehicle.

So there we were, in that field, with dandelion seeds flying all around us.

I looked at the Bhikkhu, very pleased with myself that I had the strength to come out of shock and lift my foot to stop the car.

He looked at me in disgust and said, "What did you stop for?"

She Wouldn't Bow for Anyone! (Vancouver, 1967)
Daisy Heisler

After leaving the Dharma Centre, I arrived in Vancouver with my children in August, 1967 as a single parent. The following spring when my mother was visiting, a nun arrived, traveling ahead of Ananda Bodhi.

During the day or two we had together before he arrived, she explained that on their recent trip to India, he had been made a lama and would have a new name. During his brief stay in my home he wore his new robes and the tall hat of a lama.

My mother was visiting from Regina. When I told her that people get on their knees and bow to him, she told me she would never do that for anyone!

A couple of days later, my mother happened to be kneeling near the front door, picking up some of my children's toys when suddenly the door opened and there stood the new lama, towering over her.

A Warp in the World (Toronto, November 1968) *Rab Wilkie*

One morning the Bhikkhu seemed late for class. Extraordinary! He was usually sitting in his chair by the front window when we arrived at nine o'clock. But everyone was quietly waiting, sitting on the floor in front of his empty chair. I was too until it occurred to me that this was absurd. If he didn't show up we'd still be sitting there the next morning — like sheep!

"I'll give him another minute."

A minute passed. No Bhikkhu.

"Right, well that's enough for me. This is a test I'll bet. He's not coming today and I'm not going to sleep here!"

So I pulled on my jacket and headed for the door. As I stepped down onto the street I came face to face with the Bhikkhu, his eyes wide with surprise.

"Leaving so soon?" he asked.

"Uh, no, no. Just thought I'd step out for some air," I replied, sheepishly.

While following him up the steps I glanced at my watch: 9:00 am.

Walking back into the room I felt a warp in my continuum straighten out.

Tony Will Be in Charge (Toronto, 1965) *Lama Sonam Gyatso*

On September 23rd, three of us arrived in Toronto — the Bhikkhu 'returning to his roots' with me and another student, Barry Goulden — entering Canada as landed immigrants. Barry generously paid all three fares to make the trip possible. (When Barry passed away in England many years later, he left a generous endowment to the Crystal Group in England that was used to support centres in Ireland and Wales.)

We formed the Dharma Centre which became official at the founding meeting on May 2, 1966 after a group began to develop. The Bhikkhu gave classes three days a week. He still had a group of loyal students in the U.K. who gathered in Eskdalemuir, Scotland at Johnstone House — the centre he founded and subsequently handed over to Trungpa Rinpoche and Akong Rinpoche. It was re-named Samye Ling and became the first Tibetan Buddhist centre in the West.

That April, he asked me if I would take over all the teaching in Toronto for a while. That was my second teacher training experience. I had returned to lay life in order to work at a job to support the Bhikkhu and was known in those days as Tony.

We had started a newsletter called 'Dharma Notes' which we know today as 'Dharma News.' Before leaving, he wrote a message: "I'm going to Scotland to teach and while I am away, Tony will be in charge and will give the classes. You will receive a more sympathetic hearing from someone nearer the struggle."

I Am Not Your Teacher (Vancouver, early 1970s) *Daisy Heisler*

I last saw Namgyal Rinpoche in the early 1970s at a Diamond Wisdom Ceremony he conducted. I did not know many of the people attending, but was asked to take part in making the arrangements.

I borrowed a long Tibetan horn that was part of a display in a store window. The owner of the store was delighted to lend it if he could join us in the ceremony and be assured of keeping his horn safe.

At the last minute after all the stores were closed, I was asked to provide a pure, never used, white sheet for the altar. I scoured friends for someone who had a new white sheet in their closet and found one.

I also was asked to bake the cake for the ceremony. I baked a giant three-layer cake with each layer a symbol of the Dharma when put together, looking at it from the top. I used fresh blueberries between the layers and lots of whipping cream.

The ceremony was great. I took my children to it and they already knew how to behave in these ceremonies. As a closing thought, Ananda Bodhi asked all of us to be mindful of our dreams.

I attended the meeting the next morning and had three disappointments. The person renting the apartment was extremely upset because Ananda Bodhi had encouraged people to throw cake around at each other — a cake fight! And now the light-coloured rug was completely stained with blueberries and she was worried about her landlord's reaction.

Also, the sheet I had borrowed had been packed up with the other ceremonial objects and was gone. I would now have to buy my friend a new one. Finally, that morning we each had a private few minutes with Ananda Bodhi. I entered and told him I had not seen him in my dream the night before.

"I am not your teacher," he advised.

I was stunned. I wondered how long he had not been my teacher. Was I being punished for not being a forever supporter of whomever he sent my way to be fed, housed and catered to? Had I not been asked to do all this work and at my own expense to provide things for the ceremony? There was no further explanation.

I never wanted to see him again and I quit being involved with the people among his students I considered users taking advantage of others. Yet I came to realize years later that he was right. I had other things to do and would have a lot of learning ahead of me on a new path.

And my new path took off immediately in the following months as we went to live in the Canadian Arctic, at Puvungnituk. When I came together with Kehnroth Schramm, M.D. and took the path into medicine, I realized I had met the teacher I had been waiting for all my life. My late husband has been, and is, my true teacher and partner, in this life and beyond.

Ananda Bodhi finally came to me in a dream two years after he died, when I heard from my son, Marcel, about the stories being collected for a book about interactions with Namgyal Rinpoche. In the dream he was handing out potted green houseplants to various people and handed me one that was a little plainer than some but very nice, symbolizing to me that he appreciated my work but some people had done even more.

What really mattered was that we looked at each other and there was a clean slate. He looked as he did when I first met him, face very clear and young. So that is the story and I would do it all again. It was all worth it. My life has been as I would have it.

This lifestyle of wandering and camping is an important aspect of this teaching. It helps you to overcome your old patterns, to free yourself from clinging to any one environment. There is no place you can permanently abide.

Right Livelihood and Other Foundations of Enlightenment, Kinmount, Bodhi Publishing, 1996; p. 74. Used with permission from Bodhi Publishing.

Voyage to India (December 1967 to February 1968) A series of 5 stories by *Henri van Bentum*

The Hunting of the Snark

In the autumn of 1967, Ananda Bodhi asked students to put their names on a list if they were interested in joining him on a pilgrimage to India by freighter. I was asked to find a ship for the voyage and secured a Dutch freighter that could carry ten passengers, sailing by early December from Western Europe to India.

From the 27 students who had shown interest, the Teacher chose eight, plus himself and Tony, his attendant at the time. We sailed from Montreal to Southampton on the Russian vessel, *Aleksandr Pushkin* and arrived nine days later, with time to explore some of England.

In Southampton, we hired three cars. We visited Stonehenge in the rain and after Stratford and Canterbury Cathedral we wound up that evening in Lyme Regis, a fishing village in Dorset. By now it was dark, foggy and cold and everything was closed, but we found a small inn and rang the bell. The kitchen was closed, so no warm meal was available, but the innkeeper served us tea and scones.

After touring England, I booked a Scandinavian ferry from Dover to France — the Bhikkhu wanted to visit the Paleolithic caves of Lascaux. I spoke French so I functioned as guide in the lead car with him. Since we had to reach Lascaux, we drove on into the evening and arrived very late. After waking half the village, I found accommodation for us all, but again all the kitchens were closed.

Early next morning I inquired about access to the caves. A guide was found who was given permission to take us on a private tour. Thus on a cool November day, ten of us entered the ancient realm and came face to face with the art of the shaman-artists. Everything the guide said I translated, but Ananda Bodhi already knew intuitively the meaning of these works and how they had been created.

"Those who painted these images were definitely not primitives," he told us. "The grace and elegance of the animals, rendered with such confidence and directness of line and form, are proof of a refined and intelligent mind behind the hand."

We visited a grotto filled with stalactites and stalagmites. There were no cave paintings but the experience was uplifting in its display of natural wonder. The visit to these caves and natural cathedrals stayed with me.

From Lascaux we drove through the Pyrenees into Spain to see the cave paintings of Altamira. We stayed in several *paradors* (restored monasteries and other historic buildings converted into hotels.)

Ananda Bodhi taught all the time, on any subject — history, religion, nature — for which the occasion called. We were even given a discourse on olives when we drove through olive groves.

We arrived in Le Havre the first week of December. Our ship, the *Giessenkerk,* was anchored next to nothing less than the legendary *France*, a colossal ship that dwarfed our freighter. We were welcomed aboard our ship by the Friesian captain and officers and shown to our roomy, comfortable cabins, all with large portholes and fine woodwork of oak and mahogany.

Ananda Bodhi and his attendant were given the owners' cabin and the rest of us paired up in our own cabins. There was a spacious recreation area, complete with bar and stools.

Departure was delayed for another day or two, prompting the Teacher to suggest I take the train to Paris to see an exhibition by the great master Henri Matisse. I was not keen on the idea. What if the Captain decided to lift anchor earlier and I didn't make it back in time?

I did go, enjoyed the works by Matisse and returned in time. The following day our ship lifted anchor for our long-anticipated voyage.

Ananda Bodhi had instructed us to bring construction paper, glue, crayons, sketchbooks, watercolour paints, pads and brushes, scissors, balloons, as well as playing cards and games like chess, checkers and Monopoly.

We had only three records: the "Rite of Spring" by Igor Stravinsky, "Afternoon of a Faun" by Claude Debussy and "Carmina Burana" by Carl Orff. A misunderstanding had caused the meagre musical selection.

Reading material included *Alice in Wonderland* by Lewis Carroll which contains *Hunting of the Snark*. This became a very important part of our journey. We discovered we were going to 'perform' this poem and would have to memorize our respective roles. I was to be the Baker.

Our first port of call was Genoa, Italy. By then we had all been introduced to the crew, the cook and officers. We had meals at our own table in the officers' mess which contained the recreation area.

The officers and Captain heard so much Stravinsky, Orff and Debussy that it drove them out of the mess room sooner than they would have liked. Our free time ashore in Genoa was spent sightseeing and enjoying a seafood feast at a picturesque restaurant near the harbour.

Our next port of call wouldn't be until Colombo, Ceylon. No wonder Ananda Bodhi made us bring along all those arts and crafts supplies. In preparation for Christmas, the Teacher gave us an assignment to make a greeting card for each crew member and for our group. This kept us going for awhile.

The captain and crew were very touched when they were presented with individual hand-painted cards on Christmas morning. We sailed by Cape Town on Christmas Day, sighting the legendary Table Mountain and, not long afterwards, sailing by Madagascar.

The food aboard ship was wholesome, tasty and varied. Every day we played our small but fine selection of records, while in the evening we played board games and — oh yes — bridge!

The Teacher was a wizard in contract bridge and woe to those who were partnered with him. One was given a lesson in bridge — and awareness — amongst other things. Talk about mindfulness, memory, decision-making and not doing anything stupid. The game of bridge is a discipline for awakening! Needless to say, Ananda Bodhi usually won — sometimes through sheer bluff! In the course of this eventful voyage, we were all given turns as the Teacher's bridge partner.

There were daily meditation sessions on deck at night and very early in the morning. The days were always filled, with the three classes given by the Teacher, artwork, crafts, or giving our meditation and dream reports.

One day the Bhikkhu and I were called to the Captain's cabin. Since he was from Friesland and spoke Dutch, he complained to me that one of the girls in our group had been wandering about during the night in her nightgown, in the crew's quarters! That was too much for our Calvinist skipper. He told us he was very satisfied with the way we filled our time and that we didn't bother the crew or officers, but could we possibly stop playing that strange music for awhile? Also why did we sit cross-legged on deck, morning and evenings?

The clear, starry nights while sailing the Indian Ocean provided many a night of celestial teaching. As was his nature, Ananda Bodhi not only talked about the constellations overhead but wandered off topic to discuss the early stargazers and astronomers, from desert dwellers and the Egyptian pharaohs, to the first star-guided navigators.

He then moved again onto gems, such as the star ruby and star sapphire. He emphasized that each of us should get acquainted with our birthstone, so that when shopping we would all recognize and buy at least our own zodiacal gemstone. The discourses were eclectic, always full of surprises and enriching. Now, many years later, I think of these as the 'honey nectar' or 'spiritual banquet' moments.

New Years came and went at sea and we began in earnest to learn our roles for the upcoming production of Hunting of the Snark — for which we used the whole ship! In the end, after much rehearsing, we pulled it off. Even Ananda Bodhi was pleased with the result and that says something!

Prior to our arrival in Colombo, he introduced a week of semi-fasting, the tradition of Theravadin Buddhist monks, with no meals served after noon. During that time we crossed the Equator, with the traditional Neptune ceremony for *pollywogs*.

By then our supply of water had run low, prompting the Captain to issue the following request: "Due to a shortage of water on board ship we kindly ask you to shower with a friend until further notice. Thank you."

The lettuce was now treated with a disinfectant, but the pantry still had apples from Europe. We were keeping some apples aside. Ananda Bodhi told us they would be much appreciated in Ceylon.

We were now entering the waters where the Indian Ocean and the Laccadive Sea meet before reaching Colombo. A surprise lay in wait for us: the Captain announced there was a dock strike!

A Pilgrimage to Ceylon and the Gem Mines of Ratnapura

The week before our scheduled arrival in Colombo was in many respects the most disciplined up to that moment in our voyage. We had eight-hour meditation sessions and daily discourses on Buddha Dharma. The Bhikkhu shared more of his vast expertise and knowledge about gemstones — now the moment of truth was about to arrive.

We were going to visit the mines of Ratnapura on the island of Sri Lanka (then still called Ceylon) our next port of call. Both my grandfathers were diamond-facetters in the Netherlands as was my father so I was aware of things such as carat weight, spectrum presence and durability. This, combined with my familiarity and experience with colour as an artist, made these unique discourses on gemstones and their connections with the ancient Mysteries more than just a passing interest.

As we approached Colombo, cargo ships and small fishing boats appeared on the horizon and as we anchored offshore to wait out the dock strike. More than ever, food and water had to be rationed.

No sooner had the anchor dropped than several small boats surrounded us. They belonged to merchants and vendors with all kinds of wares and treats for sale: brandy, whiskey, cigarettes and woven, painted or batik fabrics. Even gemstones were offered.

Bargaining was conducted from the deck to the noisy and eager vendors as merchandise was raised and currency lowered in woven baskets. Tempting as this was, we waited until going ashore. The crew did some shopping and fresh Asian vegetables were snapped up by the ship's cook.

After two days of looking at the port of Colombo while at anchor, the Captain negotiated with the strikers to have his ship tugged to the dock, under one strict condition: no unloading or loading of cargo until permission was granted. He was given the privilege of docking due to us ten passengers.

This unexpected strike allowed us bonus time on Ceylon. Not only would we go to Ratnapura, but could also visit Kandy and the temple of the Tooth of the Buddha, crisscross the beautiful island and relax at remote beaches.

At this point, Ananda Bodhi donned his robes for the first time on our voyage — much to the surprise of the Captain and crew. Soon we had firm land under our feet for the first time since Genoa.

We rented cars with Buddhist drivers — so noted by their long white skirts. The Sinhalese paid respects to Ananda Bodhi, now in his Bhikkhu attire, as did the ambassador from the Burmese embassy when we were applying for visas to visit his country. Our Teacher's first aim was to visit the monastery where he had previously studied. As a courtesy to the Order we had to get there before noon since no meals were being served after that time until the next morning.

The apples we had saved went to good use. The taxi drivers got a few and were grateful. Never in our experience had just a few apples been so warmly received! On our way to the monastery along a hot dusty road, Ananda Bodhi ordered the cars to stop by a fruit stand. I had the honour to bite into what he called 'the local apple.' It was like biting into a layer of fine, sour sand. I spat out my mouthful, much to the delight of the Bhikkhu and our group.

"Now you know," he said, "why I asked you to keep those apples."

We reached the monastery in time, allowing the Teacher to have lunch with the other monks. We had to wait until they'd all finished, following which we were served a frugal but nourishing bowl of food — but in a hurry, it was almost noon.

The Bhikkhu would make up for it when we had a delicious lunch the next day in Kandy, tasty but very spicy. (I can still feel the tears in my eyes.) Cool beer helped a bit, but more so the patties and yoghurt.

While visiting Adam's Peak, we spotted many elephants bathing in rivers, saw giant fruit bats hanging in trees and continued to sample the local cuisine at breakfast and lunch, but now we were more adapted. It was like travelling into the past, in the time of Rudyard Kipling, through many quaint villages and the lush green interior. We rested and bathed at deserted coconut-palm beaches before heading to the gem mines of Ratnapura.

We arrived at Ratnapura on a hot humid day. Gemstones there are mined from clay deposits in gravel pits and riverbed sediments and workers spend endless hours in scorching heat scooping clay into flat baskets. They tossed them up the riverbank to their overseers, the 'connoisseurs' who emptied them onto heaps of dried earth. After drying in the baking sun, raw gemstones were separated from the ordinary pebbles with the speed and ease of chickens pecking amongst gravel at kernels of grain.

The deposits bring forth an abundance of stones. Tourmalines, in their wide range of colours, are the most commonly found, but many of the world's finest gems can be found at Ratnapura, including the exotic *Padparadscha* (Sanskrit for 'lotus blossom',) with its lotus blossom colour. At the time of our visit this gem, unfortunately, was not available.

The raw gemstones were facetted and polished the ancient way by foot-driven wheels and then they were selected, weighed and put on sale in a large showroom. The huge ceiling fans tempted us to go inside, a welcome relief from the heat. A mixture of precious and semi-precious gems, along with imitation stones, was laid out on a long table covered in white linen. Visitors were closely watched by security guards and of course, salesmen.

Ratnapura was one of the few places on earth where the rare alexandrite and chrysoberyl cat's eye gems could be found. Visitors were left to their own devices without advice in selecting their gems. Ananda Bodhi was understandably the first one to review the vast collection and select from it. Alexandrites, tourmalines, zircons, garnets, chrysoberyl, sapphires and more were all displayed.

We all had our turn. I selected a beautiful, large blue-sheen moonstone, a 'one of a kind' that I later gave to the Teacher as Dana (a gift,) a peridot (my birthstone,) along with a chrysoberyl cat's eye and some tourmalines. Buyers were totally responsible for their choices. This is what made the Ratnapura experience so unusual and unthinkable today, when regulations require everything to be labeled indicating type of stone, carat weight, price and so forth.

After being exposed to this variety in such quantity and quality, upon leaving the showroom, my eyes flickered still from all the colour and glimmering stones.

Among our purchases, there were blunders. One student got an artificial alexandrite and a synthetic star sapphire among his stones. Even after all the discourses on gemstones by the Teacher, including what to look out for, it was possible to be hoodwinked by a fake, right at the source where real ones were found! Later, when Ananda Bodhi made him aware that all the other gems he had were genuine, the student was so pleased that he promptly gave a few of them as dana to the Teacher.

Another person in our group was approached at the crowded Colombo market by a 'money changer.' (The black market offered more rupees than the bank rate.) She changed $US 50 into rupees but when she tried to use the money, she was shocked to find that only the first and last two bills were real. The rest in the bundle were all fake. Such befalls the unalert in the Teaching of Awareness. During the evening prior to our departure for Rangoon, we all shared our newly acquired possessions, prompting Ananda Bodhi to give us more profound insights into the gemstones we had purchased.

The strike was over, the cargo taken care of and the anchor was lifted.

Burma and India

Now the Teacher's focus was on our next port of call: Rangoon, Burma, the Shwedagon Temple and, of course, his teacher and mentor, U Thila Wunta Sayadaw. He told us we should watch for the golden dome of the Temple which glistens from afar, whether one sees it in daylight or at night.

Meanwhile the onboard classes concentrated on dream and meditation reports interspersed with enlightening discourses on one special precious stone: the ruby — Burma being the realm for rubies. Ananda Bodhi stressed that the pigeon-blood hued were the very best and told us to be aware of the difference between a spinel and a ruby, since at first glance they look very similar.

He did not speak much about his teacher U Thila Wunta, but we knew that he was looking forward to seeing him soon. We approached the Burmese coast in the morning and indeed the glowing dome glittered in the sun from afar. We all looked in awe.

After the usual formalities with immigration, we went by taxis to the home of Ananda Bodhi's patron and sponsor, Yogi U Thin. This was a surprise, since he hadn't mentioned it, but a pleasant one. We were very warmly welcomed and the Teacher was pleased to see his benefactor again. Likewise, his patron was delighted to see Ananda Bodhi, along with his students. We were served a delicious meal: a traditional and elaborate breakfast of *mohingar* — a spicy fish broth with noodles and lime juice. Each one of us received a gift of a length of silk cloth.

Following this, we visited the Shwedagon, an enormous complex with many Buddha rupas that can hardly be described in words. We placed incense at several shrines, while the Teacher explained to us in his unique way all the symbolic images and rich history. In 1956 he had received the Higher Ordination here and been given the name Ananda Bodhi Bhikkhu.

Since our stop at the port of Rangoon was a short one, en route to Calcutta, and we had spent quite a bit of time with the Teacher's patron, just a handful of students in one taxi accompanied him to visit U Thila Wunta. I missed out on this due to my wanderings about the Shwedagon; "The camel that sleeps misses the caravan!"

Back on ship we heard all about this auspicious occasion of the visit with U Thila Wunta, then not much more was spoken about it. The next day after breakfast, we lifted anchor and sailed away. Ananda Bodhi now began discourses on Bodhgaya, the place of the Buddha's Enlightenment, and about Calcutta and India in general, preparing us for what to expect — although he sometimes deliberately left things unsaid, to test our reactions to the unexpected. Always teaching of course!

We sailed up the Ganges River on the way to our dock in Calcutta, where bloated corpses of cows, sheep, dogs and human beings floated past as well as raw sewage and whatever debris that can be associated with a city like Calcutta. The colour of the Ganges was a drab grey-brown, not the crystal-clear waters of this holy river at its origins in the Himalayas.

Where we docked, youngsters dived for coins into these filthy cadaver-infested waters. The coins were thrown for them to retrieve by crews, from our vessel and from many other cargo ships we were alongside. Some threw slices of bread, anything. These kids dived for whatever hit the water. What an introduction to India!

Travelling inland, we saw scrawny cows, black water-buffalos, white zebus, three-wheeled rickshaws; also women clad in brilliantly-coloured saris, some with two or three copper pots on their head and beggars — with or without limbs — often on little platforms with wheels so they could get around.

We were warned not to give any *baksheesh* since we'd end up causing uproar as others rushed to get coins. In those days, 97% of the population was poor while the other 3% controlled all the wealth and was often fabulously and lavishly rich.

The Bhikkhu was seemingly untouched by it all, but we knew that his compassion spread out to them. He didn't have to say a word. He had been in India before, but it was our first taste.

My first question was, "Where on Earth are we going to spend the night?"

But, as usual, he had planned this long before — there was an oasis in town called the Maha Bodhi Society. We arrived, rang the bell and were let inside. At the Society visitors may stay no longer than three nights and payment is made on the basis of Dana.

It was an oasis alright. Inside the walls no city noise or smells penetrated. Our rooms were simple, clean and welcoming. Meals were also provided, and true to the tradition of the Buddhist Order, no warm meal was served after mid-day. Upon leaving, with a 'Namaste' and giving a donation, we thanked the abbot, who was the caretaker, and his humble staff for their hospitality.

In the early morning, the first thing you hear all over India is the "Caw! Caw!" of the crows. When you go out, everywhere you see the holy cows. (We wondered where the bulls were.)

When you encounter the first open cremation it's a shock. But soon this too becomes part of the daily experience — along with the scents of spices, combined with every imaginable odour. And colour! The whole spectrum of pastel and brightly hued saris alone is a feast for the eye!

I said to the Teacher, "No need for a filmmaker to go through all the preparation and trouble of making a movie; one just has to hang a camera around their neck, let it roll and voila! You'd have the most splendid, dramatic and exotic documentary."

"Phenomena and distraction, Henri," was his reply.

Delhi

The teacher had arranged that other students would join us in Delhi, so we set out for there by train. Coming out of the station, he made a great impression in his robes and mala, head shaven and in sandals.

Although they did not know him, soon people were hanging garlands of flowers around his neck. When people asked the name of our Guru and we told them Ananda Bodhi, they said "Oh Ananda!"

While in Delhi we met with the Maharaja of Sikkim and the Canadian High Commissioner, Sir James George, then went on to Bodhgaya where Leslie George Dawson had joined the Sayadaw U Thila Wunta in 1956 and received his novice ordination.

Shortly after we arrived, Ananda Bodhi gave a discourse under the Bodhi tree where the Buddha attained Enlightenment. The group had grown to 28 or 30. This became routine for the Teacher — to travel for awhile with the group, then be on his own for a few days, accompanied only by a very few students. The rest of the larger group would disperse and travel in smaller groups on their own.

Back in Canada, he had spoken of the houseboats of Kashmir and now I had a feeling that's where he was heading after Bodhgaya. This he did, with a few students, for a rest. Some students went back home or stayed on in India on their own, as my partner and I did.

Epilogue

This first pilgrimage with our beloved Teacher will stay with me, as the most memorable, educational and spiritual journey of all the travels that followed. And there were many! He would become the 'Hero of a Thousand Places.' It was during this journey that he set the wheel in motion for all travels to come.

It was a great privilege and honour (sometimes it seemed like a dream) to be in the presence of the Teacher and to witness his compassion and wisdom in action. Not only did he relentlessly and sometimes ruthlessly, share his wisdom and insight, but his ever-present humour and Irish impishness made him at once an ordinary human being as well as a saintly *Arahat*.

The Pali word *bhikkhu* means wanderer in English. Buddhist monks spent three months of the year teaching in one place (during the monsoon season) and during the rest of the year they wandered. This, the Bhikkhu Ananda Bodhi also did and in the process of wandering created numerous centres worldwide as a natural result of his endless wisdom and compassion.

In the past, a few individuals here and there throughout history have emerged and unfolded and passed on their teaching. In the future, the quantum leap will lift all those who desire to be uplifted. It is in a state of love that we will make this quantum leap together. For it is from Divine Love that we came, it is love that enables us to intuitively grasp what Divine Love means, and it is love that finally brings a being through to fulfillment of his task.

The Vision and Other Essays, Bhikkhu Ananda Bodhi, Toronto, 1971; p. 14. Used with permission from Bodhi Publishing.

The Third Blessing (Sikkim, 1968) *Lama Sonam Gyatso*

The night before we were to meet His Holiness the 16th Karmapa, we were in the small town of Gangtok, Sikkim. The Bhikkhu was wearing his monk's upper robe over ordinary clothes and I had a red blanket thrown around my shoulders.

We were strolling around the town when suddenly a great many Tibetans appeared out of nowhere. They came up to the Bhikkhu and started bowing in front of him one by one for a blessing and he was putting his hand on their heads and blessing them. Then they started coming to me and I looked at the Bhikkhu and said, "I'm not a monk or a bhikkhu or anything, what should I do?"

He just looked at me and said, "Bless them." So I did.

That was my third lesson in learning to be a teacher. It's a real teaching for everybody. If they come, you should bless them.

Even on the issue of purification of the being (Vajrasattva) it's important to be gladdened first. If you are depressed and you want to turn on the 'junk genes' which gladden the being, access them through the senses and enrich the being.

Hope should spring eternally in the human breast.

Namgyal Rinpoche, Teaching Dharma, Dharma Centre of Canada, 2003

Letting Go and Going Forward (Toronto, Yukon and India, 1970-72) *Wesley Knapp*

The Venerated Karma Tenzin Dorje Namgyal Rinpoche became my Root Guru in 1968, when he was known as the Venerable Ananda Bodhi. The instant we met I was captivated and simultaneously set free by the realisation that I was neither crazy nor alone in this world. He showed me sanity and set me free.

At our first encounter he generously gave me a private, 'sacred afternoon.' I did not know then that he kept afternoons as 'his time.' I gave him the traditional offerings, lifetimes of love and my astrological birth chart. We pored over this and after many explanations he announced that I was a healing therapist and dharma teacher destined to establish a new school. This was big news to me because at that time, age 23, I was co-owner of a rock and roll club in Toronto's Yorkville entertainment district.

We lived in the three story building, had a terrace roof garden, swimming pool, restaurant seating a hundred in the summer; and a lounge, sauna and showers in the basement. I rarely felt a need to leave Yorkville and was immersed in the exploration of the young people's culture of change, hosting some of its luminaries such as Jimi Hendrix's band, the Butterfield Blues Band and Led Zeppelin while I ingested vast quantities of texts from the Theosophical library a couple of blocks away.

In the fall of 1970, in response to my request for life guidance, Rinpoche recommended I give up the rock & roll life and balance it with wilderness living, make some money, then travel to India with him. He sent me to Yukon to help found a Dharma community and I was there for two of the most magical years of my life just as I had lived in Yorkville for two years — balance.

In the Yukon that first winter I met Angela my partner-to-be, then in 1972, travelled to India with Rinpoche and a large group of his students. We experienced private encounters and many transmissions with His Holiness the 41st Sakya Trizin, his Guru, HE Chogye Trichen Rinpoche and with His Holiness the 16th Gyalwa Karmapa.

Rinpoche took us to meet the Karmapa at the Bhutanese Embassy in New Delhi. When it was time to make our offerings to him, I shuffled forward on my knees to his table to present the traditional white scarf. I was mindful, as ever, of Rinpoche's instructions — in this case not to go 'all holy' on the lama. "Look him in the eye, keep your senses alert, receive everything that's going on."

I looked His Holiness straight in his smiling eyes as he effortlessly placed his hand on the crown of my head. Without any change of expression on his part or any visible effort he began to press. As he smiled at me lovingly, his hand became like a one-ton weight.

The effort of trying to maintain eye contact by keeping my head up became too much. The muscles in my neck, shoulders and eventually back let go and as I collapsed forward His Holiness heavily drove my forehead into the coffee table — a direct teaching on the wisdom of letting go!

Focus on the heart to heart relationship to the outer teacher rather than an intellectual one.

Namgyal Rinpoche, Dharma Centre of Canada, 2003.

The Dead End Goose (Toronto, 1968) *Rab Wilkie*

Zen Buddhism and the practice of Koan contemplation (dead-end speech) was the topic during one series of teachings that the Bhikkhu gave in Toronto. While in strict retreat, the meditator had to ponder and answer an impossible question — or else.

"There's a goose in a glass bottle with a very narrow neck. How do you get the goose out, uninjured and alive, without breaking the bottle?"

"Quick! What's the answer?"

"Well —" a student with furrowed brow responded. "Let's see — if you used a highly effective acid on the glass, say on the bottom, that wouldn't be exactly 'breaking' the glass, now would it?"

WHAP! "Go stand in the corner."

"Oh! I know, I know!" another student intervened. "Starve the goose for a week and then you could pull it out. I mean, she wouldn't be dead yet and not really injured?"

Some more experienced students, unable to contain their glee, chortled in anticipation of the next response from the Bhikkhu — a Zen Roshi for this lesson that will surely devastate a clever ego. But he just shook his head and captured every mind in the room with his gaze.

"You are trying too hard and not hard enough. Do you really want to know how it's done?"

"Yes, sir," all heads nodded; eyes focused on him, the question peaking.

"Picture this: there's a white goose stuck in the bottle. It has already been in there for a few days, so it has to come out now. It's a very nice goose. It's the goose that lays the golden egg —"

"And there's no acid around for miles! Besides, the bottle is a very fine and rare bottle. It's an antique heirloom."

Some brows are knit so tight the cranium seems about to explode.

Some eyes are as wide as flying saucers.

"But sir," someone ventures, on the brink of despair, "This is an impossible challenge. It's not a fair question!"

"Exactly so, but you MUST get the goose out. And I will tell you how it's done."

Meanwhile, I was wracking my brains. I'd read Suzuki and knew about koans. I liked the frog one. "The green frog jumps into the emerald pond — plop!" And maybe I read the one about this goose?

"How do you get the goose out of the bottle?" — Pause.

SNAP! (Finger snap.) There — it's out!"

Every being has a teacher inside that is struggling to get out. Outer lamas are there to give history, methods, context and meaning.

Namgyal Rinpoche, Dharma Centre of Canada, 2003

In The Lion's Den (Brock University, St. Catherines, Ontario, 1969) *Henri van Bentum*

The Venerable Ananda Bodhi had been very interested in Western psychology and had studied the subject at the University of Michigan before his ordinations. One of the earlier highlights of his career as a meditation teacher after returning to the West was his participation as a speaker at the Fifth International Congress of Psychotherapists in London where he met Anna Freud, R.D. Laing, Aldous Huxley and other leading psychologists.

So, several years later in Canada, when invited by the head of the Department of Psychology at Brock University to be a guest speaker, he accepted. His presentation was about meditation. For this occasion, he had donned his Bhikkhu robes, a rarity. The auditorium was circular, with seating rising in tiers, like the classic lecture halls at medical schools. There were fifty people in attendance and Ananda Bodhi spoke from a lectern about the benefits of meditation and what psychology should be — a life of practice, not mere preaching — as taught by the Buddha.

He began with one word: "Consciousness," then asked, "What does it mean? Meditation is a very personal exercise. It's not theory, but practice. It's doing — not reading or gathering 'knowledge' about Buddhist ideas. Without practice, our potential will not blossom. Only what we've experienced through practice has the possibility of staying with us. Most, if not all the rest, easily fades. That's what makes meditation such an important factor, since such exercises bring one closer to oneself through personal, individual experience. This in turn refines and sharpens our consciousness and meditation is the best method to achieve this goal."

At this point the Teacher left the lectern and moved to the centre of the floor to take questions; he answered every question — most were about Buddhism and meditation. While answering, he would turn and look up to face the individual asking the question.

The Bhikkhu had obviously upset the applecart for some with his remarks on what we in the West term psychology as an approach to mental healing.

"We have left out compassion and true healing! In the West, we're experiencing a compartmentalized style of education and living. Psychology should not contribute to this depersonalization. If courage and self-confidence could be bought in bottles, there would be no need for psychologists or psychiatrists."

"Churches and schools teach conformity rather than a love of discovery. However, at the same time anti-conformity can lead to mental disturbance and madness. Children are forced into unnatural patterns until they are smothered and silenced. The child thus conforms, but will not be loved and protected, nor will the child trust anyone but rather have a pseudo or pretend accepting. Then fear enters and distrust. We are made into wage slaves so we can fit into society. Humans become machines. No wonder we go mad!"

"In our culture it has become a must to know everything and anything but oneself. Meditation is the vehicle for self discovery. We do not, with our preoccupation on diet, notice that a mental diet is also needed."

"You're all charlatans," one student remarked.

To which the Bhikkhu replied, "Hmm — but what if we're not?"

There were other comments as skeptical and sometimes it felt as if we were in an ancient Roman Colosseum, but instead of fighting lions, the Teacher was verbally challenging paper tigers. Each person who put a question to him was answered while he put some of the more clever ones into checkmate with his unique calm and clear way.

. . . to refer to this teaching as "Buddhism" is not correct. There is no such thing as "Buddhism." There is, however, Buddha-Dharma which, in an orderly way, explores the laws behind the dharma of awakening.

Body, Speech & Mind, *a manual for human development,* Kinmount, Bodhi Publishing, 2004, p. 13. Used with permission from Bodhi Publishing.

Zen Jerusalem (Dharma Centre of Canada, 1969) *Rab Wilkie*

One week into a month-long Zen retreat I decided it was time to pack up and leave. I'd done a retreat before, for much longer, but this was different — more disciplined. Some discipline was fine but this was a bit much. And besides, it was spring. There were more interesting things for a 23-year-old to do in the city.

Yet after my interview with the Teacher, I thought I might as well see it through to the bitter end. He didn't seem to mind if I quit or not, which was nice, but said, "Ah, so you are thinking about rolling up the mat?" reminding me that what I was going through was typical. I had read about stages of resistance and this was one of them. Being 'typical' was the last thing I wanted. I returned to meditate.

At night the honeymooners in their tent carried on as usual and when they left the next day I was surprised that my spirits lifted — without even wondering why the Bhikkhu had given them permission to camp out, *together,* for a few days in our midst. (And right next to me!)

As it turned out, Ananda Bodhi cut the retreat short by a week — just as I was, if somewhat robotically, meditating 18 hours daily and probably about to experience a sense of accomplishment. After the last session, with relief I trundled away from the temple. Deep constraint and frustration lingered, but inwardly I heard music and drumming as red Dakinis danced.

As I approached Main House, with other meditators mindfully straggling along, the Bhikkhu was leaving. He got into his roofless green jeep and made a triumphant standing exit, waving goodbye as Blake's hymn to the New Jerusalem rose to a crescendo sweeping over the greening land.

The Bhikkhu must have told his attendant to turn up the volume on the symphonic hymn. At first I thought I was hearing things — an astral choir of angels. At the close of a Buddhist meditation retreat, Jerusalem was the last thing I expected. It was West meets East.

That wasn't Ananda Bodhi in the departing Chariot of Fire but the Baptist preacher Leslie Dawson.

As Blake said: "And did those feet in ancient time walk upon England's mountains green?"

I'll bet He was doing the walking meditation, too: 17 paces back and forth: ... lifting   ... moving   ... placing.

Namgyal Rinpoche on the Road, Egypt, 1972

Galapagos Voyage: To the "Enchanted Islands" (May, 1969) A series of 4 stories by *Henri van Bentum*

Blowing In the Wind

We flew from Miami to Cali, Colombia where the Teacher gave several discourses and visited an art colony. My task was to find transportation to Guayaquil, Ecuador where we'd embark aboard the *Cristobal Carrier* en route to the Galapagos. I succeeded in hiring a new Mercedes bus and driver. After establishing the fare, our group of 36 students was on its way. Rinpoche had stressed that under no circumstances would drugs of any kind be allowed.

He was seated at the front of the bus, I was next to him. So far, so good. Then the happy group began to sing songs by Bob Dylan and the Beatles, such as *Lucy in the Sky with Diamonds, Hey Jude and Yellow Submarine.* And why?

Well, the answer was Blowin' in the Wind. Yes, the bus had become engulfed with the unmistakable aroma of pot.

This merry-making went on for some time. Finally, Rinpoche asked me. "What's going on here?" He then instructed me to tell the driver to stop the bus.

"Everyone out!" Rinpoche commanded. "Empty your pockets and shoulder bags!"

A good harvest of Acapulco Gold, Mexico's finest marijuana, mixed with Colombian, was soon uncovered. The bus had halted at the edge of a steep ravine. Rinpoche collected all the goodies and gracefully disposed of them over the edge of the ravine while singing:

"The pot, my friends, is blowin' in the wind; the pot is blowin' in the wind."

Inca Pirca

We reached the border of Ecuador and went through Customs and Immigration. This went smoothly and our passports were duly stamped, but our Colombian bus — our beautiful Mercedes — would not be allowed into Ecuador. A recent soccer match between the two countries had led to an uproar and the Ecuadorians were not on a good terms with their neighbours. We continued our journey, this time in a dilapidated Ecuadorian bus with metal seats.

Always on the lookout for something different, the Teacher said he'd like to visit Inca Pirca which he'd read about. "*Es muy pequeno*," our driver said. (It is very small.)

We started to ask about the location. The people at the first three places we asked had never heard of it. Finally, at a small post office, one person knew about Inca Pirca and laughed when we said we wanted to visit the site.

He pointed to a postage stamp and said in Spanish. "That's how small it is!" And that we'd need jeeps or horses to get there.

"Henri!" said Ananda Bodhi. "Get me four or five jeeps!"

That took some time but we did corral them, each with a driver. After negotiating the fare, we were on our way. Inca Pirca was not a tourist attraction — not like Macchu Picchu and other famous ruins in Peru and the Andes. Only one of the drivers knew where Inca Pirca was located.

Torrential rains put an obstacle in our path — a washed-out bridge. The jeeps could go no farther. So we continued our journey on foot, criss-crossing ice-cold Andean creeks. The rains did not let up.

"Henri," said the Teacher, "see if you can find us some horses." Off I went, into nowhere.

Amazingly, I encountered two riders on horseback. I told them our dilemma. They were able to get us eight or nine horses. I negotiated a deal, which included horses and two guides.

Ananda Bodhi rode ahead of the pack. Some of us had to carry on by foot because there weren't enough horses for all. The day was getting on by this time and every minute counted if we wanted to get back before dark. After some time, we made it — drenched but happy.

The site was just a rubble pile of unremarkable stones and without the guides we would have ridden right over it. Nevertheless, it felt like a great adventure in the high Andes. The scenery was magnificent. In the distance there was a snow-capped volcano, nearer to us were waving tall grasses and grains and once in a while the sun peeked through rainclouds creating rainbows. We made it back to the jeeps by dusk.

The drive through the Ecuadorian Andes was unforgettable and when we finally descended to Guayaquil on the coast, the temperature had changed gradually from 5° C to 32° C, with high humidity.

Galapagos, here we come!

A Fistful of Fives

In Guayaquil, we all booked into the Humboldt Hotel. The boat that would take us to the Galapagos Islands was the *Cristobal Carrier*. The vessel had been making the trip for 30 years and was a legend.

The Bhikkhu, another student and I went down to the dock to look at the craft. It was an old wooden vessel painted dull grey. Ananda Bodhi, ever-mindful, said as soon as he spotted the ship. "There are not enough lifeboats. Henri, tell them."

Besides our big group there were also many locals, chickens and all sorts of cargo. Somehow I managed to get the ship's agent to arrange for two more boats to serve as lifeboats. It was a Saturday and we were scheduled to sail at 1700 hours. By 1900 hours we were on our way, with much fanfare and cries of "Adios!" as we lifted anchor for what was to be another routine sailing for the venerable *Cristobal Carrier*. The two upper decks were reserved for us. All cabins had upper and lower bunks, while Ananda Bodhi had a single-bed cabin.

These 'Darwin' islands, the world-famous Galapagos, lay ahead and our group, a motley mix of Dharma bums, artists, ballet dancers, architects, writers and so forth, was happy. We had a magnificent clear, starry night above. Everyone's spirits and expectations were high and soon we'd all retired for the night.

Then, sometime between dusk and dawn: BOOM! I was thrown out of my bunk and was suddenly wide awake. 'What on earth could that loud noise have been?' I made my way up to the bridge. No one was there. The stars were glittering above in the clear sky. It was four o'clock in the morning.

I looked over the railing and was shocked. Ananda Bodhi suddenly appeared. "What's going on?" (Remember, it was the Teacher who noticed there were not enough lifeboats on his first inspection of the ship.)

"It looks like we've hit an island and we're shipwrecked!" I replied. "Would you believe it? The ship's bow is one-third up onto the rocks."

"Where is everyone?" I asked. "No captain, no pilot or officers on the bridge — in fact, nobody is here."

By dawn everyone was up and about. The captain had left the ship and was sitting on a rock with a bottle of rum in his hands, shaking his head. The ship began to list. I went below to get my passport and luggage, as did a few others. Just in time, as the ship began to list heavily to starboard. The tide was low and Ananda Bodhi ordered us to get to the highest point of what turned out to be not a very high island. Children were crying, roosters were crowing. Then I spotted some triangular fins jutting out of the water, telling us not to go out for a swim!

In the meantime the radio operator, the 'Marconi man,' had contacted the mainland and sent out an SOS for help and some boats. Our hopes of seeing the Galapagos were now smashed. Ananda Bodhi told us to stay calm.

Being the Spanish-speaking member of our group, I was in communication with the officials. A large schooner would come soon from Posorja, a fishing village, to fetch the women and children first. If no other vessel were available to rescue us, the schooner would return for the men.

The schooner, with terracotta-coloured sails, appeared to everyone's relief. All the women, children and the chickens were boarded and set off. Many hours later, the men were also picked up and transported to Posorja where we found all the women and children huddled on the floor of a large fishing warehouse — but not for long. The local people soon disappeared and we men in turn sat down on the floor with the Dharma women.

Our luggage was forwarded to the Humboldt Hotel and Ananda Bodhi told me to arrange transportation to get our group back to Guayaquil. However, it was a Sunday afternoon. Using my best Spanish, I managed to get a big truck which was used to transport fish. We negotiated a price with the driver and were told it was about a five-hour drive to Guayaquil. The teacher and I sat in the front and everyone else got into the back of the half-open truck.

By now it was getting dark, there were no lights and the rain began. After an hour the truck came to a halt, pitch black around us. I asked the driver, "Que pasa?"

"I'll take a look," he replied, getting out of the vehicle. He lifted the hood and appeared to be studying the engine.

Ananda Bodhi looked at the fuel gauge on the dashboard which showed an empty tank. "Now what? No gasoline, in the middle of nowhere!"

The rain became a downpour and half our group in the back of the truck was soaked. The Teacher was not amused and asked me for some swear words in Spanish.

"Caramba! Bandito!"

"Henri! Get out and hitchhike. I am not sitting and waiting here all night!"

And I got out and stood in the pouring rain on a road to nowhere with only the headlights on our truck lighting a few feet of the road. After awhile, a car stopped. I couldn't believe it — a black Mercedes! A well-dressed gentleman opened the window slightly.

"Que pasa?" he asked. It turned out he was the former mayor of Guayaquil. When he heard we were the hapless victims of the *Cristobal Carrier* he immediately became helpful — he had already heard of the calamity. Realizing we were stranded, he invited Ananda Bodhi and me to get in the car. I was in the back, the Teacher in front. My companion in the back seat was a large German shepherd dog who growled at me until the Señor ordered, "Calma!"

The Señor knew friends who lived further up the highway who might be able to supply us with some gasoline. After awhile the Mercedes stopped at a metal gate. I was told to go ring a long iron cable, which I had to pull several times. It must have been around 1 a.m. by then. Finally in the distance two dim lights appeared. I could see two lanterns, carried by what looked just like a Chinese man with one long braid swaying in the wind and rain.

(I was not hallucinating! Many Quechua Indians of Ecuador look so Asian that their friends call them "Chinos." They are born with the same Mongolian blue spot at the base of their back bone that many northeast Asians are born with, indicating a common ancestry.)

He was not amused that someone had awoken him at this hour but when I pointed to the Mercedes, the Quechua Indian with the braid seemed satisfied. He knew the Señor. I asked for some gasoline and he slowly turned around and went back along the long path to his house. It seemed like hours, but 15 minutes later he returned with a large yellow can, full of gasoline.

"Cuanto?" I asked. (How much?)

"Nada, el Señor nos paga un otra vez." ("Nothing, the Lord will pay us another time.")

It seemed we had stepped into the twilight of some fairy tale. We returned to the truck where most of the students were asleep, but once they saw the can of gasoline they gave a huge "Hurrah!" and applauded. Our driver was astonished.

Ananda Bodhi and I carried on in the Mercedes and arrived at the Humboldt Hotel very early that morning. During our ride in the car, the radio was repeatedly broadcasting on the national news the disaster that had befallen the legendary *Cristobal Carrier* en route to the Galapagos. The former Mayor seemed pleased to have had a hand in getting us all safely back to the hotel.

After breakfast, Ananda Bodhi called an urgent meeting. He wanted all the money that we'd paid for the voyage, about $450 (US) per person, returned to us. And he wanted the money in small notes! Another student and I were delegated to get this done. Mission impossible? First, we had to find out who owned the *Cristobal Carrier* or who the ship's agents were.

Meanwhile, both local newspapers had published a tear-jerker story. "It was a foggy night and I could not see my hand in front of me," the captain was quoted as saying. Foggy? The stars were sparkling in a clear night sky. And when I got up to the bridge, there had been no one there. Furthermore, there was a lighthouse at each end of the island. So I called the media and two reporters, one from each local newspaper, showed up at the hotel. We told them the real story — which they printed.

Now, mission money. It turned out the ship was registered under various names and we had a difficult time trying to find the responsible party who could authorize the refunds.

By now, nobody believed the captain and second mate. The print media were on our side, so was the radio. Cornered and nowhere to turn, the owner's representative arranged for the local bank to return all our money — mostly in five-dollar bills (as Ananda Bodhi had requested.)

I bought a large leather shoulder bag and stashed it full.

The Da Vinci Boat and Sun Train

Now, what to do with all our extra time? People had return flights home but not for awhile. I had noticed a sign somewhere that the *Da Vinci* an Italian passenger ship, would be in port the next day en route to Lima, Peru. Ananda Bodhi told me to find out if there was any space aboard the ship. And there was — for six passengers.

The Teacher said we would go from Lima up to Cuzco and Macchu Picchu, so six of us sailed on the *Da Vinci*. The rest travelled by bus and we all met in Lima from where we took the train up to the final stop in the Andes: Huancayo.

This train ride was something else! At least three dozen times we shunted back and forth in order to gain the higher altitudes. The zigzag railway was a superb feat of engineering.

The train was called *El Tren del Sol* ('The Train of the Sun') because two hours of out Lima, we were over the clouds into a sunny blue sky and clear air. Due to the altitude the train carried oxygen tanks. From the station we took a bus to Cuzco with its amazing walls built of huge boulders fitted perfectly together — still a mystery today.

After visiting Cuzco and Oleobamba, we took another train to Macchu Picchu — a new world, an older era. This was 1969, long before the site became the heavily-visited tourist destination it is now.

After Macchu Picchu we all separated. Most returned by train to Lima then connected back home by air. Three students accompanied the Teacher from Buenos Aires on a freighter around South America. Thus ended an extraordinary journey.

The world is shrinking. We can respond positively to this or not; by opening up our being and reaching out to others, or by withdrawing into our defenses. Those who do not really want anyone to reach their core and be penetrated and communicated with are committing psychological suicide. We have powers that still lie dormant within us. But we must throw off the conceptual hypnosis that keeps us isolated from each other in terms of religion, class, race, ideas and chosen-people-ism; and that keeps us as individuals from exploring ourselves and our outer world.

The Vision and Other Essays, Bhikkhu Ananda Bodhi, Toronto, 1971; p. 3 Used with permission from Bodhi Publishing.

The Journey (Mexico, 1969) *Peter Dederichs*

When I was nine years old, my mother and I went to Mexico with Ananda Bodhi and a group of his students. We drove and I remember very clearly being cramped in a small car which belonged to an older woman who was a long time student of Rinpoche and later became a Nun. She was always very determined to keep up with Rinpoche's car and it was funny at times to see how she would just miss a turn or all of a sudden see the Bhikkhu in his Land Rover passing us by in the opposite direction, chuckling and waving at us.

I have many stories which I can only describe as magical. There were many times when things were scary or even life-threatening but incredibly it always worked out. Once, I lost my wallet which I loved so much and later Rinpoche gave me a present. When I opened it up, there was my beloved wallet!

The Hat in Mexico (Mexico, 1969) *Steven Gellman*

Rinpoche and a group of about 20 of his students were travelling in the Mexican highlands. We were walking across a small village square when he spotted an elderly woman in traditional native Mexican dress sitting on the corner begging. Rinpoche immediately took off his hat and went around the group asking us all to put money into it. If we put in a dollar he would say "more!" In fact, no matter how much we put in he would ask for more. When the hat was full he put it before the woman and indicated, "This is for you."

The woman beamed with gratitude and awe. I don't imagine that she had ever in her life been supported so generously.

The Buddha said that all beings desire happiness. You have to see if your actions are happy actions. It's as simple as that. The whole teaching comes down to: "Cease to do evil, learn to do good, purify the mind." That is what it is. Get on with it! May you be well and happy.

The Womb, Karma and Transcendence, A Journey towards Liberation, Kinmount, Bodhi Publishing, 1996; p. 213-214. Used with permission from Bodhi Publishing.

Telepathy (Toronto, 1969) *Rab Wilkie*

A few of the Bhikkhu's female students lived above the Fifth Kingdom bookshop, near his house on Harbord Street. One evening I decided to visit them, taking with me a pack of cards devised at Duke University for telepathy experiments. The Bhikkhu had mentioned ESP recently and had encouraged us to explore such things, so I thought that maybe the ladies would be interested in a little experiment.

After arriving and chatting for a bit I began to suspect that my idea was not going to cut it. I wasn't sure why not, but my friends seemed to have other things in mind. One of them produced her Tarot cards and did a reading. This was fair enough but seemed tangential.

I wandered off towards the kitchen, wondering if I should leave, just in time to see the downstairs door open and the Bhikkhu walking up the stairway.

"Goo-ood evening. Are we all at home and receiving visitors? I wonder if I may borrow a cup of sugar."

It was a transparent and gracious ploy. There had been no knock and he had simply appeared, reminding us that there were no doors in The Kingdom.

A pot of tea was hastily prepared as we sat or stood around the small kitchen table with Mr. Dawson — as seemed to be his persona that evening: the visiting neighbour, yet still the Teacher.

"And what brings YOU here this evening?" he queried me, sitting opposite.

I was beginning to ask the same question of myself, but rather than sink into unknown waters, I presented my telepathy cards.

"Well then!" he said. "Give them to me and let's see how telepathic you are."

He shuffled the deck and blew on it gently.

For the first round, he gave the deck of cards back to me. I was to look at seven cards and he would guess what they were. The images on the cards were simple: a square, a star, a triangle and wavy lines were some of them, and they were easy to visualize.

I was impressed that he got seven in row correct. Before I concentrated my gaze on the last card, I began to suspect that his wavering over the first couple of guesses might have been a playful sham.

"Try the whole deck, now," he challenged.

After the first ten correct answers, my concentration lapsed. But even as I limply gazed at a shape, he knew what it was. He wasn't guessing, he simply knew.

"Very good," he said.

"You know, there are *senders* and *receivers,* he told me, "most people are better at sending or receiving, but not both."

"Now I will send to you."

I passed him the deck.

He shuffled and looked at the first card.

"Square!" I said.

"Yes." He showed me the card and then looked at the next one.

"Waves?"

"Yes — and this one?"

"Hmm — triangle?"

"Yes."

I was losing confidence yet still managed to answer correctly. All I had to do was say whatever came to mind and not second guess it. I made it to the seventh card without error, yet after the fifth try I threw up my arms in disgust.

Somehow it wasn't fair — not to be able to make a mistake! It wasn't my telepathic prowess, but his. How was it possible to learn when he ran the show?!

But when it came to the last card I was laughing. By this time I'd made a couple of mistakes, but I knew how to get it right and that was better than getting it wrong.

For telepathy that is beyond words, (although words may sometimes pop out,) it is necessary to be familiar with the other people involved, to 'wear people easily' and be mentally relaxed.

Any ego trip spoils rapport. Friendship is the best thing.

Namgyal Rinpoche, Toronto, 1971.

Stardust (Toronto, 1969 and Oak Ridges, Ontario, 1996)
Graydon Clipperton

It was springtime and I was 15 — exploring, energized, with lack of direction finding and making up what I could. I knew the realization of mustard seed and mountain through direct experience and had no discipline, no full knowledge of what to do with it, if anything. My sister told me of a 'guy' who gave teachings and personal mantras. I thought that's just what I needed. One day I went with her to a house in Toronto. There seemed to be cool people and the atmosphere felt familiar. I remember 'The Bhikkhu' and I remember that this was important and felt good. Then I didn't pursue him, but pursued the teachings.

Twenty-seven years later, after marriage, four children, several professions and much life experience, my wife heard a teacher was going to be nearby and we decided to go. It felt like it was not a choice. The event was in a private home in Oak Ridges, Ontario, again in springtime. People sat everywhere, some seemed to know each other and a spot appeared to be reserved.

I recognized him when he entered and turned to my wife and said, "I think I've seen this fellow before." My insides fell into place. It was beyond relaxing, beyond knowledge and my inside stories drifted and dispersed. The Rinpoche instructed that we were made of stardust, billions of years old and that a lot of work had gone into preparing us to be who we are today. "So, get it right!" he exclaimed.

Everything vibrated in my body and I knew he had gotten it right. He was truly one of the most encouraging, loving, compassionate and correct people I've ever met. He ordained me later that year, continued to give instruction through his remaining years, including telling me all too clearly to teach Dharma; and I continue to revere him and the teachings every day. May all our joys multiply to all ends of the universe.

In the womb, first you are floating (a moon-air experience,) then comes birth and the crush of gravity. You fight your way through that to freedom, enlightenment, terrestrial consciousness, beyond gravity.

The entity is then its own master with its own capacity and vibration. All it takes in affects its responsiveness.

Namgyal Rinpoche, Toronto, 1971

. . . we must come to realise that even though we raise questions about the life flow, it still keeps flowing. In other words, this flow exists as an objective fact of the universe. Although we each may have our perception of the flow, it is merely a perception "of" and is not the flow itself. Our task is to come into harmony with this flow, so that we are this flow. Most beings spend most of their time resisting the flow and call this resistance "Life."

The Vision and Other Essays, Bhikkhu Ananda Bodhi, Toronto, 1971; p. 7. Used with permission from Bodhi Publishing.

Further Journeys: The Bhikkhu Becomes a Rinpoche

In the 1970s Ananda Bodhi travelled and taught and encouraged students to establish meditation centres around the world. He would teach at these centres and invite students to travel with him or meet somewhere exotic. While in Sikkim with many students in 1971 to meet His Holiness the 16th Karmapa, Ananda Bodhi was recognized as Namgyal Rinpoche.

Meditation is useful to develop confidence and strengthening. To go in and out of meditation you can take refuge in the traditional forms or rupas. Arupa 'without form' is the full opening of awareness.

Namgyal Rinpoche, Dharma Centre of Canada, 1996.

Boiled Eggs and Mixed Nuts (New York to Thessalonica, Spring, 1970) *Henri van Bentum*

Ananda Bodhi and nine male students were bound for Greece. I had booked two freighters — one for women and one for men. Ours was a rusty old tub while the ladies had a brand new ship! On our ship, meals were nutritious but bland and repetitious. Each morning they served fried eggs swimming in olive oil. After a week of fried eggs, Ananda Bodhi lost patience and asked the chef if he had ever learned to be creative and do more with eggs than frying them in olive oil? This helped a bit. Every day for the rest of the voyage we had boiled eggs!

A student gave the Teacher a big box labeled 'Mixed Nuts.' Taking the label as a sign, I remarked, "That's us, Sir! Mixed nuts alright!"

Later that day, Ananda Bodhi found me alone on the deck. He was carrying the now empty box. "Henri," he said, "have you looked at the other side of the box and seen what it says?"

"No, sir."

He turned it over and pointed to the name of the producer: "Golden."

The Young Mothers of Invention (Greece, Spring, 1970)
Pamela Hyatt

When I recently heard that Wangchuk, a long-time student of Rinpoche, had retired from active Dharma teaching and moved back to Ontario from Saskatchewan, an image sprung to mind. I had known her some forty years ago as Anna McDonough and I suddenly saw her grinning gleefully from a deck chair on the foredeck of the Hellenic Lines freighter, *SS Livorno*, as we crossed a cold Atlantic, then a warmer Mediterranean, bound for Piraeus. We were a gaggle of Dharma dames and kids, aiming to chase the Bhikkhu around Crete.

The Atlantic was rough that early April — major storms, not fun. What a treat to steam through the gentle Straits of Gibraltar one sweet sunny evening, Morocco to our right, Iberia to our left. Damned if the silent lounge radio didn't leap to life with the Beatles' *HERE COMES THE SUN*!

Arriving in Piraeus, we three mums clambered into a large cab with our various sons and daughter, asked the driver to take us to a downtown, inexpensive hotel that welcomed children — the Hotel Minerva, with a huge suite including cribs and ample beds. Rumour had it the Bhikkhu was up on Mount Athos with the inner circle of lads and eventually they'd be coming to Athens.

Two weeks into our Athens sojourn word whipped round the Dharma gang that the Bhikkhu's group went directly to Crete — so MOVE OUT! We did, that night, on the overnight ferry to Heraklion - inside cabin (no porthole, arghhh.) The cabin's stuffiness propelled my blond son up to the main deck where he curled up in a big stuffed chair and slept soundly.

Heraklion at last! Lovely days on a beach, nifty explorations of the charming Knossos Palace and of course, we wondered WHERE WAS HIS NIBS?! At last, word filtered through the grapevine. "Rinpoche is at Sitia! GO!" Everyone raced to rent cars. Our rented Volkswagen beetle had problems. It kept cacking out then resuscitating itself. The final straw was when it gave up the ghost going up the last hill. A pickup truck approached, three lads leapt out, pushed us UP and — pointing waaaaaaaaay down towards the seashore, shouted 'SITIA,' gave a final heave and down we drifted — allllll the way and came to rest in a parking spot by the beach.

Uncoiling ourselves from that midget vehicle, sweating like stuck pigs; we were startled to hear a familiar voice from above and behind us. "Well, Pamela, it took you long enough!" There stood our teacher, on a small balcony, grinning down at us, Cheshire cattish. "Come up here and see what I've painted!" Right away, he spun our heads in a new direction — away from the hassles we'd just experienced.

That night I was sitting on the beach with my sons, Zack asleep in his Snugli on my chest, Carson's head on my lap. Almost a hundred students were listening raptly as the Bhikkhu, perched on a large rock, spoke of karma, touching on so many aspects of it. Pitch black sky above, festooned with brilliant stars, planets, wandering satellites; Aegean Sea lapping softly beyond us, mournful horns of distant freighters, a balmy night — utterly wondrous!

Of course, the next day was nuts. Where's the teacher?

"FOLLOW! FIND HIM! DRIVE!" he said. So we packed fast, leapt into the Bug, drove east until we located his car at a motel, checked in, flung ourselves into bathing suits (he was often in the water) and joined the group. I cannot tell you the names of the villages in which we stayed with the exception of the final one, near the western end of Crete: Chania — such a sweet curved harbour. The town had strong Venetian influences, along with a deserted minaret.

On Crete, after swimming one day, I asked the Bhikkhu if he knew what the oozing red sore above my right breast might be. "Shingles," was his reply. I winced; remembering my dad once had a horrendous case, years ago. "It's an indication of something you haven't taken care of emotionally. It's a warning. Be grateful it's on your surface - better than something interior and more serious." Those words have enabled me to view the periodic recurrence of that unpleasant itchy stuff with gratitude and awareness.

The Bhikkhu announced he was off to Egypt. Whoever had the money to join him was welcome. As much as I wanted to explore the pyramids with our teacher, my son had become ill and we needed to head for home.

I discovered on that journey that I was a very competent individual, capable of finding shelter and food for my sons on a daily basis and I did not need a man to direct me. It might sound trite now, in the 21st century, considering all that women are able to do on their own, but I was born in 1936. I'm from a generation that was taught that a woman MUST be led by, approved by, a man. This trip was extremely empowering for me.

As far as the Order goes, there is equal opportunity for both man and woman. This has been long established. However, the cyclic function can pose a problem for women, if nothing else does. Both men and women must remember constantly that both sides, male and female, must be developed and integrated.

Namgyal Rinpoche, Toronto, 1971.

Slices of Liver (Toronto, circa 1970) *Henri van Bentum*

I used to spend most of the morning at Rinpoche's house on Palmerston Boulevard, going there with him after the morning class. I'd stay on and often help prepare lunch. For one of these lunches, Ananda Bodhi sent me out to get a few slices of liver and also some marrow bones, leeks and potatoes for a soup he had in mind. When the time came for me to prepare the soup — after the bones had slowly simmered to make the stock and the potatoes and leeks were added and cooked into a broth — I looked around for the liver. It was nowhere was it to be found.

"Looking for something?" said the Teacher.

"Yes, the liver. I'm sure I put it in the fridge."

"Why liver?" he asked.

"Because you told me," was my reply.

"What made you think it was for the soup?"

I took it for granted the liver was for the soup. "Where is the liver?"

He laughed. He had cut it into very small slices and without my noticing, fed it to the cats. (In those days, Ananda Bodhi had beautiful Burmese cats and a Siamese.) The following week for one of my shopping errands for his lunch, he told me to bring spinach, barley, marrow bones and liver. When the soup was almost ready, he came into the kitchen, looked over his shoulder to me and asked. "Where is the liver?"

"I thought it was for the cats."

"Did you ask?"

"No, sir," said I.

"Well, you took it for granted again, didn't you?"

Happily, liver doesn't take long to cook, so I got the liver out and cut it into slivers and added it to the soup. Again, he chuckled, in that unique way when his 'Irish imp' was performing. That was the first time I ever ate spinach, barley and liver soup! And delicious and nourishing it was.

Sunyata is based on Anatta 'no-thing-ness'. There is no-thing to be spoken about. All is impermanent and in conflict. There is no moment when you can stop and say, "There it is."

Namgyal Rinpoche, Toronto, 1971.

The Photograph (Toronto, Autumn, 1970) *Rab Wilkie*

Ananda Bodhi announced that he was travelling to India again in the spring and would anyone like to accompany him? Was there any hand, other than my own, that didn't go up? Such a journey had little interest for me and even if I'd had a burning desire to see India, it was far beyond my means. As the class ended I noticed a new photograph on the mantelpiece in the dining room. It stood beside the smaller one of Rinpoche's mysterious Burmese teacher, the Sayadaw U Thila Wunta, whose face was turned and hidden in shadow. By contrast, the face in this other photo was frontal and with a familiar gaze that seemed to permeate the room. As if he were 'one of the guys' — in disguise as a Tibetan lama. When I asked who it was, a fellow student, looked at me in amazed disbelief and whispered, "Karmapa."

Ananda Bodhi and a small group of students had met His Holiness the Sixteenth Karmapa at his monastery in Sikkim in 1968, two years prior. At some point along the way the Bhikkhu had, at a special moment, said that he would grant every student one wish. So they all thought deeply and seriously and came up with very fine wishes such as Enlightenment, Wisdom, an end to suffering, and so on. One student said all he wanted was a pink Cadillac.

As we were about to leave Rinpoche's house after the class that evening, heading for the curb and the student's pink Cadillac, Rinpoche asked me if I'd signed up for the trip.

"Umm, no," I replied.

He seemed taken aback, and considered this peculiar response for a moment before boring into me with what felt like more than a suggestion: "You — are — going — to — INDIA!"

"Uh, well, okay," I said, shrugging.

Several months later, I was on my way. To get money, I'd landed a miserable job as a mail-room junior, a long commute away in a drug and chemical factory, but found how to make it interesting by tracking the outward flow of mail and comparing it with the lunar cycle. (The mail peaked just after the full moon.) By August, I was sleeping on the floor of the Karmapa's monastery.

'Spiritual' means free-moving. Evolution is on about greater complexity. The development of consciousness is part of this.

Namgyal Rinpoche, Toronto, 1971.

The Feeling of Enlightenment (Toronto, 1970) *Byron Stevens*

It was a typical grey and timeless Toronto day that could have been summer, winter, spring, or fall. The class was held on a weekday morning in the front room of Ananda Bodhi's house on Palmerston Boulevard.

He was in a relaxed and jovial mood and announced that since it was such a grey day we would abandon the usual format and he would just take questions. The mood in the room was informal, spontaneous and light. We were all enjoying it. Cecilie, a long time student, put up her hand.

The teacher, with a gleam in his eye and glance over the top of the perpetual coffee mug said, "Yyyeeesss?" in that long drawn-out and mischievous way that immediately set us all to laughing and to silently congratulating ourselves on not being the one who put up her hand.

Cecilie, unruffled, asked, "Sir, what does it feel like to be enlightened?"

Sitting in the back of the room, I thought. "What kind of question is that?" I would not dare ask such a question knowing too well what usually results: the not so esoteric teaching on the form and function of the flying coffee mug of awakening!

Expecting quick retribution from the Bhikkhu, I was surprised to see from his face and manner that he was actually going to answer the question!

I looked at the students around me. We are all on the edge of our cushions with anticipation. "I can't believe it! He's actually going to tell us what it's like? Oh my god!"

"Well, it's like . . ." (long pause.) It's like . . ." he look upward as if searching for the right words.

There was total silence and full concentration from everyone in the room. "It's like . . ."

I couldn't take it any more — please tell us!

"Naaahhh! It's no good. I can't tell you. It would be impossible and would lead you astray from the path!" said the Teacher.

The whole room erupted in disappointment and release of pent-up expectations: a chorus of. "Please Sir, please." Pleading, laughing and pleading again! This was fun in a fish-on-a-line sort of way.

Rinpoche smiled, pretending to drink his coffee while observing the pandemonium.

When calm was restored, Cecilie, undaunted, asked a second time. "Please Honourable Sir; what does it feel like to be enlightened?"

He immediately replied that it was no good and the look on his face indicated that it was over.

Then, just as we were all reconciling to having to take the usual path of work to discover what enlightenment feels like, he relented and looking at the ceiling said, "Well maybe, maybe if . . . " and paused long enough to make sure the hook was well and truly set.

Again the room was as silent and intense as if our lives depended on the next utterance.

"Well it's like, hmmm, like . . . Naahh! Can't do it! It would lead you all astray. No words can even come close. Anything I say would be so far off the mark that it would interfere with your awakening."

He laughed hard now.

The chorus was loud and desperate and we were on the hook and unable to let go. "Please Sir! Oh please, pretty please!"

Cecilie, unbelievably for the third time asked, "Oh please Most Noble and Honourable Teacher — what does it feel like to be enlightened?"

Now nearly collapsed from laughter, hope and disappointment, I looked at his face and vaguely remembered something about asking a teacher three times, but had no hope we would get anything but a playful response.

"Well it's like . . ." (Here we go again.)

"It's like . . ." he looked serious this time. Could it be?

The Bhikkhu, very thoughtful and with deliberate delivery, said:

"It's like you have one foot on solid rock . . .

                                    . . . and the other foot over the abyss."

It struck me like a massive thunderbolt and I'm happy to say I've never recovered.

A mystic, experiencing the transcendental, is in the experience of utter beauty and complete fear. How could you not have seen the all pervasive intelligence and sense a connection to it? Its light on your life makes you feel like a miserable beggar. We are fake, caught in a pretense. In a way we are forced to be this way since worldly affairs and the like are all not real.

Namgyal Rinpoche, Dharma Centre of Canada, 1993.

Meant to Be (Trip to India, 1971) *Peter Dederichs*

I was on the second India trip in 1971. My mother told me Rinpoche asked her whether she was going to join him and the group. When she said no, there was no way she could afford it, the Rinpoche asked how much she could afford for the boat trip and seeing her hesitate he asked if she could come up with $300 for the two of us and of course she said yes. The rest was provided.

This was an incredible gift and the funny thing is, when we got on the ship we ended up with a first class cabin and my mother overheard other people grumbling that there must have been some mistake. They paid for first class but got third class.

It was pure teaching all the way with Namgyal and I am very fortunate and honoured.

The Soccer Game (Spain to India, 1971) *Henri van Bentum*

Ananda Bodhi was a mirror par excellence. On one occasion he broke through my overly enthusiastic emotional state which, as usual, was a waste of energy. We were playing table soccer on deck.

During these games one tends to become very involved, as I would, shouting excitedly at every move. In the middle of the game with him, I was all keyed up, hollering this and that.

Then he started mimicking me, in the very same voice, until I suddenly noticed that it was 'me.'

I calmed down after that and put a little more awareness and less emotion into the game and even scored some goals!

Rather than coming into contact with their feelings, there are beings who like to dramatize everything, who would rather be on stage than watch the stages of the human being. But in order to open your eyes, you will have to shut your mouths.

Body, Speech & Mind, a manual for human development, Kinmount, Bodhi Publishing, 2004, p. 355. Used with permission from Bodhi Publishing.

The Marrakesh Express (Morocco, June, 1971) *Rab Wilkie*

Six passengers recovering from shock stood on the dock in Casablanca. Their cruise ship was drifting away, its gangway withdrawn. Could they get back on? A portal at dock level was open and Henri stood grinning in the opening. Beside him, hand stretched out stood Sonam. But the captain, not so happy, lurked nearby and drew back into the shadow.

The gap between dockside and ship was only a yard or so, but the distance was rapidly increasing. Henri shouted above the grumble of the ship's engines, "Hand me your crutches" then, after taking them, stretched out his long arm to grasp the hand of the first victim, Rochelle. It looked easy. She was small and light. And the dusk was kind — one hardly noticed her bandaged forehead and blood-stained robe —

Several months earlier, after Ananda Bodhi showed his collection of diamonds to several guests, me among them, I'd walked up the steps into the MacMillan Planetarium in Toronto. I wasn't really searching for the Philosopher's Stone, I told myself, or even an 'Agni Mani' ('fire jewel') but that's what I found — a dark olive-green tektite.

Did the sellers know what a steal this was? Hard rain from heaven that responded to fate, that lit up from within when danger was near, or glowed when a wish was to be granted. Or maybe they thought this only a folk-tale? I had it set in a silver ring that I wore into Africa.

The passenger ship, *Asia*, Italian owned and manned — by robust young seamen with evening guitars — was late in leaving Barcelona and darkness had fallen as we sailed past the Pillars of Hercules, the myriad lights of Gibraltar glowing to starboard.

There were over seventy of us on board, on a passage to India, taking advantage of a group rate negotiated in Toronto: $250 each for a month's voyage around Africa. The Suez Canal was still closed from the 1967 Six-Day War between the Israelis and their Egyptian, Syrian and Jordanian neighbours.

Beyond lay the great unknown of the open ocean. Venture if you dare from the familiar limits of the Middle Sea. How far to the world's edge and to falling off, seduced by deep-sea monsters?

"Do you realise what this means?" I nudged my deck companions, trying to encourage some awe and wonder, drawing on ancient myths, met by puzzlement. Then another tack: "This is the night of the Great Opposition! It has been twenty years since Jupiter and Saturn last aligned like this across the zodiac. We are sailing now past the Point Of No Return."

When the *Asia* put in at Casablanca, it was behind schedule by several days so the layover was shortened. Instead of an all-day exploration of the city, passengers had to be back by noon or be left behind.

No problem, we thought, as we rented a small Renault, squeezed six of us in and, aiming inland for Marrakesh, zipped out of the city on a good highway. The distance was 136 miles - a couple of hours each way would get us back in time.

"That's not much time to shop," one woman protested. "I want to buy some real leather sandals." Shopping hadn't occurred to me — I just wanted to visit the Kasbah and find a cafe crowded with French Legionnaires, belly dancers and spies.

"Sandals! You could buy them right here in Casablanca. You don't need to go to Marrakesh for that," I observed.

"Silly. This is a port city. Everything will cost a lot less away from here."

Aah, the indisputable logic of a seasoned shopper. Can't argue with that; and off we went. Our friend driving was delighted to be going — anywhere, leaving potential arguments in the dust.

We rushed about. Finally, after haggling deals for rough cotton robes and leather sandals in the marketplace, it was past time for leaving. We'd have to push to get back to Casablanca before the ship sailed.

As we ran to the car, I happened to glance at my silver ring with the tektite and noticed a dull red lustre. A warning of danger, according to the legend I'd heard about such *Agni Mani* stones. It's reflecting the sun, I thought, and hurried on.

There was no speed limit sign on the highway and we seemed to be making good time. The gauge read 70 mph soon after we rounded the bend out of Marrakesh and drove coastward. In the distance, to our right, a small green truck stopped at a highway intersection. As we sped towards it, someone in the back seat wondered out loud if Moroccan road rules included right-of-way.

Apparently so — wasn't the truck waiting for us to pass? Apparently not.

The truck suddenly pulled out in front of us and with a glancing crash our car was tumbled into the ditch on the opposite side of the road. The two passengers in front, sitting beside the driver, felt the full impact of the collision and as their door swung open, they were flung out and sent rolling together down the middle of the highway.

I grabbed a woman in mid-air to protect her back before we hit asphalt. As we uncurled from our beaten dyad as a human cannon ball, I had a very sore rump and I saw that her head was scraped and bleeding, but otherwise she seemed all right. There were no broken bones and she was talking — between groans.

We stumbled over to the wrecked car to see how our four friends were. Aside from shock and bruises, they'd survived intact. The Arab truck driver was worried and doting and somehow, within minutes, an ambulance showed up and took us to a clinic.

Three of us needed stitches — the woman's head and my back for sure — and since our clothes were in shreds, we donned our new ankle-length djelabahs. With the help of crutches, we became mobile but as we thanked the clinic staff we realized that a more terrifying fate loomed.

What time was it?! When was the ship sailing? — in ten minutes and we were still two hours from port. One student, the least scathed, succeeded in contacting the ship's captain. "Sorry guys, we've missed the boat. They're sailing without us. The captain says we can fly to Cape Town and get back on there."

Right. As if we could afford that. Some of us had barely enough, (or not enough,) to spend during our planned month in India. Our driver phoned the ship again, asked to get word through to the Bhikkhu, and got his point man on the line.

"Sorry, the Teacher says there's nothing he can do. The captain has his schedule and hundreds of other passengers to think about."

We were shocked and stunned and starting to bleed through our djelabahs. We were at a loss, totally. Stranded for life — abandoned. After a few minutes, the clinic phone rang. It was Rinpoche's assistant. "The captain will wait for two hours. If you're not here by 5pm, that's too bad. He's sailing on the dot."

We hooted and hugged each other and the staff in incredulous celebration then realized we no longer had a car. Quick! Call a taxi! How do you say 'faster' in Arabic?

It was almost dark as we finally reached the dockyard entrance and maybe we were too late. The gate was closed and guarded. Our cabbie drove up to the guardhouse and spoke with the armed official.

"Sorry, docks closed at night," and our cabbie began to drive away. Ah, this driver is not trying hard enough. We MUST get to the ship!

Having persuaded our driver to try again, he circled back around and this time claimed victory. The gates creaked open and we raced through — discovering that these were pretty big dockyards and we didn't know where we were going.

Then at the far end we spied familiar tan-coloured funnels. "That's the *Asia*. It has to be!" Bob in the back seat whacked our driver's shoulder and, pointing at the funnels, yelled, "Go! Go!" And off we sped — suddenly downward on a dry-dock ramp heading for water.

Screech! Oops, wrong way.

The ship's clinic was a dungeon deep in the bowels of the vessel. Engines thumped as we steamed away from the African coast. The ship's doctor was a sadist and not often sober. Gloating, he told us that we'd each need a tetanus shot and gleefully prepared his long needle.

Afterwards, feeling stung and drowsy after the day's ordeal, a distant part of me was amused and grateful for the captain who entered the room that evening with a chocolate cake and a bottle of rum. For this, we happily sat up in our cots. This was good.

Until then we thought that the captain bore us a grudge. And why not? We'd delayed his vessel's departure by several hours. We'd had our shots, rum and cake and lay on our cots unable to sleep. It was late when the doctor announced that we had visitors. The Bhikkhu walked in to see 'the patients.'

The Bhikkhu was very sympathetic, especially about what had greeted us when we had hobbled to shipside. Our Economy Class friends, arrayed on the lower deck, were cheering, but the blue blazered, white-slacked South Africans on the higher decks were jeering — indignant that we'd delayed their departure.

"Never mind," he said. "I've come to tuck you in," and he did so.

The women giggled; Rochelle squealed — and leapt out of bed, while I groaned, eyes to ceiling and Heaven.

Before leaving, Rinpoche turned and said gravely, "You know, some students — will do ANYTHING to get my attention."

. . . beings with two feet have to do things in the correct order. The correct way, the one direct way to liberation from suffering, from Dukkha, is by inculcating awareness in the being, but in a certain blossoming, in a particular order. First is the development of awareness of the body. You must always move from crude to subtle understandings — not that the body is crude, but certainly the way it is perceived by many beings is crude!

Body, Speech & Mind, a manual for human development, Kinmount, Ontario, Bodhi Publishing, 2004, p. 8. Used with permission from Bodhi Publishing.

The Gift (Toronto to India, Summer, 1971) *Peter Dederichs*

Once upon a time there was a little boy and his Good Mother who lived a simple, religious life. She prayed every day and saw her spiritual Teacher as often as she could. She taught her son that praying was good and soon he was praying each day with his mother and she brought him to see and hear the Teacher, the Bhikkhu, who was very wise and respected by the little boy and his Good Mother.

A few years went by and one day the Bhikkhu asked the Good Mother if she would come on a trip across the world to India to see very holy and great teachers, one of them being His Holiness the 16th Karmapa. This was no ordinary trip. It was a journey of spiritual learning, sometimes physically dangerous, sometimes mindfully blissful. The Bhikkhu led the way and the boy and his mother followed with a number of other students.

Finally, after many adventures and teachings, The Bhikkhu and his students were nearing their destination, Sikkim, where one of the highest teachers lived, namely, the Karmapa. The approach through the Himalayan Mountains was incredible. As the students neared they began to hear some beautiful sounds. The closer they got, the clearer the sounds became and they could see what looked to the little boy like a fortress, with monks high atop it blowing very long horns. It sounded like they were greeting lost heroes returning home. Awesome!

The students were greeted by the Karmapa and there were teachings and many blessings. At one of these blessings, the students were lined up in front of the Karmapa. The little boy was about three people away from receiving his blessing when he noticed that everyone else was giving a white scarf or flowers and he did not have anything. He reached into his pocket and pulled out a medallion that he had found along the way. The medallion was worthless really but the little boy treasured it very much and considered it lucky. Since it was the only thing he had to give, he placed it at Karmapa's feet. The Karmapa looked at him and gave a big smile. The little boy felt a little embarrassed but also very warm and good. He knew that he gave from his heart a true gift.

Later on, at the time that students were receiving spiritual names from Karmapa, and when Karmapa recognized the Bhikkhu as a Rinpoche, the Karmapa's personal assistant signaled to the Good Mother and the little boy to come for a personal interview with his Holiness. That's when the Karmapa gave the name Karma Tinley to the little boy.

"But we already have a Karma Tinley," said Sister Palmo, the Karmapa's translator.

"Then this will be the second Karma Tinley," his Holiness replied, smiling.

"And My Blind Eyes See It Not" (Indian Ocean, 1971)
Henri van Bentum

During a month-long voyage around Africa aboard the *Asia* en route to India, Ananda Bodhi devised a daily program of classes, exercises and meditation sessions for his students. Many of these were done on the deck in plain view.

Aboard ship there were also passengers not part of our group. One of them was a rather intense, tall young man in his late twenties. He would often run a few times around the deck each morning or do brisk walking exercises.

On one of these occasions he came across Ananda Bodhi who asked the young man. "Where are you off to when we arrive in India?"

"Oh." he replied, "I am going to seek a guru!"

"Ah, I see," said the Teacher in his most innocent manner.

Later, as we approached Bombay, Ananda Bodhi and I, along with a few other students, were standing at the rail of the ship watching our entry into the muddy brown waters of the harbour. Near us stood the young man.

The Teacher turned to him and said, "Goodbye then, and success with finding a guru."

To which the young man replied enthusiastically, "Thank you, I hope I will."

We never saw him again.

You have to be aware of your body since your body interacts with nature. Remember, there is as much space within your body as without. Experience the vastness of space. Pay attention to Nature around you then turn your attention within. Go into the space within — the Hollow-Body Practice.

By hollowing you are hallowing — like Christ crucified, descending into Hell, purifying and then the resurrection and ascension. You can get the feeling that within this body is the universe. The guru principle is also within.

Namgyal Rinpoche, Dharma Centre of Canada, 1996.

The Darjeeling Demon (India, Summer, 1971) *Russell Rolfe*

Lightning flashed constantly in the distance as our caravan of pilgrims drove towards the foothills of the Himalayas. We didn't have thunderstorms like this back home in Santa Cruz, California. It was the monsoon season and we were on a pilgrimage to Sikkim to see His Holiness Rangjung Rigpe Dorje, the 16th Gyalwa Karmapa, for three days of initiation culminating in the rite of the Vajra Crown.

As we headed into the core of the massive storm, the scintillating entrancement that gave me goose flesh was soon replaced by awe and terror. The bolts were now striking so close to the cars we had hired in Siliguri that I feared the vehicle's electrical system would short out.

And the rain — no, this was way beyond rain — this downpour was like being in a carwash but instead of a smooth concrete track underneath, our little Ambassador car was lurching over a road that was being washed out. Watching the rivulets of water streaming down the glass as we bounced along,

I longed for some covered wayside service station with clean facilities. Not only was it impossible to stop lest we get stuck, but there was also an excellent chance of being struck by lightning. Mud was everywhere. Foundering in deep holes of liquid dirt was almost as nightmarish to me as electrocution.

We had hoped to board the famous toy-train in Sukna that afternoon and puff our way up to Darjeeling for dinner. However, as with so many expectations in India, reality put on the brakes.

When we arrived at the small inn in Sukna late that evening, we were blessedly between thunderstorms. I imagined our Teacher already tucked into Darjeeling's Windermere Hotel cozied up by a nice toasty fire. Our inn was snug, dry and mercifully free of bedbugs.

As it began to rain again I wondered if landslides would put the train out of commission, not to mention the road, and if we would ever get to Darjeeling.

The dawn breathed in the mountain mist which soon burned away. At the train station, I was amazed this tiny engine would take us up to Ghoom, the world's highest station for a steam locomotive.

We were informed it crossed the main road, Hill Cart Road, 177 times with over 500 bridges, four complete loops and six remarkable Z-shaped curves where the train must go backwards at a tortoise-like pace.

Finally we were in Darjeeling. There were Indians but even more Tibetan refugees. Their faces manifested the worry and hardship of a long and dangerous trek into India from their homeland.

My hotel, a relic from the era of the British Raj, assigned me a huge, high-ceilinged suite. I was amazed at how reasonably priced the accommodations were - about the same as overnight car-parking at home.

I soon discovered that it didn't include heat. Attempting to lift the temperature above 14°C by building a fire in the baronial fireplace with damp wood was like dropping a brick into the Grand Canyon to dam up the Colorado.

Someone mentioned a settlement above Darjeeling that was almost entirely Tibetan where one could purchase religious items and artifacts recently brought over the pass by refugees. It was suggested we do our shopping up there since the prices were lower and the money would go directly to the refugees, avoiding the more expensive shops in Darjeeling.

Later that afternoon, I walked up the trail to the village where I became lost in the view of distant and beautiful Mount Kanchenjunga, mystically appearing and dematerializing through cloud windows.

I purchased a rosary, Dorje and bell and a pair of small finger cymbals connected by twine. The cymbals had a high pure tone that lasted almost a minute.

It was getting late and, since this was our first night, there was a meeting of our group to discuss the entry of all 80 of us into Sikkim. I found the track back down to Darjeeling, grateful for the full moon. The trail wound steeply down through dense forest and boulders.

I was walking along, my mind going lickity-split over how exotic it all was, then wondered why there were no houses or even any people on the trail. But how extraordinary and novel this trip was! Was this a forest or a jungle? — It didn't matter. It was so unlike anything I had ever experienced in my native Sierra Nevada Mountains.

Suddenly, a slight hint of fear arose. This certainly wasn't the California foothills and anything could be out there hiding behind that black wall of foliage; even enormous snakes.

At the thought of snakes, I heard a distinct long hiss behind me to my right, coupled with the sound of movement through the undergrowth. Instant panic! As I picked up my pace the hissing became formidable, with the sound of large bushes and branches being shoved aside. Whatever it was, it was big and it wanted me.

I began to run as fast as possible, stepping on rocks and weaving in and out of the boulders. A monstrous black presence now made heavy crashing sounds and its whiffing melded into the sound of something dinosaurian.

The terror was so complete my body took over as I ran flat out down the rough trail through the boulder field as the dark presence loomed larger and I heard a growl that was a force of nature. I was close to tripping and passing out.

Finally I rounded a bend and street lights were just ahead. Relieved, I found myself in the uppermost street of Darjeeling. The nightmarish presence was gone; vanished as if someone pulled a switch. Deeply shaken,

I walked towards the brightest lights of 'downtown' Darjeeling. What animals or reptiles did these hills shelter? Whatever it was it didn't like light or open spaces. I went straight to a hotel where friends were staying and excitedly related my plunge down the mountain. "Oh, you didn't hear?" they asked in amazement. "The Bhikkhu didn't want us to be on that trail after dark. The Rinpoches informed him there was a demon, Maujjung, who lived near the main trail."

The demon manifested and fed on human fear. Since we students had barely started to subdue our fears, he had announced for word to be spread that anyone who ventured up to the village was to return to Darjeeling before sunset or take a taxi the long way around.

Some were dubious but chose to return just before sunset anyway because the light was perfect for photography. My friends now realized that Himalayan demons are not to be taken lightly.

When I told Rinpoche about this he said, "Well if you had turned around and faced it in the natural state of love, it would have instantly dissipated. But nooooooo. You (or what you identified with as you) gave it a nice hearty meal!"

How do we dissolve fear? Dissolve fear by moving ahead, by doing that which one is afraid of. Are you afraid of disease? The solution is walking. Eat, drink and be merry for tomorrow you may live!

If someone has an anxiety attack, give them a drink of water and have them move and do something. Walk, dance, do the Highland Fling! Go to a movie or have a beer. Do! Unparalize!

Namgyal Rinpoche, Dharma Centre of Canada, 2001

Avalanche (India, Summer 1971) *Russell Rolfe*

We learned that our permits to enter Sikkim, so generously secured by the Canadian High Commission, were not going to be accepted. Permits in India can be of dubious value at any time but especially so in 1971 when the country was at war with Pakistan. This necessitated our sending an emissary to Delhi and, through the Commissioner, another request would be made, this time directly to Indira Gandhi.

The group would wait in Darjeeling until new permits were secured, this time from the top. When the phone lines were working, His Holiness the Karmapa was also advised of our delay.

Our anticipation grew as the days wore on. I believe it was over a week but time was compressed as we explored the Tolkeinesque trails with their hidden abandoned relics of the British Raj in the misty forest. One had the sense of immense changes colliding with an ever-reluctant past.

We couldn't imagine being turned back now, especially since the Karmapa, the Black Hat hierarch of Tibet, honored as a Living Buddha in sixteen successive incarnations, was aware of our plight at his doorstep. There was little surprise when the permits came through. What was astonishing was how they were secured.

The Prime Minister, Indira Gandhi, was presented the petition at the behest of the Canadian High Commissioner, James George, but she had little inclination or time to worry about a large group of foreigners in a sensitive border region close to China. There was a war on with Pakistan over Bangladesh and, despite the nearly hysterical political clamour that surrounded her she would, as always, remain in control.

She passed our request on to her Minister of the Interior for his decision. This minister had just had a close relative pass away. He was a Hindu and, as such, was bound by tradition to grant the very first request made to him after the death of a close relative. Our request reached his desk the very day he learned of the death in his family. Death is the essential condition of life and human life consists of mutual service with death.

It took several more days for our large group of Westerners to hire every available four-wheel-drive vehicle in Darjeeling. Then, early one morning, miraculously we were all off at once, a fleet of jeeps that resembled some of the endless military convoys we had seen on their way to the front in West Pakistan.

The 20 kilometers from Darjeeling to the border of Sikkim commenced at a snail's pace. The unpaved road had been severely eroded by the monsoon rains and was being tested beyond its limits by our fifteen vehicles.

We were in the clouds crawling through enormous steep landslides where it seemed there was no track at all, only slanting mushy scree listing off to impenetrable depths on one side. We ground to a halt.

This wasn't just another of the many passport checkpoints though. Many of us, like me, were standing on the back of our Land-Rovers hanging onto the canvas roof frame the better to jump off should the mountain ooze away underneath.

In fact, that is precisely what had occurred just in front. Our drivers were keeping themselves at least 300 yards apart in order to preserve what little remained of the road and not cause a landslide. About 100 yards of road had reverted to steep mountain slope just ahead. We were awe-struck that none of our vehicles had been present when the land gave way.

Now we waited. We could see large rocks coming out of the mists and rolling down back into a cloud — we wondered how far down. I had seen enough Indian mountain roads to know the bottom was very likely a roaring river appearing from our heights as a tiny silver thread.

We got down from our vehicles and began to mill about. It was apparent that we wouldn't be going anywhere soon. Every couple of minutes another boulder came tumbling down across the washed out section, seemingly out of nowhere, and bounced off into the abyss.

Yet another singular occurrence in India is that no matter how remote you may find yourself, people will promptly appear. Our caravan of four-wheel-drives filled with Westerners had a stunning effect on the local population. After the tenth vehicle passed they just stood staring, mouths agape. They had never seen anything like this and were very curious.

With their instinctive entrepreneurial nature, a tea shop appeared in short order. I have no idea where the chai and biscuits came from but there they were just where the road gave way several rovers in front. It was manna from heaven.

I then heard the unmistakable sound of a large piece of equipment being started off in the distance. Soon an enormous bulldozer appeared, coming out of the fog. It was listing fairly heavily down the hill but as the driver worked back and forth the list subsided and he could proceed once again leveling out some semblance of road.

The roads in these mountainous border regions are maintained by the army. Perhaps they had been put on alert knowing we were coming and that the road was perilous?

In less time than I thought possible the driver had graded a track across the gravelly moraine. After several more passes by the dozer, it was safe to proceed.

On closer inspection, it was not a soldier at the controls. No, it was one of our own — putting his experience with heavy equipment to work attacking the scree! He had noticed an abandoned bulldozer nearby with the ignition key still in it, I later learned.

Boulders and rocks continued to come hurtling down between us out of the cloud; any one of them large enough to overthrow a Land Rover and send it crashing down into obscurity and oblivion.

Perhaps I had learned a lesson from my earlier night flight from 'the monster', or perhaps it was the belief that we were now in the realm of the Karmapas and no harm would come to us. There was no fear.

As we pulled into the forecourt of Rumtek monastery, the mists cleared. The light took on the crystalline quality found only at higher elevations in the Andes and Himalayas. Monks were excitedly dashing about finishing their preparations.

We were given the choice of a couple of rooms outside the main assembly hall or sleeping in the hall itself. I chose a shared room that was just off the kitchen and closest to the outside shower.

Others wondered why I would miss the opportunity to sleep in the temple which had never been used as a dormitory. I was told I would miss a rare opportunity to sleep in the presence of hundreds of ages-old sacred Tibetan relics and Buddha rupas.

I just wanted first dibs on the shower.

Break out of rote! Meditators in rote practice are not in real inquiry. Move beyond theory — when you are crossing a busy street you have to deal with the traffic as it is.

Be like a handyman with a bag of tools or like the many handed deities in the thanka paintings and visualizations with different implements in each hand. Develop and use your capacities!

You never know what situation you will come upon. More important, you never know what beings you will meet.

Namgyal Rinpoche, Dharma Centre of Canada, 2001.

My Inner Purity (India, Summer, 1971) *Russell Rolfe*

Travelling with Ananda Bodhi, we were the first large group of Westerners to be given the initiations and teachings we received at Rumtek in India. It was the beginning of the transfer and preservation of what had previously been secret Tibetan rituals. It was all so strange and exotic; clouds of juniper incense, hundreds of small oil lamps, peculiar deities framed in silk hanging from intricately decorated ceiling rafters, multicolored umbrellas and banners.

One whole wall was a great glass case filled with what appeared to be boxes covered with yellow and maroon cloth. At first I thought these held the ashes of departed lamas but soon learned they were sacred texts recently brought out of Tibet. The monastery, though completed several years before our visit, seemed as if it had been there forever.

In the morning we were to experience the special ceremony of the Vajra Crown. Our teacher, Ananda Bodhi, had told us about this magical black hat ceremony on board the ship to India.

From my notes I re-read that the crown was presented to the Fifth Karmapa by the Chinese Emperor Tai Ming Chen. Its origin goes back to very ancient times, when the Bodhisattva Avalokiteshvara received it from other Enlightened Ones. It was said to be made out of the hair of 10,000 Dakinis or goddesses.

The Karmapas are an emanation of Avalokiteshvara and custodians of this black and gold Crown, the mere sight of which is believed to ensure Liberation within one lifetime.

There was no way I could enter the temple for this sacred event in everyday travel attire. For this very day I had saved a white outfit: shirt, pants, socks sealed in hotel laundry plastic in a separate zippered compartment of my suitcase. I had even saved a pair of white tennis shoes. However, I discovered they were not as pristine as the rest of my turnout and much time was required meticulously scrubbing off every visible earthy blemish.

Finally I was showered and dressed. I stood in the grimy kitchen whose stoves consisted of petrol drums with fuel-holes cut out of their side for the dung patties. The yak dung chips were stored just outside the door.

There was a little shiver of excitement and pleasure standing in the squalid kitchen as I anticipated entering the assembly hall in spotless whiteness, a true manifestation of my inner purity.

Amidst all my grooming, I had lost track of time. How long ago now had I heard those long Tibetan horns? I dashed outside and saw only a few monks wandering over to the men's toilet.

My God, it had already started and everyone was already inside! And now I had to go to the bathroom.

I rushed to the men's facilities just outside the courtyard wall. Well, to be honest, they weren't really facilities but simply a dirt-floor room with a trench cut out next to the wall. The trench was filled with the offal of the entire monastery.

I decided to squat. If I relieved myself standing, it was certain to splash on my undefiled whiteness. The trench was about a foot from the wall, which required placing one foot on the ledge to straddle the trough. I very carefully balanced myself, not wanting to touch the wall or anything in that room. The ledge was slick, compacted mud.

My left foot suddenly slipped off the ledge and before I had a chance to dig into the wall with my fingernails in a futile attempt to keep upright, I was in the trough, literally floating on my back in human waste. I lay there, frozen in shock as two monks turned to see what had caused such an enormous splash. I must have presented the most bizarre sight they had ever seen — a Westerner, dressed all in white to make himself whiter, lying on his back in a deep trough of dark excrement.

They convulsed with stifled laughter, running out before they had finished, peeing on their own robes as they ran.

I climbed out on all fours in a state of complete stupefaction. Could this really be happening? This was no time for paralysis. I ran back towards the kitchen to a waste-fire burning in a petrol drum, undressing and throwing in my clothes. I chuckled to myself as I bolted naked back into my room.

This was like one of those dreams where you find yourself publicly exposed without any clothes.

As I threw on the Levis and travel clothes that everyone else would be wearing I thought this was the authentic self, without the urge to establish a persona at odds with reality. Finally I realized that all this preoccupation with clothing was pretension, a weakness for worldly display.

As I entered the assembly hall, His Holiness the 16th Karmapa looked up and gave me a sublime warm smile as I slunk to my seat.

You must do the inner work first. You can't get sight by viewing only the outside. You must view what is doing the viewing.

Namgyal Rinpoche, Dharma Centre of Canada, 1998.

Enthronement at Green River (October, 1971) *Rab Wilkie*

The evening air was crisp and cool and the stone path covered with fallen leaves as we walked past a barn to the house, looming white amidst great dark trees. For some students, after another summer adventure, this time dodging bolts of blue lightning in the monsoon drenched foothills of the Himalayas, the occasion felt like a quiet afterthought.

Of the 108 pilgrims gathered at McLeod Ganj in July to meet the Dalai Lama and of the 80 who then jeeped the avalanched mountains beyond Kalimpong into Sikkim to visit Rumtek Monastery, most had returned to Toronto by various routes from mid August to September. Others had dispersed to other parts of Canada, the United States and Europe. Our Teacher came back in October and classes began at his house on Palmerston Boulevard. By then we were scattered about the city, looking for work and dwellings, staying with friends or friends of friends.

Then word went around that there would be an enthronement, according to tradition, at a country house in the hamlet of Green River. The Venerable Ananda Bodhi had been recognised by His Holiness the 16th Gyalwa Karmapa as a Rinpoche and had received a Tibetan name. The crowd was large and the living-room small, but it wasn't a long ceremony that began after dusk, with candles glowing.

The new maroon-robed Rinpoche sat on a simple wooden chair, Western style, while Karma Thinley Rinpoche conducted the ceremony sitting on a carpet in front of him. He was the only other lama present. Tibetan Rinpoches in Canada were few in those days and Karma Thinley was the only one we knew. He arrived the previous March with the first contingent of refugees to settle in Canada. Several of us from the Dharma Centre greeted them at the airport, after which they were cordially welcomed by our Teacher and other students at the Centre's retreat property. Karma Thinley's ritual and chanting was followed by an Amitabha puja and meditation. The warmth was deep and all-pervading.

Afterwards, Rinpoche joked about getting "off the throne" and "getting on with it," as if this had been mere protocol. Yet we all knew we had participated, however briefly, in an historical event — the installment in the West of the first Western Rinpoche.

The ideal relationship to the Teacher is based on friendship not on awe.

Namgyal Rinpoche, Teaching Dharma, Dharma Centre of Canada, 2003.

Memory Test (Indian Ocean, 1973) *Lisa Elander (Adamson)*

On a voyage between Bombay and Mombasa I was called out of bed one night to form a fourth for a game of bridge. I did not want to play, feeling tired and not at all bright. Rinpoche sat to my right and I was playing the hand.

I had taken three tricks, when suddenly Rinpoche covered my tricks with his left hand and moved them over to his right side, saying, "What are you doing with my tricks!"

Knowing that now I was in for it, and feeling everything reeling, I replied, "Those are my tricks, sir!"

"They are not!" he said.

Immediately, I knew I could have them back, if I could tell him what was in each trick and what card I had taken it with.

However, my mind turned to soup and I simply wished that I had stayed in bed. Leaving my tricks with him, I played two more hands.

When he saw that I was not going to engage with him, he pushed the tricks back to my side, saying disgustedly, "Then keep your tricks!"

What did I learn? That my mind was in no way clear under pressure.

You are beginning to attend to detail, to identify phenomena and individual species. Remember as much as you can of what you notice.

As you make clearer distinctions, become more aware of how the many different forms relate to each other — how the species interact as the whole community of the coral reef — as an ecosystem. Notice how you are related to it.

Awareness naturally expands into greater detail and onto more levels.

Namgyal Rinpoche, Dive Ship near Komodo, Indonesia, 1997

The Money Tree (Toronto 1972, Japan, 1973) *Heather Rigby*

It was 1973 when I arrived to study Rinzai Zen for the year at Ryosenan Temple in Kyoto, Japan. Following a flight from Toronto to Tokyo and a ride on the rapid train, I met my close friend and fellow student of Namgyal Rinpoche, Nobuo Kubota. Nobuo was preparing to leave following a year's study with his teacher Nanrei Kobori. My timing was perfect as upon arrival I was introduced to Kobori Sensei just as a small group was beginning to study the *Shinjinmei*.

> *"The Perfect way knows no difficulties*
> *Except that it refuses to make preferences;*
> *Only when freed from hate and love,*
> *Does it reveal itself fully and without disguise?*
> *A tenth of an inch difference*
>   *and heaven and earth are set apart;*
> *If you wish to see it before your own eyes,*
> *Have no fixed thoughts either for or against it."*

Hsin-hsin Ming (Japanese: *Shinjinmei*) — *On Believing in Mind*, by Seng-Ts'an, (Sōsan) 7th century Third Chan (Zen) Patriarch

The above verse is the beginning text from the *Shinjinmei* — *On Believing in Mind*, a lengthy poem I studied each Sunday for the duration of my stay. Below is a short story of how I miraculously arrived in Japan from Toronto through the generosity of a simple gesture by my Root Guru, Namgyal Rinpoche.

In 1972, I was offered an interesting full-time job in an animation house working as an artist in the production end of making animated commercials.

At the same time eight friends, students of Namgyal Rinpoche were beginning a three-month retreat in the west-end home of one of the students. I found myself pulled in two directions: one was to continue to survive in the *Relative* world of making a living and the other was to explore the *Absolute* through a more contemplative life.

I harboured a deep longing to join the group on the hill at Ellis Avenue. In an appointment with Namgyal Rinpoche, one sunny winter day at his home, this dilemma was resolved. As I explained my job offer and deep longing, Rinpoche suggested we drive over to meet with 'the meditators' to see if there was any 'room at the inn.'

Before I knew it I was moving in and having my head shaved! A short time later I took my Samanera vows and went into retreat for three months.

The first two months were spent at the Ellis Avenue Vihara with eight other practitioners. We began with intense Kasina work — focusing on a mandala — followed by Vipassana or insight meditation.

For the last month, the nuns traveled to the Dharma Centre in early spring, practising pure Insight in the forest cabins. At the close of our retreat many Dharma Centre members gathered around our beloved teacher in the Main House for informal teachings.

He requested that someone bring a large tree branch into the house. The notion of the nuns traveling to the East had been initiated by one of the female students and encouraged by our teacher. (I had an interest in Japan and knew that Nobuo was getting ready to leave.)

As we gathered at his feet, Rinpoche spoke about Dana (generosity.) To my utter surprise, at the end of his talk this small cluster of students had donated hundreds of dollars in money and pledges which were hung on the tree to help support our trip. The beautiful looking branch, once bare, now glistened with the prospect of travel and deepening our explorations in meditation practice.

This was a truly magical time for us all. When I reflect on this auspicious day, I recall Rinpoche's luminous laughter and presence radiating into everyone in the room. As the pledges continued to flow in during the following days, a new level of understanding about the power of Sangha (community) began to open my heart.

I remember Japan and sitting in the candle-lit zendo with the Ancients in the evening spring rain. I can still hear the sound of the shinei (wooden sword) as it hit my shoulders. I vividly recall another windy day when I swept leaves off ancient moss in the graveyard next to the temple.

Of course as I am much older now, my legs sometimes remind me of the grueling five-day *sesshins* — touching the heart-mind through walking, sitting and chanting meditations that 'the four nuns' participated in at the temple on the mountainside.

These are mementos of a pivotal experience Namgyal Rinpoche initiated through his generosity. He took any opportunity to work toward the awakening of all beings.

Out of this experience and many others I continue to unfold into the wisdom that generosity isn't just about giving but is also about being able to receive.

For this I am grateful.

A Lesson in Love (Mexico 1973) *Peter Boag*

We were the lucky four. Chosen from the whole group to ride with Rinpoche up the coast from Mexico to Vancouver, we were indeed fortunate, but also very mistaken in thinking we were in for a joy ride.

One by one Rinpoche engaged us and systematically left our egos in tatters. There was no escape from that station wagon. We were all frantically searching for a chance to show him that his lessons were not lost on us — that we were great little Buddhists. Maybe then he'd go a little easier on us.

That chance came when we stopped at a small market town for a quick rest stop. Just before ordering us all back into the car, Rinpoche pointed out a vendor who was selling parrots in rough wire cages.

"Let's buy one and set it free in the countryside!" someone said, echoing all our thoughts.

Rinpoche, after ensuring that the added cargo in back would not impede his leg-room up front, agreed. Night was falling and Rinpoche rarely liked to travel at night, which demonstrated to us the importance of our rescue mission.

We drove into the night, until Rinpoche motioned to pull over at an overgrown papaya plantation. "This seems to approximate the natural environment of that bird, don't you think?" he asked.

We all agreed and soon we were gathered part way up the grove, standing beside the cage.

"Ok, let him out," Rinpoche ordered.

The bird slowly hobbled from the cage and tried to flap his wings. It tried again and again but it could not fly. Its wings had been clipped. The parrot just hobbled around in small circles. There was a big problem with our plan!

Somebody grabbed the bird and was about to put it back in the cage.

"What do you think you are doing?" Rinpoche boomed in a fierce voice.

"But Sir, the bird can't fly and the predators will get it for sure," came the timid reply. All our heads nodded in agreement. After all, we were here to exercise compassion, weren't we?

Another voice tried to say, "We could give it back to the vendor. At least it will be fed and kept alive that way."

Rinpoche crushed those words in mid air. "How dare you lay your fear trip on this creature!" he thundered. "The bird finally has a chance at freedom, to let his life take its proper course!"

Rinpoche's voice was getting even louder. "Have I wasted my time, have I taught you lot nothing?"

There was a momentary silence as we all shook in our boots.

Rinpoche resumed, this time with a voice so primal, so savage, that time seemed suspended. "If I had to trade places with you lot or that bird, I'd choose the bird! At least he is free, if only for one night! You lot are prisoners of your fear, your comforts, your 'pretty' illusions!"

"You hear me? I would rather be that bird than you!"

There was no way that Rinpoche's voice could have gotten any louder, so at this point his tone changed. His words cut, his words tore, his words chewed — his words clawed through whatever hasty ego defenses we were trying to erect against this onslaught.

"Freedom! Have I not been teaching you about freedom — the infinite potential of a single moment of liberation? Who the hell do you think you are? Who the hell do you think I am?"

"Have you not been paying any attention at all, or were you just looking for some pretty fluff to protect you from your own illusions that love has to be nice? That your lives are nice? That you understand anything at all?" Rinpoche was stamping his foot, just to make sure we got it.

We were devastated, crushed, speechless, shaken. We could not move.

Rinpoche waited in silence till at least one of us got the point and could show it by heading back to the car. One by one the others followed, leaving the bird flapping around in the dark grove.

Nothing further was said. Nothing needed to be said. Only the wild sounds of nature, the rushing of a nearby creek and the light of a million stars remained.

As we drove off, even the reflections of those stars were swept away by the rushing water, leaving only the scene illuminated by the inherent light of our own minds, or darkened by our own fears.

It was our choice . . .

This practice is difficult or unusual — but you need the universal.

Namgyal Rinpoche, Dharma Centre of Canada, 2001.

The Rolling Rinpoche Gathers No Dross (North Africa, 1974) *Melodie Massey*

A student who knew Namgyal Rinpoche only by attending his classes in the city, never having accompanied him on one of his 'field-trips,' might have thought him to be a sedentary monk, very knowledgeable, but rarely active in a physical sense.

After all, he had spent most of his adult years in monasteries then teaching, often in quiet retreats, and even when travelling around the city he was chauffeured because he did not have a driver's license.

The farthest he walked, it seemed, was half a block from a car to the place of a class or talk.

So, as such an urban student, and verging on elderly at that, I had a few surprises in store when I agreed to travel to Africa — the first surprise being that he'd even suggest that I go on a drive across the Sahara Desert!

During the trip Rinpoche decided to learn to drive. Terry took him down to a flat part of the desert where we had spent the night, so there was nothing to crash into.

Later that day, as we stood atop a dune surveying the endless sea of sand, Rinpoche suddenly crouched, curled into a ball and rolled to the bottom. He was amazing. He virtually flew all the way down.

Each of us tried but could not roll the way Rinpoche did. Even Terry, who was much younger, was nothing like Rinpoche who was so unbelievably flexible.

Sitting here now at the age of 86 so many things pop into the mind — surprising experiences that became wonder-full! However the most wonderful experience of all is that there is no separation from Rinpoche.

I continually feel blessed to have such marvellous beings in my life that guided and are a part of this incarnation.

I pray the next time around, the formation I call 'I' can be of benefit to more beings.

The play of universal consciousness has infinite manifestations. If you try to make any of the phenomena permanent, you have suffering.

Namgyal Rinpoche, Dharma Centre of Canada, 1993.

Faith in Empty (Morocco, 1973) *Lisa Elander (Adamson)*

I was to drive Rinpoche to Agadir from Casablanca and was late leaving in the morning. One of my daughters was sick so I decided to take her with me.

I knew the gas tank in the van was almost entirely empty but I decided to pick up Rinpoche first then fill up. That was the wrong decision (or the right one!)

When I arrived Rinpoche chastised me for being late. When I said we had to stop for gas, he said that he had no time for that; I was just to drive on. I objected and was instantly shut down.

So we started to drive, with my mind very much on the gas gauge which was dead on empty. On the highway, I saw what seemed to be a gas station and started to swerve in.

This time, he howled at me. "Drive on, have you no faith!"

I really couldn't answer him, because I did have faith that he could get us there. What I did not have faith in however was the possibility that he would simply allow us to run out of gas, step out of the van himself and flag down a large Mercedes, leaving me with a child and an out-of-gas car on a highway in Morocco. This was not possible to give voice to.

We did however arrive in Agadir, drew up to his hotel and he got out and very sweetly said, "I hope you make it to a gas station!"

There was one next to the hotel and I made it. The gas tank was totally empty.

I don't believe in the transcendental as something you fall into a trance to experience, leaving your body to fall wherever it will. This world IS your home and the transcendental is not elsewhere. You ought to believe more in the reality that life is created by evolution. It is actually much simpler to fulfill the spiritual life than many of you make it out to be. This is not poetic; this is the actuality.

Paleochora Discourses, Part I Exploring the Language of Liberation, Part II Healing, Faith and Karma, Kinmount, Bodhi Publishing, 2009, p. 23. Used with permission from Bodhi Publishing.

The Unexpected Gift (Haliburton, 1974)
Karma Chime Wongmo

In the autumn of 1974, Namgyal Rinpoche led a series of retreats at Deer Lodge in the Haliburton area, where the large number of people could be accommodated. The retreats began with the Women's Week, followed by the Men's Week, the Family Week and lastly, a retreat on *Mahamudra*.

At the conclusion of the first retreat, Rinpoche announced he would give a talk that evening which those of us who hadn't left yet could attend, along with those who were arriving for the retreat starting the next morning. Just before dinner I noticed one of the new arrivals go in to see Rinpoche and caught a glimpse of a gift in hand.

"Was that a Kewpie doll?" I asked myself, somewhat incredulous. We were aware of Rinpoche's wonderful sense of humour — and the lengths to which some students would go to amuse him — but bringing him *a Kewpie doll?* Good grief! Designed to resemble a 'cute' chubby child complete with a tummy that stuck out, a single shock of hair atop its head, an impish smile and a twinkle in its eyes, the Kewpie doll epitomized all that was supposedly 'adorable.' Various versions had been around for decades but in the 70s they were mostly remembered as a prize awarded at carnival games. Thankfully, and by choice, my life had managed to stay free of direct contact with one. Until that evening . . .

After dinner we gathered in the lounge, only partly illumined by the light of a single floor lamp placed by the comfortable armchair Rinpoche would sit in when teaching — the forty students sitting on the carpet barely discernible in the soft shadows beyond the lamp light. There was an expectant silence as we waited for him to appear.

As Rinpoche approached we rose to respectfully greet him. As he entered and walked past the students standing nearest the door, a sudden burst of laughter erupted and quickly rippled through the room as he made his way into our midst. The cause of the laughter became evident. There, in one of Rinpoche's arms, was — *the Kewpie doll!* Obviously enjoying himself he sat down and placed the doll in his lap so that it stood directly facing him.

While he waited for everybody to finish paying their respects and sit back down, the rest of us looked it over. Because I was sitting back and to the side of Rinpoche, I had a good view of him and a really good view of the Kewpie doll.

This doll was quite unlike any I had ever seen before. While it definitely had all the attributes of the Kewpie genre, this one had several more. It was much larger (at least two feet tall) and free-standing. Its balloon-like hollow-body was made of soft, yet firm, translucent material to which the lamp light gave a radiant glow seeming to magnify its size and enhance its other features giving it, I admit, a surprisingly captivating charm. If this weren't enough, an additional and quite remarkable distinction would soon reveal its magic.

When everyone was settled we joined with Rinpoche in chanting the traditional ancient Pali verses of Homage. Then, after a brief pause while calmly surveying those present, he began his talk. I can't recall the words of that evening's discourse; but to this day I clearly remember what it was about and how it unfolded.

The first several minutes were devoted to an overview of the teaching of the path of liberation and the aspiration necessary for awakening. Rinpoche soon followed this by pointing out — as he occasionally did — one of our shortcomings on the path. On these occasions we had learned to listen to what he was saying while trying our best to maintain whatever equanimity we could muster. If what he said struck a chord or pushed a button that caused us discomfort in any way, we definitely knew what we had to let go of and what we had to learn.

This evening, however, he added an unexpected dimension to make his point. Having brought one of our shortcomings to our attention, he suddenly punctuated it with a swift fisticuff to the Kewpie doll's solar plexus! *BOP!* Back down and away from him rocked the doll on to its back!

To our further amazement — and delight — the Kewpie doll immediately rocked back up and faced Rinpoche again as quickly as it had been knocked down! Still smiling impishly, eyes a-twinkle, hair tuft securely in place and body all aglow . . . as if nothing at all had happened. Its hidden attribute now gloriously revealed: un-stay-down-able-ness, made possible by a weight cleverly positioned within the base of its feet.

When the laughter subsided, Rinpoche went on to point out yet another of our faults, again punctuating it with a quick deft clip to the Kewpie doll's midriff — *BOP!*

Back down it went again . . . and back up it rose to face him again. This time the laughter was a bit quieter and subsided more quickly. It didn't take us long to recognize that not only was the Kewpie doll our innocent stand-in; it was also this evening's scapegoat for our shortcomings on the path. And so the discourse continued. Rinpoche, with the perfect skill and means of a master, patiently enumerating:

our sins — BOP*!*

our faults — *BOP!*

our failings — *BOP!*

our lacks — *BOP!*

our dullness — *BOP!*

our missing the mark — *BOP!*

On and on and on — BOP! BOP! BOP! BOP! BOP!

Each noted shortcoming punctuated with a well-placed jab to the solar plexus — *BOP!* — and the Kewpie doll was knocked back and down, again and again and again. And, without fail, immediately came popping back up, again and again and again and again — still smiling impishly, eyes still a-twinkle, tuft still in place and still insouciantly, translucently aglow.

With each named fault, each *BOP!* each time Rinpoche knocked the Kewpie doll down and away from him — it popped back up to face him again. We continued to listen and watch . . . with amusement, yes, but more and more we listened and watched in silence . . . wonder . . . suspense . . . and question: Where was this going?

What would be the final punch line? Would it . . . ? How . . . ? . . . . ?

And we gradually let it go, dissolved at last into unformed, unspoken question: openness beyond words or thought.

At that moment of deep, expansive silence — just as the Kewpie doll was rising back up one more time — swifter than the blink of a twinkling eye Rinpoche reached out and gathered it into his arms and, settling back into the armchair, completely and lovingly embraced it firmly to his heart — while silently, radiantly, beaming over its shoulder at all of us . . .

In the palpable fullness of that unexpected, engulfing beyond-words-gesture, we were all transported, transformed by pure, naked love demonstrating beyond any doubt the truth of where we were and always are: in the indescribable, unconditional, unborn and undying boundless adamantine grace of the lama — and a Kewpie doll.

If you don't have an impossible task you're an impossible human being. Every being should attempt what is impossible, what is beyond them. Supreme Awakening?

. . . As far as the ego is concerned? . . . Impossible!

The Song of Awakening, A Guide to Liberation Through Marananussati, Mindfulness of Death, Boise, Idaho, The Open Path Publishing, 1979, p.22. Used with permission from Bodhi Publishing.

Motherhood in the Desert (North Africa, 1973)
Lisa Elander (Adamson)

We travelled with Rinpoche through North Africa in a caravan of three vehicles — Rinpoche with three others in his vehicle and two Volkswagen buses. Sometimes Rinpoche's vehicle would take off alone and go somewhere else.

One time we all stopped for a quick picnic lunch just off the road and I was busy making peanut butter sandwiches for a group of clamouring hungry children.

Rinpoche came over and expressed interest in also having one of the peanut butter sandwiches.

I said, "Just as soon as I have given the children theirs, Sir."

He said, "NO, ME FIRST!"

I got it.

I knew he was not disparaging looking after children, but was giving me a very clear message that if I wished to awaken in this life, I would always have to put the teaching first, and the teaching at that moment was standing by the van in the shoes of my teacher.

He got his sandwich instantly.

In Iceland the winds blow strong and constantly and as a result the trees grow lower to the ground. They are often gnarled and bent away from the prevailing winds to reduce their wind resistance as they do the best they can to be trees.

People around you have similarly been affected by challenges and difficulties in their lives. Notice that even with their sometimes seemingly neurotic patterns, what they have done is adapt to their environments and cope as well as they could.

Rather than resist them, you could understand and be tolerant. With compassion and loving kindness, you can seek to provide a more favorable environment for them to develop and evolve.

Namgyal Rinpoche, Dharma Centre of Canada, 1993.

Faith and Light (Rotorua, New Zealand, June – September 1973)
Steven Gellman

During a three-month meditation retreat at Lake Rotoiti, Namgyal Rinpoche would take a day off periodically and on one occasion I was his driver and attendant. I was driving him between Lake Rotoiti and Lake Taupo when I asked him, "Sir, I have read the stories of Milarepa, Marpa and Naropa and I am struck by their absolute faith in their Teachers. Maybe because of the modern era we live in, maybe because of Western society's individualism, I am finding it quite difficult. I really wish I could have that kind of faith!"

He answered, "Steven, in this teaching faith comes from experience."

I became quite concerned about my level of faith and trust. We arrived at the hotel on Lake Taupo and I helped him get installed in his room. Towards evening I knocked on his door to ask him what he would like for dinner. He said that he would prefer Chinese, as there was a Chinese restaurant not far from our hotel, so I happily obliged. An hour later I returned with the food and knocked on his door — silence. I waited and knocked again — silence. I was about to leave when I thought I heard his voice from afar. "Yes?"

"I have brought your dinner," I answered. As I opened the door I suddenly experienced a distinct chill in the room temperature. The room was filled with a cool blue light and was charged with an otherworldly energy. The Rinpoche was sitting cross-legged on his large bed. He said quietly, "Leave it there and go." I did.

The next day while driving him I asked, "Sir, what was that?"

He replied, "You aren't my only students you know."

It is said that the teaching is beautiful in the beginning, beautiful in the middle and beautiful in the end. It is especially beautiful to hear now because it provides some sensibility in the midst of this charnel ground of modern society. It is even more beautiful with practice, particularly with the practice of loving-kindness, which brings an immediate state of joy and goodness. The result is also beautiful — the realization of the true nature of the universe and all universal dharmas.

Suchness, the Diamond State of Realization, Teachings on the Diamond Sutra, Kinmount, Bodhi Publishing, 2006, p. 15. Used with permission from Bodhi Publishing.

Slackers (New Zealand, 1973) *Lisa Elander (Adamson)*

Often, during a three-month retreat in Rotorua, I drove Rinpoche around. Every day he would visit the campsite where those who had not yet completed their Foundation Practice were living, as they were not allowed into the retreat itself. Although we were parents with children, we had finished our Foundation work and were allowed to take as much part in the retreat as we could manage.

One day, Rinpoche asked one person, who by nature was quite laid back, how many prostrations he had done the previous day. He answered that he had taken the day off. Rinpoche went ballistic and totally demolished everyone present.

When we returned to the Volkswagen bus I got into the driver's seat, very shaken.

Rinpoche heaved himself up into the front seat beside me, rocking the van with his weight, gave a hugely satisfied sigh and said with great relish."Aah! There's nothing like one good rage a day!"

"Who are you?" (New York City, circa 1974)
Lama Sonam Gyatso

I drove Namgyal Rinpoche to New York from where he soon would be embarking on a boat trip. Arrangements had been made to meet Chogyam Trungpa Rinpoche while we were in the city. We went to the hall where he was giving teachings. As I walked along the hallway in my robes, a short bearded man greeted me. "Om ah hung, who are you?"

"I'm Sonam. Who are you?"

"I'm Alan Ginsberg — nice to meet you."

We went into the hall where organizers had set up two thrones. By this time, Namgyal Rinpoche was recognized by the Karmapa as a Vajra Master, so one throne was for Trungpa Rinpoche and at the same height, was one for Namgyal Rinpoche.

I sat in the audience. Around me were some students skeptical about a Western Rinpoche. During the question period a student stood and asked Namgyal Rinpoche in a rather off-hand way, "How do you know a true teacher?"

Rinpoche looked him straight in the eye and calmly said, "Ye shall know them by their works."

Awareness (Piraeus to Crete, 1975) *Bryan Upjohn*

Our beloved teacher, as most people who met him know, would use any and all occasions to teach and talk about the sublime Dharma. My first trip with the teacher had been in 1974 when about 100 of us had gone to Mexico for 'therapy.'

I had managed to avoid Rinpoche in Mexico as I really didn't think that therapy was 'my thing.' He had tricked me into coming. When he asked me if I was coming to Mexico, I had responded that I didn't really feel that I needed therapy.

He replied, "Well then, come and help the people that do need it." (Little did I know.)

A year later I found myself on a small ship crossing from the port of Piraeus in Athens to Hania on Crete with Rinpoche and a lot of 'old-time' students. I only knew a few people so I felt like a bit of an outsider but one student in particular was kind and included me.

I spent the early part of the voyage in the bar drinking Pepsi and ice. I figured I could avoid Rinpoche in the bar as I assumed he didn't drink. He wandered through the bar a few times and jokingly referred to my drinking habit to which of course I pled innocent.

Later that day, as the sun was going down into the ocean, I was sitting in a deck chair by the railing with three of Rinpoche's students. One of them, Richard, was into massage and I had just gotten my license as a massage therapist so we were talking about bodywork.

I went for a brief walk and came back to where I had been sitting. Richard was sitting in the chair I had just vacated, beside someone I didn't know. By this time it was getting dark. I came up behind Richard's chair and placed my hands on his shoulders and started to give him a shoulder massage as we both looked out over the railing.

I had given a lot of massages by this time, so I noticed that this pair of shoulders felt quite relaxed compared to 99% of the shoulders I was used to massaging.

"This is different," I thought, so I really started to get in to it. I worked my way firmly up the neck and put my hand on the forehead to gently massage the points where the neck muscles insert at the bottom of the skull. "No tension here either," I thought.

Then I slowly worked back down the neck to the shoulders and then over both shoulders to a pressure point on the upper arm that relieves tension in the entire shoulder. At this point I picked up on some odd energy coming from two women students who were looking over at me with a combination of panic and bewilderment. I wondered and looked down at who I thought all along had been Richard.

Leaning back and looking up at me was the face of Namgyal Rinpoche. I think that was the only time in my life when I actually had the experience of time standing still.

"I'm sorry Sir. I didn't know it was you," I said quietly.

"NEITHER DID I," he replied, in his very direct way. "SIT DOWN."

People scrambled to find a chair for me to sit on.

"I don't mind that you gave me a massage," he said. "What I do mind is the fact that you were unaware."

He then proceeded to give the four of us the most amazing discourse on awareness.

Why not just be aware of what is happening around you rather than work with an exotic meditation exercise?

Namgyal Rinpoche, Dharma Centre of Canada, 1996.

Star Birthing (New Zealand, 1973) *Susan Cowen*

On an arduous three-month retreat in New Zealand, when we were meditating 20 hours a day, Rinpoche would scan the crowd during the inspirational talk he gave each morning.

He would spot those students who were on the edge of breaking — either 'down' or 'through' — and select them for what he called a 'star-birthing' experience.

That night he would take us to a nearby hot spring where, under the brilliant stars of the southern sky, we would float spread-eagled in the steaming pool.

Rinpoche would move around the pool grabbing hold of the nearest big toe and twirl each startled student in slow circles as they looked up at the starry sky.

In the womb of the hot spring with our gaze on unfamiliar constellations our spirits felt free to soar into the vast expanse of the infinite.

The Secret (Crete, June, 1975) *Rab Wilkie*

Rinpoche was teaching in the land of *Zorba The Greek* and after a dire warning to 'certain students' about not turning up at class again with smelly socks, he continued to manifest the Seven Rays of Healing and hinted that he might soon reveal the 'greatest secret of all.'

We were in the middle of his course on healing and our daily hikes to his small villa on the hill had become a strenuous habit that peaked in easy glory as we sat round his chair every afternoon on the stone patio overlooking the sea, a few miles to the perpetually sunny south. The course lasted only a week but what was brought forth seemed the essence of a curriculum based on more than two thousand years of experience. He had begun, three days earlier, by saying that in the Mystery Schools of ancient Greece, the original gymnasia, healing was taught through seven levels or grades, beginning with food and diet and culminating with stars for graduates — real stars, and breathing in their rays.

We were the privileged few. Only those with a 'professional' interest in healing were allowed to attend — if we already were, or seriously intending to become a qualified medical doctor, counsellor, chiropractor, or therapist of one kind or another. We were a small group, drawn from the larger crowd attending the first Teachers Training Course. Healing was just one subject among many: astrophysics (black holes,) theatre (Oedipus Rex,) homiletics (sermons,) creative writing (science fiction,) politics (Evolutionary Marxism) and Vajrayana Tantra were some of the other topics, with a surprise sing-along to stir Canadian passions from their state of Hyperborean cool.

After lunch, the long march of Healers up the winding road was livelier than usual and some of us, despite the heat, took a shortcut, racing along goat paths that led up the steep hillside to Rinpoche's rented villa. It was Friday and Saturday would be the last class on healing. As Rinpoche brought the class to a close, he shone like Pythagoras.

"To retreat from the world is no longer possible. You must go forward and evolve by encouraging the idea of exposure. Anything else is not only hiding from others but from yourselves because you are, like the Roman god Janus, facing two ways at once, inwards and outwards."

"Your only hope for a safe path, for refuge, is in exploration, by becoming extroverted. The life within must be in accord with the outer life and the inner secrets should become as accessible as the outer secrets. Explore everything. Be a detective."

"Avoiding secrets gives rise to ill health. Refusing to see or recognise secrets is called, in Pali, *Avidya* — ignorance or not seeing. The goal of this teaching is total seeing and total health. All healing depends on greater and greater exposure."

"Is this the Greatest Secret?" someone asked.

"Ah, this has yet to be revealed!" he responded, "and that's for tomorrow."

Back in the seashore village, students dined at various restaurants. There weren't many in Paleochora, yet there seemed to be more than when we first arrived. The villagers weren't accustomed to visitors and mothballed cafes were dusted out while the fishermen and gatherers of arid hillside thyme were kept busy. Every meaty dish exuded this herb. It held us in thrall; we salivated at the slightest whiff.

The Healers, especially during the last few days, had been congregating separately from those who were not making the trek. It was not quite apartheid. During coffee time, after moussaka and salad, our table was joined by a non-healer. He asked, "What have you guys been hearing up on the hill?"

After giving our several accounts, there was a hush as a Healer implied a revelation to come — but about this naught could be said. It was a secret. "Wow, that's great!" the interloper proclaimed. "We'll ALL be in on this."

"Huh? What do you mean? It's — um — private!"

"Not any more. Rinpoche has invited EVERYONE tomorrow."

During the following afternoon the inland road was crowded with pilgrims, most ascending to Rinpoche's villa for the first time. There was much shaking of heads and laughter. The Joker had struck again!

It was a short class and the Teacher soon got to the point as a student finally asked about the most important thing in healing — the Greatest Secret. The whole group became one big ear.

"It's quite simple, really, as all secrets are. If you want to be healed, you will be healed." The ear dissolved and there remained only hearing, hearing, hearing — the distant surf, then silence and wellness beyond being.

You need to drop words as you experience totality. Words can't get you there. The mystics dropped long prayers and said, 'Oh God' or just 'Oh!'

Namgyal Rinpoche, Dharma Centre of Canada, 1968.

The Dance of the World Serpent (Paleochora, Crete, summer, 1975) *Jacques Varian*

During six weeks in Crete Rinpoche taught many things but when he tried to teach Meditative Movement, after ten minutes he was disgusted and cancelled the class. We were hopeless. He'd told us to become trees and I guess there were too many saplings turning into giant oaks in three seconds flat, or rootless willows prancing.

"Trees are STILL!" he thundered. "And they grow s-l-o-w-l-y! Go take a shower or something. Just get out of my sight."

The sun was setting and our café meal was finished, leaving only salt-whitened peanut shells beside tiny ouzo glasses, all empty.

Then Jorgos, the owner, seeing his chance, came to our table with news that the outdoor cinema was up and running and the movie tonight would be *2001: A Space Odyssey*.

After weeks of immersion in Rinpoche's Teachers Training Course, the idea of a short break was attractive, especially with the summer solstice approaching.

The screen was small and barely capable of doing justice to the 'Blue Danube' in orbital space, but it was framed by palm trees, the blue sea behind, stretching darkly into the star-twinkling distance. And from the arid, thyme-fragrant hills, the sea-seeking breeze wafted over and around us, fondled fronds in passing and caused the unsilvered screen to tremble.

The air calmed and I was entranced once again by Kubrick's realm and lost in cosmos until near the end when the climactic syzygy births three orbs from one during the triumphant cadence of *Zarathustra* — Yah Dum da-DA! Doo-ee — as from behind the blue marble Earth in space, the white-mirror Moon is extruded above, then suddenly the sun blazes forth, pulling one's gaze higher; but my gaze kept going — drawn right off the screen in a leap beyond to the real moon in the sky, floating exactly in line with the pale, tripling image below.

Zing! — from image to reality.

When the movie was over, the night was still young as we sauntered back from the stony shore into the village and just past Jorgos's cafe we came upon tables, set out all over the street. A party was just beginning. A couple who owned another café was passing it on to their son.

The Serpent of Hermes manifests in some of the oldest forms of the village dance, particularly in Crete. The black-frocked, tall-hatted priest starts it off, dancing alone to the clarinet, and then invites an old woman, a matriarch also in black, to take his hand as the bouzouki joins in.

Then, in due but languid course, another of the family and another, takes the white kerchief raised in hand until the whole community — sitting at tables variously strewn across the dusty street — has joined the dance: a growing chain of quiet celebrants that spirals in and out and weaves with dignity towards midnight and a firm, ancient ekstasis that makes dry hills sigh and the full moon weep with joy over the glistening Livikon Sea.

This was not a night we danced. We were audience. We sat. But long after my companions left, I remained, stubbornly waiting out a tide of boredom.

A village dance is not rock'n'roll, and to a stranger from the wild New World, or even I suppose to a youth from Athens, it no doubt can seem old-fashioned and tame. There were no raised voices, no thumping drums — just bouzouki strings and a clarinet. No drunken revelry and no voracious, chugging bodies.

The continuum of rhythm and tune and dancing pulsed without ceasing, but calmly and in an orderly manner, on into the night. There were no highs and lows, neither in the passage of time nor in the collective mood. And it didn't feel like it was GOING anywhere.

Then folk began leaving. My boredom peaked. I wanted to see how it ended, but it didn't. There was no end. There was no "So long, that's it." No bong or bell. No announcements, no ritual salute.

I expected some kind of — signal. But people just kept leaving, gradually, until only the immediate family remained. They began taking the tables from the street. Then there was just the husband and wife. They locked the front door of their cafe and vanished, but the ground in front remained warm and musical, throbbing inaudibly.

I was puzzled; stood there alone, scratching my head. Something had happened but I wasn't sure what. Yet I was in the midst of the most confident, stable, solid high that I'd ever felt.

This must be a clue to Crete — as in 'concrete' and 'discrete' I mused. I'd missed the build-up, subtle despite its strength.

I was not familiar with this gradual empowerment, ingrained over thousands of years as habit in a people who had always lived here, living the land. There HAD been a climax, but one so gentle, so present, that it had caught me unaware.

Was this what Rinpoche had tried to teach us — the movement of Nature?

That night I slept deeply in my white-washed room with a cool marble floor — a family's spare upper-room for visitors and my waking before dawn was extended for hours as the all-night chirping of tree-frogs outside the window was joined in measured sequence by the distant crowing of a rooster then dogs barking, donkeys braying, birds whistling; each animal voice in turn saying something different, simple and profound.

The volume of the chorus built slowly towards dawn, my room aflood with sunlight as voices of being human sprang upward from the street below.

"Eh? Pavlo?"

"Stavros!"

"Kalimera! Kalimera!"

Good Morning, indeed, one and all.

Spin a world globe slowly. During a year the zenith Sun traces a spiral upward from the Tropic Capricorn to Cancer and back down. This is the solar serpent, coiling and uncoiling around its world-egg: an Orphic Mystery.

But go slowly, naturally — one dance-step at a time. Feet together to start. Wait — feel what that's like. Then one step forward. Wait, feel that. Next foot forward, the other back and behind, forward again; now back, back, swing and return. Wait after each move until you are exactly where you are.

The Greek Welcome Dance. If you get it right, you'll never forget: introduction and greeting without talk. Just body, gesture and clear empty mind; rooted and growing slowly like a tree — leaves unfolding among stars.

You move through so many field forces that are constantly pressuring you, and yet you have to forget them in order to focus. At this stage you are not meant to be aware of all these levels: the gravitational pulls and the electro-magnetic fields. They always influence you but in general you are unaware of them, and for a reason.

Paleochora Discourses, Part I Exploring the Language of Liberation, Part II Healing, Faith and Karma, Kinmount, Bodhi Publishing, 2009, p. 89. Used with permission from Bodhi Publishing.

Ass Backwards (Samos, July 1975) *Peter Boag*

The problem with clinging is that until you let it go, either you cling to it or it clings to you. Either way is suffering. Here's a story of my own clinging that spans more than twenty years.

Namgyal Rinpoche once sent me on ahead from a course in Crete to find accommodations for him and close to one hundred students on the Greek island of Samos. This was an impossible task, according to conventional wisdom, as it was the height of the tourist season and there would be 'no room in the inn' on that small island.

However, after many adventures and a lot of haggling, everything fell into place by the eve of Rinpoche's arrival.

He seemed pleased with the small, previously mothballed hotel that had been re-opened just for him.

He was less pleased I intended to stay there that night until the students arrived the next day. However, he relented, after making it clear that I would clear out in the morning.

That night I couldn't sleep. I kept thinking of a rumour circulating among the students that Rinpoche never slept. I decided to find out once and for all if this were true.

So, about 3 am, I silently crept down the marble hallway in stocking feet. The door to Rinpoche's room had an old-fashioned keyhole which would be quite sufficient to peek through. Just as I crouched down to get a good look, the door suddenly opened!

At well over six feet, Rinpoche towered over me, even more than usual, with me in the most subservient of postures.

"Yes?" he enquired.

I was quickly trying to find my wits. "Sir, I was just putting something to the test." I said, referring to a favorite phrase of his.

"Very good, carry on," he said, closing the door in my face.

The next day at the first lecture he threw me out of the class, in circumstances that left me with a bitter feeling. I couldn't help but wonder if he were getting me back for my indiscretion of the previous night.

With each passing year the memory of this event faded, until I completely forgot about it. Or so I thought.

Many years later, during Rinpoche's last year of embodiment I knew he was seriously ill and that his death was imminent. Still, he kept on travelling and teaching. Early that year I was invited to Guatemala by a student who had offered Rinpoche a place there to rest and recharge. Everything was in place for me to see him there and maybe do a retreat.

Yet I could not shake the feeling that I had no right to take any more of his dwindling energy. He had already given me lifetimes worth of work to do. The more I contemplated this, the more I was convinced. As a result I threw away my non-refundable ticket and stayed away.

A few months later, I heard Rinpoche would be teaching in Idaho, a two-day drive from where I was staying. I decided to head up to Boise to see him one last time.

When I was about two hundred miles from Boise, in the mountains of Nevada, I was overtaken by his presence and experienced what can only be described as the full-on Namgyal Crystal Cave empowerment.

I never previously had that Wongkur and the experience did not seem to be the result of any practice I had done.

When I arrived at Boise, Rinpoche was a shadow of his former physical self and was teaching to a large group of students, many of whom had never met him and wanted to make a connection. Once again I decided to keep at arm's length out of concern for his diminished energy.

During my drive home, in those same Nevada mountains, time warped, shapes shifted and it was as if Rinpoche was in my passenger seat, saying. "So, what about that thing that has been bugging you all these years?"

Somehow I knew immediately. He was referring to events in Greece, decades ago. "You threw me out of your class!"

Rinpoche said, "Shall we examine this? Remind me!"

"Well Sir, the previous night I had spied on you."

"And?"

"The next day you gave us an exercise to draw our parents naked and then you took off to get a cool drink."

"As I recall it was sweltering hot, was it not?"

"Yes sir, it was almost unbearable sitting in the sand in that sun."

"And when I returned?"

"Well Sir, I had completed my drawing and suddenly understood the whole thing. I looked around at the other students' drawings and they confirmed my thoughts. The notion that we are partially products of our parent's own inadequacies was brutally obvious, but also so absurd I couldn't help laughing!"

"Yes and when I returned, a bunch of you were laughing like hyenas. And when I asked who was laughing to stand up, only you stood."

"That is why it was totally unfair of you to have banished me and let everyone else stay!"

Rinpoche was beside himself laughing. "You still don't get it, after all this time?"

"I guess not."

"What did you do after I tossed you out of the class?"

"I went down to the sea and had a cool drink under a tree."

"Yes, while the rest of us had to sit in the hot sun for a few more hours! And you call that punishment?"

Rinpoche went on. "People think they have been banished from the Kingdom of Heaven, while the opposite is true. Peter, all these years you have had it ass backwards."

Our thoughts are like fire ants on the tree — to keep us from being eaten. But we have defenses for threats which no longer exist.

Namgyal Rinpoche, Dharma Centre of Canada, 1993.

The Light Goes On (Peru, 1976) *Lisa Elander (Adamson)*

We were doing star-group meditations in an old monastery in the Urubamba Valley. We also did meditation with kasinas — focusing on a disk or hoop with earth, water, air, fire or a colour in it to calm the mind.

One day Rinpoche found out that one student was using a light bulb instead of a kasina and staring at it.

Rinpoche got into a thundering peroration about not following directions and rounding to a climax he bellowed, "AND IF YOU THINK YOU CAN GET THE TRANSCENDENTAL FROM A LIGHT BULB —"

And then, because he could not tell a lie, his voice suddenly lost its thunder and very calmly he said, "— well, you can."

Morning Coffee in the Andes (Peru, 1976)
Lisa Elander (Adamson)

In Cuzco, at one of the sites during a six-week retreat in Peru, Rinpoche came to the house each morning when he was in that city. One morning he asked me to make him a cup of coffee. I went to the kitchen.

In Peru, there was only one way to make coffee: with boiled water, instant coffee, sugar (if taken) and powdered milk. I made him the usual cup of coffee and took it back out. He took one sip and spat it out all over the floor.

He said it was disgusting, that I did not even know how to make a decent cup of coffee and then lit into me, tearing me to shreds as only he could do.

I spent the rest of the day in despair, crying on and off, trying to understand what this was all about.

The next morning he came again, looked at me and asked me to make him a cup of coffee.

With a feeling of dread I returned to the kitchen and looked carefully at the ingredients for making coffee: boiled water, instant coffee, white sugar and powdered milk.

So I made exactly the same cup that I had made the day before and offered it to him with great trepidation.

He smiled, took it, said, "Thank you," and drank it without a word.

Hoops of Space (Cuzco, Peru, 1976) *Susan Cowen*

One day in Toronto, Rinpoche announced we were going to the Andes 'to meditate on Space,' and off we went, imagining sitting on mountain tops and gaze into the distance — but it was not like that.

After a voyage through the Panama Canal to Lima, we arrived at our accommodations on the outskirts of Cuzco. Rinpoche had a room in a Cistercian monastery where Simon Bolivar, 'the Great Liberator,' had once slept. I stayed with other students in a convent a few kilometers away.

As our meditation practice, Rinpoche had us hang wooden hoops, woven with rainbow coloured threads, from the ceilings of our rooms. He instructed us to sit and focus our minds on the space between the threads.

We quickly began to discover that space had characteristics radically different from what we had previously assumed.

Twice a day, we met in the monastery courtyard where Rinpoche taught. We walked back through the mountains to our convent. One night, leaving late and winding up alone,

I passed a store where watchdogs were normally tied up during the day. In the dark I didn't see a band of wild dogs gathered around. As I imagined myself bleeding to death by the side of the road, a car drove up and rescued me. Looking down I saw the wild dogs had only ripped my dress — a testament to the power of prayer!

The next day back at the monastery, Rinpoche gave a blessing in the courtyard surrounded by brightly coloured hoops hanging from the branches of trees around him, scattering rose petals all around.

The Master Mariner (Norway, summer, 1976) *Peter Bergerson*

We were in a class outside Rinpoche's tent in a farmer's field in Norway. One of his first students, G.K. Chorpel Dolma (or Beatrice Raff) sat, as she always did (being somewhat deaf,) as close to his right foot as she could get. I was sitting beside her. Rinpoche had been on her case pretty consistently and of course, he relished every opportunity to take it further.

This time, however, another female student, who was sitting quite far back in the large crowd, right in the centre, stood up and very clearly and eloquently took Rinpoche to task for his treatment of the elderly nun. She said that Chorpel was her teacher and she thought that more respect should be shown her.

In a pregnant pause, we all waited for the thunderbolt. He looked down and an impossibly sweet smile came to his face. When he looked up to answer, he said:

"You must understand this lady and I go back a long way. The relationship reminds me of a yachting magazine I was looking at recently. On the cover, was a picture of a grand three-masted schooner, white sails fully inflated by a strong wind, cutting through the bright blue sea. Across the corner of the cover was a banner which read, 'She's a spirited craft and it takes a great mariner to sail her!'"

It has occurred to me often since that day, that however much one might sometimes feel ridiculed, put-down, or abandoned, the compassion of the Teacher's intent was never ultimately in doubt — maybe only to be made obvious just 'round the next bend.'

The Black Saint (Assisi, Italy, 1977) *Melodie Massey*

I first met Rinpoche in Italy where he was teaching on the Christian mystical life - something I had read a great deal about. I had met an artist in Port Hope, Ontario, who told me she had a shrine room where she meditated. I had a small Russian Orthodox chapel in our house, so it was wonderful to meet someone who was practising. I went to her house and up to her shrine room. When I sat down and saw the picture of Rinpoche on her shrine, I knew he was my Teacher.

The woman sent a telegram to Rinpoche and he told her to come to Assisi and bring me. We arrived in Italy and, even with the wrong address, eventually found the convent where we were meant to stay. We met Rinpoche near the little church Saint Francis built which now has a huge cathedral built over it. In the church square my friend introduced me to him. I immediately thought I had found Jesus and while we were walking behind him I stepped as close as I could, as if I were walking in His footsteps, until my friend said quietly to me that I was too close and Rinpoche wouldn't like it.

The Teaching was wonderful and to have found my Teacher even more wonderful. It was quite different from anything I had experienced. My friend and I would go for coffee with Rinpoche at the hotel nearly every night. I often asked him questions. Some he answered, some he didn't.

Rinpoche wanted me to see the body of Saint Clare in the crypt beside the convent bearing her name. As I looked, I saw that she was black.

Rinpoche asked, "Do you know why she is black?"

I said, "No." He told me it was because she died of the fire of love.

There is no real dichotomy between doubt and faith. In fact, as the doubt increases, so does the faith. How is this? You may say "But if we must continually raise questions, how can we believe in anything?" First, we must be careful to distinguish between faith based on blind dogma and ritualized formulas and faith based on question, on seeking to know. In other words, we must become aware that we were created to doubt, to explore, to extend our consciousness. This is precisely what we have faith in! Faith in the universal flow of process.

The Vision and Other Essays, Bhikkhu Ananda Bodhi, Toronto, 1971; p. 6. Used with permission from Bodhi Publishing.

Motel Vigil (British Columbia, 1970s) *Byron Stevens*

Three of us were driving Rinpoche back from Whitehorse to Jasper in the Canadian Rockies via Prince George. My friend and I came to the teaching through a few of those worshipful and no doubt highly embellished stories in those many Guru books that were so popular at the time.

On the trip, we got it into our mischievous heads to see if enlightened beings slept. As it happened, I drew the short straw.

I was acting as Rinpoche's attendant that night and shared the motel room with him. We decided I would stay awake and report my findings to him in the morning.

Rinpoche and I watched some local TV and I turned over, ostensibly to sleep, but was determined to keep awake.

My last waking sight was of Rinpoche lying on his right side with his back to me, his head propped up on his right hand, leisurely smoking a cigarette.

(Yes, he occasionally smoked "to relax" he told me, but only occasionally.)

Valiantly remaining awake (or so I thought,) my next conscious observation when I awoke around 3 am, was Rinpoche still lying on his right side, his back to me and head propped up on his right hand, leisurely smoking a cigarette!

I was so tired from all the driving that I just gave up and decided to get some real sleep.

When I awoke, everyone was up and about, packing, and getting ready to hit the road. To this day I still don't know whether he slept that night or not.

Curiosity is the key! INTEREST in a solution leads to integration — beyond subject/object and beyond 'buts'.

Namgyal Rinpoche, Toronto, 1971.

A Rose Garden (Assisi, Italy, 1977) *Prue Vosper*

I was a student who from the first meeting with Rinpoche would ask questions. They would pop out of my mouth spontaneously, with no fear or hesitation. Somehow his presence released that in me. The questions were neither always on the subject, nor always with a respectful attitude and sometimes he had to stop this in order to keep his flow.

Following a family disaster, a suicide of a 19-year-old, I had brought three people from France to a small course in Assisi that Rinpoche was giving. One day, they all stayed home and when I arrived for class alone, he turned to me and said, "Oh, this morning is not for you today. Go and wait outside!"

What a thing to say! Did I need a break? But of course it provoked a nest of coiling vipers! Yet, I went to the garden with all good intentions, wondering what would be the most appropriate way to use this time. Well, of course, I could meditate. Only I couldn't. I kept thinking, "What could he possibly be talking about this morning that he didn't want me to listen to? Higher teachings? What was I missing? Why couldn't I be there? And why is it that I can't just sit and meditate?"

So I tried enjoying the garden. But it wasn't very interesting, just roses formally laid out with paths and I certainly don't remember the flowers. (Surely they must have been flowering; it was summer time!) As my feet repeated the circuit around the garden I was hopelessly entangled with these repetitive questions while only a little distance away the others were enjoying his presence.

It was the most uncomfortable morning of my life. I was excluded, like a naughty girl at school, only I didn't know what I had done or why I couldn't be there. I spent an hour reliving all the feelings of a four-year-old who has been wrongly (or rightly?) accused of breaking the rules, like ringing the gong too soon before lunch.

Eventually these feelings subsided and towards the end of the class, a student was sent to call me in. There was no hint of what I had missed or why I was now allowed to rejoin the class. I sat there not knowing what to think, in wonder.

Come to love through differences. Separateness, duality, ambivalence, question and struggle - all lead to love. The greater the struggle, the greater the love.

Namgyal Rinpoche, Toronto, 1971

Inside Passage (Yukon, 1970s) *Michael Brine*

After one of Rinpoche's visits to the Yukon and a visit to my bush home, he decided to leave on the ferry that sailed down the Inside Passage to Prince Rupert, so I drove him to Haines, Alaska to catch the boat.

You had to book if you wanted a cabin, otherwise you'd be out of luck. I had already tried to book in Whitehorse, unsuccessfully, so when we got to Dezadeash Lodge I phoned once more. But again — no cabins.

Rinpoche was not in the least perturbed so we drove on.

When we got to the ferry, I went on board with him and he said he wanted to get a cabin. I explained again that I'd tried but there were none.

He dismissed this and simply said, "It's okay, Michael — just hold my bag."

So I went with him into the line-up. Others ahead of us were told there were no cabins available. When he got to the window of the ticket office the agent said, "What can I do for you, sir?"

To which Rinpoche replied that he wanted a cabin.

The agent looked at him for a moment, looked down at his sheets and then responded, "Yes Sir, I think we can manage that. What name?"

"Leslie Dawson." While registering, Rinpoche took a quick look at me and winked.

Meditate with clear seeing — not eyes closed in ecstasy. Embrace phenomena to the best of your ability.

Ask what kind of path you are on. Adopt a victory mode — watch the effect of listening to a raga about heroes in the morning and to another one on lovers in the evening.

Most of you meditate only waiting for an accident to happen — worrying about upsets, thinking about your sins or that the lama will get you.

Set out to be victorious!

Namgyal Rinpoche, Toronto, 1971.

Caitlin's Trick (Wakefield, Quebec, 1970s)
Lisa Elander (Adamson)

Rinpoche was teaching at our house in Wakefield, near Ottawa. We were having a break between sessions. There were many people around and I was kneeling near Rinpoche, asking him about dinner.

Suddenly, amidst the chaos, nine-year-old Caitlin appeared at my left, extending a package of gum towards Rinpoche, saying, "Rinpoche, would you like a stick of gum?"

"Yes, thank you," said Rinpoche as he reached out to take the gum.

To my horror, I recognized the gum as my children's trick package that snapped your fingers as you pulled out the gum stick.

Before there was time to say anything, a knowing came into Rinpoche's eyes and he subtly changed the direction of his hand so that he would take the gum from the side, but he had barely touched it when the whole thing literally exploded and fragments of paper and bits of the spring whizzed through the air.

Everything happened in the blink of an eye. Caitlin burst into tears and ran away. Rinpoche said, in a very kind voice, "Oh dear, never try to trick the lama!"

Sitting, Waiting (Assisi, Italy, 1977) *Charlene Jones*

At the end of an empowerment ceremony I sat. Others rose, left and began to speak outside the room. I heard their voices. I sat because I knew I must.

Rinpoche talked with a few people lingering, answering their questions. I did not know why I was sitting, why I was waiting. But I knew I must sit. Was this him, or me? Did he put a mind-lock on me, heavier than the weight of his tall, full body?

Did this momentary paralysis arise from the depths of what I call my own mind? Was this an experience the two of us shared, an interference wave of energy from me/him to him/me? I liked the last one best.

After the last person left, he indicated I was to come forward.

I sat now directly in front of him and into the fullness between us he said, unhurried in this as in all things.

"You will attain . . ." (Silent, I do not move.) ". . . in this lifetime."

If Music Be the Food (Wakefield, Quebec, 1970s)
Lisa Elander (Adamson)

After returning from a long freighter trip with Rinpoche, my late husband and others were at our home in Wakefield. Rinpoche was staying in a nearby motel.

I seemed to be cooking most of the time, except when Rinpoche was teaching several times a day in our place.

Steven had been away from his beloved piano for months and all the hours when Rinpoche was not present, Steven was gloriously playing the piano, long into the night. The children went to sleep on the floor, the better to hear the music.

The last morning after everyone had eaten, Rinpoche thanked me for good meals as he was leaving. Then Steven, following on his heels echoed Rinpoche's expression of thanks.

I said, "Oh, that's nothing compared with the marvelous music!"

Rinpoche whirled, nailed me with his eyes and said fiercely, "You have your priorities wrong! Without food there is NO MUSIC!"

My response was a faint. "Thank you sir (I think)!"

I am particularly amazed by how thoughtlessly some of you are able to lay out inappropriate behavior at the table, how unaware you can be of the needs of others. The table is a place of sharing love, of nourishment, and should have a meaning, a symbolism, an atmosphere of caring.

Body, Speech & Mind, a manual for human development, Kinmount, Bodhi Publishing, 2004, p. 296. Used with permission from Bodhi Publishing.

A Thousand-Year-Old Egg (Hong Kong, September, 1978)
Henri van Bentum

Rinpoche and Terry had a stopover in Hong Kong while sailing aboard a cargo ship en route to Manila. I happened to be in Hong Kong at the time and was able to get aboard the pilot boat to meet them.

As usual the Teacher had something creative for us to do. He told Terry to get him a half-dozen 'thousand-year-old eggs,' and a couple of large beach towels.

So Terry and I hired a rickshaw and set off on our quest into the hustle and bustle of Hong Kong. Neither of us had ever heard of such a thing as a thousand-year-old egg, so we were both scratching our heads.

We tried to take the Teacher's request seriously but at the same time there was skeptical doubt — was this one of the Teacher's many high jinks? Had we been sent on a wild goose chase?

Our rickshaw driver spoke no English. The large beach towels were no problem; we got them in no time. However the elusive egg was another matter. We gestured and tried our best to describe a thousand-year-old duck egg. On a notepad I sketched a duck and an egg.

"Ah yes," he smiled and drove us from one grocery shop to another. These all had chicken and duck eggs but not the mysterious thousand-year-old variety.

And so it went, from one place to another, until finally we found someone who spoke English. I asked him to write down in Chinese calligraphy the name for what we were looking for. This he graciously did, we showed it to our driver and off we went — straight to the market.

There, to our surprise, we found the famous eggs. We discovered they are not a thousand years old of course, but preserved in a mixture of clay, ash, salt, lime and rice straw for several weeks to several months.

We bought a half-dozen as instructed. In triumph we rickshawed back to the ship. Rinpoche was very pleased and shared two of the eggs with us. The yolk was dark green with a strong odor of sulfur and ammonia, while the white was a dark brown, transparent jelly with little flavor or taste.

I cannot say I'd go to the ends of the earth for them — definitely an acquired taste. But in the process we learned never to doubt the Teacher!

Delphic Flan (Crete, February, 1977) *Melodie Massey*

After our course finished in Assisi we travelled to Hania in Crete and went into retreat, practising Vipassana with a few other meditators. I had done only one retreat before in my life and that was Christian.

This Buddhist practice was very different and although it was very cold in our rooms overall it was an excellent experience.

After the retreat Rinpoche asked us if we would like to go with him to Delphi, the ancient site of the Oracle, in the Green Hornet, as his car was called. Of course we said yes.

We had a marvelous trip, which included sampling flan and licorice. He knew I didn't like the latter. The licorice he gave me I swallowed whole.

On the way up from Athens he had us stop at a restaurant and he came out with several freshly made flans, still hot, and naturally I had to eat some. They were delicious!

At Delphi we went to the sacred spring of the Vestal Virgin. The spring area was cordoned off by a wire fence which Rinpoche got Terry to pull open so we could enter.

Rinpoche showed us the seven stone steps of initiation for the Virgins. The top steps were completely disintegrated, but he made us climb up as far as we could and when we returned he gave us each a flower.

We are bound here by 'limited love', our karmic attractions bind us.

Love is the abandonment of attachment, spirit is free-flowing.

Namgyal Rinpoche, Toronto, 1971.

Self and Others (Crete, spring 1977) *Charlene Jones*

In the small room our three bodies felt slightly cramped. My friend had insisted I come with her to visit Namgyal Rinpoche, an invitation that turned my tongue to lead and caused my stomach to boil. Yet she had insisted.

Looking at Cecilie, Rinpoche said, "I have a present for you."

She was delighted, childlike and he waited, enjoying her excitement. With that lovely sense of ceremony he conjured so easily, he pulled a pencil case from behind his back.

The lacquer top shone green, red, black and yellow. She looked up at him, beaming and he nodded to her slightly, indicating she was to open the top.

She slid the wooden slate open revealing three brand new pencils, newly sharpened. Transported in bliss, she stood transfixed and laughing with him, chatting easily.

I looked at him and what emerged from my mind was, "Where is mine? Where is my present?"

"I WANT A PRESENT TOO!"

I knew it was wrong, but I couldn't help myself. I accepted my status without self-pity: the ugly child, savage, blunt, blundering and demanding, full of a vital, awkward energy that spilled unbidden, unshaped, upon the world.

Far from the shining people he kept around him, those who glide with light and grace. I was dark, difficult and unwanted.

I cringed when my defects rose to awareness, particularly around him, yet that is when they all crowded on stage. And here, once again, the embarrassment of a wild, unruly, brutal consciousness in front of the maestro, upended the pleasantness with rude demands.

In his way of simply accepting, he said, "Oh, oh yes." turned and walked out of the room, returning a few moments later with an object he placed into my hand without touching my skin.

I turned it over and over, unable to speak or reply.

"It's very good wool," he offered, "the best."

"Yes, sir," I said into the silence. I could not utter a word more as I continued to examine his present to me.

"It's a sheep!" he pointed out, his voice tinged with that famous impatience.

"Yes, yes, I see it's a sheep," I stammered, "but it's BLACK — it's a BLACK SHEEP."

He chuckled, then delighted, turned on his toes saying, "Oh yes, it is, isn't it?" as he left the room.

That afternoon he delivered a two-hour lecture on sheep, the symbolism of the black sheep and how sheep will only follow one of their own. That is all they trust.

It took a few years for the foggy, slow conscious mind to unite with the semi-conscious memory, for the dullness to lift for a moment to allow clarity to shine briefly.

Then I recognized this symbol as central to my life, an exact replica of the way vital energy thrusts forth from and dances within, this human frame.

Compassion rose for all the backward, wrong and totally unhip, uncool moments of my misbegotten life. The symbol he gave me seemed to insist that those who are different, unusual or 'out of step with everyone else' also have something to offer.

The beginning of Compassion arose from Rinpoche's spontaneous generosity married to the unceasing clarity he manifested.

There is in awakening the experience of a universe totally pervaded with wisdom - not just intelligence but also a reason for everything. It is a universe of best options.

If you intuit this to be so, practice the path of unconditional love including sympathy for neurotic beings. Work harder to see farther.

There is a reason for everything including their neuroses — and yours.

Namgyal Rinpoche, Dharma Centre of Canada, 1993.

Don't Get Wet" (The Philippines, 1978) *Henri van Bentum*

After Rinpoche and Terry stopped in Hong Kong, their cargo ship then sailed to Manila. I flew to Manila to join them again.

Knowing that Rinpoche inspired creative action no matter what or where, I thought I'd dream up something different for him to experience during his stopover in the Philippines. I was staying at the renowned Manila Hotel as guest of the General Manager, a friend. I asked him if he could recommend an adventure for someone who would really love and appreciate it more than anyone I knew.

"I have just the thing," he said. "There is a new trip on the Pagsanjan River — whitewater rafting in hollowed-out tree trunks, called *bancas*."

That sounded exactly what Rinpoche would go for, so upon the Teacher's arrival, I told him what was planned. He liked the idea immediately and the following day, in early October, off we went in one of those psychedelically decorated taxis. The drive to the river took us through exotic villages and countryside.

Upon arrival, two guides were waiting for us by the *banca*. Rinpoche was placed aft, Terry in the middle and yours truly forward. The two boatmen were there to navigate the *banca* through the rapids, slaloming around big boulders. They remained in the water, one at the bow, the other at the stern. Both men had known these waters since boyhood. We were in a gorge. It was like being in a Norwegian fjord, but flanked on both sides by coconut palms and lush tropical vegetation.

"Under no circumstances," said Rinpoche seriously, "do I wish any of us to get wet." With that command, we set off. Although early in the morning, the sun was hot. After awhile, Rinpoche dipped his fingers into the water and dripped a few drops of water onto our hatless heads — a baptism.

We were exuberant on our ride through the rapids! The guides forward and aft had a good sense of balancing the *banca* through years of experience. Staying reasonably dry, we reached a great waterfall. The boatmen asked if we'd like to go under the cascade to a cave that was nice and cool.

Suddenly, Rinpoche hopped out of the *banca* and gave it a big push! Terry and I headed into the waterfall — and got soaked.

The Teacher laughed uproariously, along with our two boatmen.

Motivation (Dharma Centre of Canada, 1974, 1977) *Achi Tsepal*

I was privileged to serve His Holiness the 16th Gyalwa Karmapa for seven years and translated for him at many official meetings with heads of state and religious leaders.

I was His Holiness' translator during his visits to the Dharma Centre of Canada, which partially sponsored His Holiness's first visits to North America. The Karmapa named the core center at the Dharma Centre 'Karma Garchen Ling.'

Namgyal Rinpoche had a Mahakala Shrine built there and vowed to keep its great puja alive. His Holiness consecrated it and performed the great Vajra Crown Ceremony there. I was pleased to hear recently that the staff of the Dharma Centre renovated the shrine room and that students of Namgyal Rinpoche who had taken the Mahakala empowerment and done the practices had rededicated the Shrine.

Getting to know Namgyal Rinpoche and his students brought an insight to me that has remained in my mind over the years. When Westerners came up the valley in Sikkim, to the Rumtek Monastery, seat of the Karmapa, as Namgyal Rinpoche did with 108 students in 1971, they saw such beauty in the mountains, monasteries, sacred art and practice it seemed to them to be a paradise. But in my own experience, something in that beautiful spiritual place troubled me.

Many of my fellow Tibetan refugees were scarred by fighting during the uprising and their flight over the mountains leaving their homeland and loved ones behind. Signs of their trauma remained in the influence of the three poisons: greed, anger and delusion.

Some schemed for money or influence in the monasteries and circles of the high lamas. They sometimes worked against each other or harbored old grudges. For some, the practice of Dharma was a religious habit or a way to seek worldly gain rather than a pursuit of awakening.

Among the students of Namgyal Rinpoche, I met people born in the West who had opportunities and abundance — and yet chose to study and practice Dharma, not to get ahead, but to find enlightenment. I prayed more of my own people could have that motivation.

We Tibetans are grateful to Namgyal Rinpoche for being a special conduit to introduce the Vajrayana Teachings of the Karma Kagyu to the West. His deep knowledge of Buddha Dharma and his love of the core Tibetan heritage will always be cherished by me.

His Holiness the 16th Karmapa & Namgyal Rinpoche at the
Dharma Centre of Canada, 1974. Photo by Peter Deutsch

Mankind is in for more suffering and upheaval in this time due to five factors: the drain of energy resources through the overexploitation of nature; pollution; population explosions; discrepancies in the balance between the haves and the have nots (it is becoming more and more costly for the haves to have); and greed (Tanha), selling people the idea of having to have more, which leads to aggression and war. Right Livelihood is finding the way to live by truth, by law.

We want to draw a parallel for a new society. What is the right way for a human being to live to the full, an enlightened being in a fully awakened state? Not only as lived in the Tibetan Tradition, for example, but the way to live by truth, by law, in any society. What is right livelihood? The drain of energy resources is wrong livelihood; we should not be expending the food and resources of future generations. But above all, the greatest factor of the unwholesome is greed. At what point do you stop the motif of having to have more? When is this crisis going to come to a head, to a point of world revolution?

Right Livelihood and Other Foundations of Enlightenment, Kinmount, Bodhi Publishing, 2008; p. 3-4. Used with permission from Bodhi Publishing.

"Alright, Get On With It!"

At the close of a teaching Rinpoche would give a blessing such as "*Idam te punna-kamman asawakaya wayham hotu.*" which in Pali means, "May the merit of this strengthening activity, bring cessation of all defilements." He often told those assembled to "Get on with it!" The path to transcendence, he said, is not fulfilled merely listening to a teaching, receiving an empowerment, or reading a text. These blessings are helpful for turning attention toward the transcendent but what we do with that guidance in our minds and actions is what moves us toward awakening. "The Kingdom of Heaven must be taken by storm," he often said.

Rinpoche constantly reminded students that this was a path of engagement and experience. Through the practice of meditation we would begin to know the results of applying what he taught. He called for kindness and compassion in daily life, for vigorous exploration, for discipline and for a keen attention to whatever was happening — not just in our minds and personal lives but also in nature and in human society.

Good Fortune (Japan, 1982) *David Pooch*

Rinpoche was leading a retreat at Yoshino, a mountain village close to Nara in central Japan. I was on a business trip to Japan and told Rinpoche I could to stay for only the first day. I calculated carefully and knew how long it would take to run to the Yoshino railway station and the time of the last train down the mountain to Nara. It was about half way through the afternoon class. I checked my watch every few minutes and finally, I guess my mental agitation caused Rinpoche to speak.

"Oh, you have to go, do you?" he asked.

"Yes sir, I must," I replied, swelling with pride at the gentle attention.

"Well then," he said, "go and seek your fortune if you must, but remember a fortune is of value only if put to good use."

I rose, walked to the door, put on my shoes and started running. My ears burned with those words all the way down the hill and on the train all the way to Nara.

Mobsters (Boise, Idaho, September 1982) *Rab Wilkie*

I flew down from Alberta. A large tent had been erected on the grounds of The Open Path, the Namgyal centre founded by Sonam Senge and Karma Chime. When I entered the crowded tent I saw what seemed both apt and amusing for a teaching in the United States: Rinpoche as Sultan, sitting easefully in the late summer heat among many cushions as he addressed a rapt assembly. He oozed smoothness, manifesting a wealth of light and luxury. A Zambhala empowerment was in the offing.

After the Golden Wealth empowerment, Rinpoche encouraged those who were interested to create a new Christian liturgy for the 'Universal Church of Awakening.' We gathered in the house and read some passages from the Bible, shared ideas and then sang a hymn. Some of us had never been to a church service before; some had grown up with it. Familiar things took over and invention was lost in the angelic dust of a Latin hymn sung as a rondo, *Dona Nobis Pachem*. We all liked this, were taken up by the innocent joy of it, and the idea of doing anything else was forgotten.

The next day another empowerment, for Wisdom, was given inside the house. While Rinpoche was preparing within, students were outside reciting mantras while sitting, walking, or standing by a bush, a tree or the tent. The least crowded area was at the front of the house so I made my way there. A friend came round the corner and soon the entrance was adorned by sentinels, one on each side, solemnly holding and clicking rosaries that drooped toward the ground.

Rinpoche suddenly appeared, coming round the same corner, looked at us and nodded.

"We have guards?"

"Umm . . ."

"Very well, you're doing a good job, but must you hold your beads like bicycle chains? You'll scare the neighbours." Rinpoche continued his circumambulation, vanishing round the other corner.

We need to maintain a balance between serenity and thrust (exploration.) Consciousness is a struggle of life and meditation, between passivity and action, male & female. A balanced mind state is needed first and an inquiring, serene mind.

Namgyal Rinpoche, Toronto, 1971.

Green Tara (Boise, Idaho; September, 1982) *Charlene Jones*

I entered the white billowing tent erected in the spacious backyard, one of maybe thirty people seated on the ground this fine summer day. Rinpoche recited the Refuges and then began the talk.

Quickly in the stream of vast consciousness he demanded, "Can anyone here visualize Green Tara instantly? You must be able to do this, at the snap —" (he snapped his fingers)

"— of a finger, in full detail."

I raised my hand, tentatively. I had recently practiced visualizing the Green Tara, who symbolizes compassion and virtuous action. I knew I could but felt very, very insecure about declaring it.

He glared at me, "Oh, you can?"

I stammered, "I would like to try, Sir."

"I did not ask if you can TRY," he bellowed, "I asked if you CAN."

Laughter drifted up all round.

Swallow, gulp and jump. "Yes, Sir, I can."

"Oh YOU! Of course YOU think YOU can DO IT," his renowned put-down voice rattled into me.

The tent exploded with laughter. He was both forceful and humorous, rolling his eyes in exaggeration. Shame rose within, but I had already visualized Green Tara in full detail into the space between Rinpoche and me.

His eyes grabbed mine as the others laughed and he said so quietly no one else could hear, "You can't trust them to know. You must know for yourself." His tone was fully earnest and very loving. "You understand?"

"Yes Sir." I beamed at him, the lesson branded within.

The body is the bejeweled ornament of liberation. Don't say you can't visualize. You have powers of visualization; you just have lost touch with them. Don't just note that evil is occurring in the world. You can do something. One thing you can do is influence kings and prime ministers by the power of positive visualization.

Namgyal Rinpoche, Dharma Centre of Canada, 1993.

Mandala Offering I (At sea, 1982-3) *Matt Wright*

Having completed the first part of Foundation Practice, 100,000 Vajrasattva or 'Diamond Clear Wisdom' mantras for purification, Terry and I were neck-and-neck as we strove to finish 100,000 Mandala Offerings — a practice to encourage generosity and non-attachment.

The conditions were ideal: six months at sea aboard a Polish cargo ship circling the planet. At some point along the way, a sense of competition slipped in.

Rinpoche kept a close eye on our progress and when I started to pull ahead, he suddenly began to ask me to prepare tea that was served on deck above, this allowing Terry a chance to catch up down below in his cabin. The competition was fierce, as Rinpoche knew, and I would rush through my tea saying I needed to return to my practice.

Rinpoche, with a hint of a grin, would say, "What's the rush? Relax and enjoy the lovely scenery."

I'd be itching and twitching and imagining Terry moving ahead whilst Rinpoche would detain me by telling story after story with great glee. I admit I did learn a lot about tea in spite of, or maybe because of, the urge to rush off and do the practice.

The desire to do the practice grew in me and I became happier with every chance to be in the practice and observe its effects. When both Terry and I got close to 100,000, Rinpoche told us to do another 11,111!

We both arrived at 111,111 offerings at about the same time and thanks to Rinpoche, an extra dimension was added that greatly heightened the experience.

> *If there is no interest to produce wholesome activity, there is no possibility for the unfolding of the heart. First calm the body and mind, then awaken the calm. Practice awareness in daily life: the washing of the dishes is as important as giving this talk. Don't you feel more awake when there is discovery and knowledge coming through? Calm and relaxation are the first things you need. Basing knowledge on the shaky foundation of someone else's realizations is in error.*

The Path of Victory, Discourses on the Paramita, Kinmount, Bodhi Publishing, 1991, p.22. Used with permission from Bodhi Publishing.

Tea for Two (At Sea, 1982-3) *Matt Wright*

While sailing the high seas aboard the Polish cargo vessel, Rinpoche often invited one or two of the ten students on board up to the top deck to share a cup of tea. I had very little knowledge of the world of tea and he made it a challenge to teach me the subtle-'teas!'

When I was invited up for a cup, he would ask that I try to identify the chosen tea by taste. Usually I would miss the mark by great distance. At first Rinpoche would show patience and try to steer me in the right direction, but as the months passed there was little change in my success rate. As we were well into this voyage around the world, Rinpoche would gently ask, "So what do you think about this tea, Matthew?"

I would answer with great enthusiasm. "A most interesting tea," and knew what was coming next, as always: the test.

"So what country is this tea from?"

I would then answer with weak confidence that it was from one country or another, which would half of the time be incorrect.

Rinpoche would shudder, legs kicking and arms waving, crying, "No — No — No!"

The guessing would continue amid fits of laughter and his flailing would increase with his hearty, "No — No — No!"

This became a great release of tensions from the long hours of Foundation Practice down below. What compassion and fun!

Mandala Offering II (At sea, 1982-3) *Terry Hagan*

My friend Matt and I were sharing a cabin on a Polish freighter crossing the Indian Ocean. We were both doing mandala offering practice at the time, working diligently to complete 100,000 offerings.

In our daily reports to Rinpoche he casually compared our progress subtly egging on the competition between us. As I was often occupied assisting Rinpoche, I had to work very hard to keep my numbers up. As we neared the big number, Rinpoche saw the competition growing and my frustration showing. He started to delay Matt with little errands which gave me a chance to catch up. He also extended our final goal, increasing the number to 111,111 so we pressed on.

In our practice we were visualising offering up the wealth of the universe, all our worldly goods and everything precious that we could imagine in a practice of generosity. We were offering all our wants, needs and desires, yet at the same time we were looking out of the corner of our eyes to see how many offerings the other had done.

It suddenly dawned on me that I was pursuing this magic number which was somehow going to release us from — what? — relentless toil? attachment? craving? competition?

I gave up the game and began concentrating on offering each moment as a gift of untold splendor. I finished the practice with immense gratitude in my heart for this precious teaching.

Safari (Tanzania, 1980s) *Terry Hagan*

I first met Namgyal Rinpoche in my early twenties and was immediately struck by his presence and naturalness. Nothing seemed to escape his awareness and he was completely at home with all that occurred around him. The relaxed attitude combined with imposing stature in a wool shirt and sweat-soaked Australian hat. Could this be a recognized incarnation of a Tibetan lama? I was completely engaged and spent the next 27 years as his attendant travelling with him and supporting his teaching around the world.

My most inspiring memories of him are not dramatic events, but rather quiet moments when he would reveal things with the twinkle of an eye, a gesture, or perhaps a few words. These moments do not transcribe well into words so I offer a small story which has stayed with me through the years.

In the early predawn light of East Africa we scrambled out of bed, downed a cup of tea and jumped into our waiting Land Cruisers. We were about to descend into one of the wonders of the world — Ngorongoro Crater. We cruised the switchback roads down the inside of the crater, headlights shining as we rounded hairpin turns while dawn brought a red glow to the horizon.

Just as we reached the base of the crater the sun appeared over the crater's edge, revealing an incredible scene open before us. We were entering a vast plain of almost 100 square miles filled with wildlife. Up to 25,000 animals live in the crater with thin brush and trees. The early light cast long dark shadows in the trees and we watched with amazement, as suddenly what appeared to be shadows started moving and became a herd of zebras. Their bold stripes, so obvious when you see a zebra in the open, were perfect camouflage in the dawn light.

Driving through the crater we began to see many animals: gazelles, bat-eared fox, wildebeest, impala, a flock of ostriches — all bathed in glorious golden morning light. Suddenly we faced a young rhino. Irritated by the sound of our engine and our unfamiliar smell he charged our vehicle, sending us roaring off past wart-hog piglets running behind their mother with her uplifted tail.

I had read our wildlife books and was good at identifying. Standing up through the open top of the Land Cruiser, I scanned the horizon with my binoculars and proudly told Rinpoche what was around. As we saw animals I called out names or Rinpoche pointed to ask what something was. I would say, "A Thompson's gazelle." or "Hartebeest," and so on.

In the distance Rinpoche spotted something sticking up from the long grass and asked, "What's that?"

I looked with my binoculars and saw what appeared to be a curved branch of a fallen tree. "Oh, it's just a dead log, Sir," I said assuredly.

He looked at it some more as did the driver and finally Rinpoche said, "No, I don't think it is."

I said, "No Sir, I'm very sure that is just a log," thinking, "I'm the one spotting up here and I've got the binoculars."

"Let's check it out anyway," and to my chagrin we drove over to look.

As we neared, the shape transformed into a wildebeest lying on its side with one curved horn sticking up in the air. Lying in front, holding on with her teeth, was a lioness still panting from the exertion of the chase. Three young lion cubs sat beside her. Rather than feed herself, the panting lioness chewed open the belly of the wildebeest spilling out the guts and the cubs went in face first as deep as they could go.

As we pulled up, the three cubs turned to look at us like cute kids with pudding all over their faces. They busily enjoyed lapping up hot blood from the wildebeest's belly. We were awestruck by the scene less than ten feet in front of us. In the back seat an older student of Rinpoche was mesmerized by the scene. Intrigued but repulsed, she splayed her fingers across her face repeating, "I can't look!" as she stared between her fingers.

My mind reeled with the enormity of all the shifting views coursing through my mind. First I had had a view expressed as "I know where it's at, I know where we're going and I know what that curved shape is."

But when we got there, the reality was completely different. Witnessing the event there was juxtaposition between the unfortunate death of the wildebeest and the care taken by the lioness as she lovingly nurtured her offspring. Without food, the young cubs would not survive. Where is the higher view — compassion for the poor wildebeest or compassion for the young cubs or both? Rinpoche turned and chuckled at this humorous situation in the back seat, then caught my eye and seemed to say, "So what is your view?"

And that question had stayed with me through the years.

We don't notice the basics of life. For example, why do you have tears? Knowing the answer could give you a leap on the path. On the Serengeti there is a lot of dust. Beings' tears clear the vision — to see where predators are and where food is. Tears are on the way to sight; this is profound. When tears come, don't shut down, look into life. Tears are for vision. Tears are beyond boredom and sadness — Look! The Serengeti has real predators and dangers, not just those imagined by you.

Namgyal Rinpoche, Dharma Centre of Canada, 1993.

The Bastard! (Canal du Midi France, 1982-3) *John de Jardin*

Rinpoche was arriving back from a freighter trip to East Africa and a friend I'd introduced to the Teaching was a student on board. I was staying at his flat near Assisi when I got word to bring Rinpoche's car up to Hamburg to meet the ship and drive him to Worpswede, near Bremen where he would teach a short course.

When I met him, Rinpoche mentioned that afterwards he was planning a holiday — a cruise down the Canal du Midi in southern France. I had very little money and was on my way back to Canada, but he said, "Why don't you come along? There will just be the four of us. I'll lend you the money to do it." So, great! A holiday with Rinpoche — an offer I can't refuse, right?

This was near the beginning of his health problems, and just coming off the freighter, he'd been on this terrible Polish Ocean Lines diet for a while. But anyway, our hotels were booked and we drove south, got on the canal boat and took it through all the locks of the Canal du Midi — a spectacular, beautiful cruise.

Right from the start he was really tough on me — very tough. It was supposed to be a relaxed holiday and my buddy from Winnipeg could do no wrong — everything was just great with him, but I was, like — garbage. Rinpoche was annoyed with me all the time. The tension increased on him as he became ill. In fact we had to call on one of his students — a nurse who lived in Paris — to come down to meet the boat and have a look at him. He wouldn't go to a hospital.

Finally it all came to a head. One day when we were going through a lock and I was trying to tie up the boat he yelled at me, "Come on! What's wrong with you? You're supposed to be a seaman (I'd worked on and off in the marine industry for a number of years.) Can't you get it right?"

I shouted back, "I'm doing the best I can!"

He just looked at me and muttered, but it really felt awful to yell back at him like that. This was a breakthrough for me but also a terrible dichotomy. This miserable old bastard was on my case all the time and I really was trying to do my best, making this effort. I hated his guts. But he was my Teacher, my Lama!

That evening he was lying down after supper, experiencing a lot of pain, and I was doing the dishes and feeling tense. He called Terry in and I heard very clearly as he said, "Get him out of here!"

And something broke, something cracked in my being, and I just wept. It was awful. Whatever self-loathing there was in my psyche came to the surface at that moment and I felt so worthless. It broke something open in me and I let go. He was still hard on me the rest of the trip — he kept me moving — but at the very end, when we got back to Hamburg, he had me come into his room and when I was done massaging his feet, he blessed me.

He put his hand on my head and said, "Good work!"

The whole nature of the relationship shifted after that. He was never harsh with me again. Sometime later, in an interview, I said to him, "Look, I know there has been a lot of my projecting my 'father stuff' onto you and I realize that that's not what this relationship is about. It's about my liberation."

And he said, "Good!"

To love is to experience all things. But to experience without love is to live in vain.

Namgyal Rinpoche, Toronto, 1967.

On Becoming a Student (1980s) *Stephen Foster*

I first met Namgyal Rinpoche in May, 1978. I was 28, near the end of a sputtering career as an actor and two years into a cab driving stint that was taking me nowhere. I had been living in a house in the beaches area of Toronto.

Upstairs lived a colourful couple; the guy, Jeff Olson, often showed up at my door (or me at his,) armed with a case of beer and a pack of smokes, to while away an evening with stories about this amazing teacher he had travelled with across the world. His stories were of adventure tinged with Zen mystery and they were catnip to me.

Jeff was one of a number of original and inspiring people I met that year — a yoga teacher, a couple doing meditation instruction, a poet — who all led back to this same intriguing man: Namgyal Rinpoche, formerly called the Bhikkhu, who spent years practicing in the East. He had been living and teaching in Toronto before suddenly announcing he was leaving for a life on the road.

If you wanted to study with Namgyal Rinpoche, you had to catch up with him, which is precisely what I did. I bought a ticket to Greece to attend a three month program that summer.

First stop was the island of Crete, for a month-long study of the *Visuddhimagga* (The Path of Purification,) the first written meditation text dating back to the year 430 CE. Those initial few days are seared in to my memory.

Rinpoche was such a big man, so forceful, knowledgeable and visionary. I would hang around his home after his talks, fold up the carpets, help clean the teaching room and quietly watch all the activity around me: people staying for interviews, guys cooking meals and attending to him.

On the third day Rinpoche suddenly approached to ask if I was going to register for an upcoming boat trip. At that time he was doing extensive travel on ocean freighters and his plan was to book a Polish boat, leaving Hamburg for south Asia, in the fall.

I mumbled something about not wanting to get too far ahead of myself (something he had said in class that day) and he replied, "I thought all guys your age want to get out and see the world."

Well, he was right. I booked on that freighter. And after three exciting summer months of travel and teaching, in Crete, Israel and finally to Assisi, Italy, I flew back to Toronto, shut down my apartment, sold everything I had, convinced my girlfriend to travel with me after the boat trip and three weeks later boarded a Polish freighter in Hamburg, Germany for a six week crossing to Pakistan, India and Sri Lanka.

We were a party of four on the boat, Rinpoche, his attendant Terry and another new student. I had a very simple idea of what our adventure was going to be. Rinpoche had suggested we might be studying anthropology, I was going to see Asia for the first time and my gal was going to be waiting for me in Bombay. Cool!

The first moment I realized that this trip was not going to be like anything I had done before started with the discussion of a book Rinpoche had given me, by Robert Ardrey, called 'African Genesis.' Ardrey's focus is on our animal nature and the unique, innate violence of mankind. Rinpoche asked what I thought of the book.

I told him I was impressed and as I launched into deep thoughts, he suddenly grabbed the book from my hand, tore it to pieces and threw it across the room, shouting that it was complete bullshit, utter nonsense. And that pretty much ended our study of anthropology!

Shortly after, Rinpoche decided it was time we learned how to play bridge; 'the game of life' he called it. Our first game was a classic. Rinpoche dealt the cards, turned to me and told me to start the bidding.

Having never played before I pleaded that I had no idea what to say and asked if he could explain the game a bit.

"Shut up," he said. "Don't play your mummy trip with me, just bid."

I think I burped out something like, "Three hearts" and boy, did he rip in to me.

"That's such a stupid bid."

It was a tough night, though I must say I picked up the game pretty quickly.

As the freighter took on cargo in India, Pakistan, Sri Lanka and Bangladesh, our six week trip was stretched to almost four months.

Day by day I learned what service to the teacher looked like and I did not like it. Rinpoche acted as if he owned us. He had us running around constantly.

My least favourite request was, "Go to the bridge and find out where we are."

The captain didn't want us up there but every couple of hours I'd have to go to the bridge, ask the first mate to pull out the maps and show us where we were, then report the incremental movement to Rinpoche.

Most days I would be in his room, yakking and planning upcoming travels, as he lay stretched out on his bed. Often Terry would remove his socks and massage his feet.

And I'd think, "Well that's one thing I'm not going to do; I'm not groveling at his feet."

As the days flipped over, crossing the Mediterranean, passing through the Suez Canal, then chugging our way to Bombay, life seemed reduced to one long showdown at the bridge table. I grew to hate those sessions.

Once, Rinpoche started by pouring us a glass of Slivovitz as a toast, then offered the Roman salute — those who are about to die salute you — before starting the card playing shenanigans.

He and Terry were partners and I always played against him but he would never lose. He would use every shameless trick to throw us off our game — yell, scream, grab your cards, throw the table up in the air — didn't matter what; I was not going to beat that man at a game of bridge.

I couldn't bear it. I used to scour the various decks on the boat, book in hand, looking for corners to hide away in. But sure enough, Terry would always find me, to invite me back to the table. Many days I would retreat into my room, to lie on my bed and get lost in my reading. But sure enough, I'd hear a soft knock on the door and there he'd be.

What could I say? "Come in, sir."

He'd sidle in, perch himself at the desk, tell me to carry on with what I was doing, then deal himself hand after hand of Solitaire. I would lie there, ostensibly reading my book, but really only thinking about him, despising him really, thinking about how I might slip away. But what could I do?

He would sit there playing, talking to himself, humming away, till I would invariably come over to the desk, feeling I should watch him play. And of course he would miss a move and I would not be able to hold back — "The ten goes on the jack," I would point out — and he would turn with the most withering look, admonishing me to butt out. Yeah, the man would get me every time.

One sunny morning Rinpoche told us that he intended, over the following weeks, to practice 10,000 mantras for each of the forty main deities in the Tibetan system.

This was mostly fun to be around, until the breakfast when he announced: "Today I am beginning the two, four and six arm *Mahakalas*. I am no longer responsible for anything I say or do."

Well, that was the beginning of one of the tougher stretches in my life. The *Mahakalas* are demon-like protectors that one calls upon when meditating on darker, more fundamental energies (not that I knew much about that then.)

For days Rinpoche became thoroughly intense. I could literally hear his footsteps, even from the other end of the boat.

One evening he joined us on the deck, wearing his black leather jacket and arriving in an absolutely ferocious, brewing state. I said something nervously about the gathering storm, mentioned the lightning, and said that it was going to be exciting.

Well, he just reared up with this screaming energy and let me have it. He told me what an idiot I was, that so many people die at sea in dangerous storms, that I was a dreamy fool — he just grabbed my sense of myself and tore it to pieces.

I had never been roared at like that before (nor sworn at.) I thought I might crumble to pieces right then and there, though even as I wobbled there was the sense of a surprising resilience in my gut.

And then one night at the bridge table, as he screamed at me about something stupid I had done, I remember blankly staring at him, in a kind of checked-out state.

He suddenly reared back with that big arm of his (he was a good 6'4" tall) and, while telling me, "I'm going to knock that out of you once and for all," delivered a full-on whack across my face.

I was stunned; I couldn't believe what he had just done. And yet the moment wasn't really about the pain.

What emerged was a concentrated and immediate memory of how dull my eyes had just been, how my jaw had been dropped, that my flycatcher (as my mother used to say) had been hanging wide open. It was a suddenly very familiar pose: the dumb child, a strategy I had used all my life to respond to moments that felt overwhelming to me.

And in one surgical strike Rinpoche decided to knock that out of me once and for all. He did. I can't remember ever using that dumb child look again.

Several months into the trip, we found ourselves stuck in the port of Karachi, in southern Pakistan. It was the month of Ramadan, when Muslims fast all day and only eat after sundown.

Work at the port moved very slowly, as groups of men would load a camel or carry a basket across the platform, then sit down with co-workers to chat for a couple of hours. Given the amount of cargo that remained, it was clear that our freighter wasn't going anywhere for a few weeks.

Normally the boat was a good base from which to explore, but we had run in to a problem. The crew had amassed a good supply of whiskey for sale. Pakistanis at that time were not allowed, by law, to drink any alcohol.

But they would come on the boat anyway, looking to buy a bottle and figuring they would have to drink the whole thing then and there, rather than risk getting caught on shore. So they would quickly down a bottle and then roam around looking for more, banging on every door, shouting and braying, throwing up in the hallways. It was an absolutely bizarre scene.

After spending a night standing guard at Rinpoche's cabin door, we decided to head out of the city and do a little touring.

By that point I churned with inner turmoil - non-stop hating Rinpoche, resenting his imperiousness, his raging at me and his persistent assertion of control.

At the same time I started to wonder if I might be going crazy. Why am I fighting this man so much? Why do I feel so confused? Where is all this fury coming from?

Hours would pass in ongoing self-interrogation. I was carrying a heavy load, barely able to enjoy the exploring we were doing, disengaged from the lively conversation we had at mealtimes or when we were out and about. I felt so lost.

And there was Terry, prodding me, "You're blowing it man. You've got this amazing opportunity and you're blowing it."

Capping it all, the fourth guy in our group, deciding he'd had enough, fled at first landfall in Bombay. God, I wished I'd run away with him.

So there I was one day, sitting alone in my hotel room in Pakistan, feeling the whole weight of the world crushing in on me. The mantra I was running was, "What is wrong with me?" and I had no answer. I remember sitting there for the longest time, holding that question, feeling entirely collapsed.

Then something started to move; just a flicker at first. I sat quietly, following the sensation.

And yes, for the first time in weeks, I could feel the constriction easing, the pain dissolving, the dark hard knot I had been carrying beginning to unwind.

I don't know how long I sat there; I just remember the feeling, of heaviness transforming into a kind of weightlessness, of this sudden expansive sense of freedom and space and unending possibility.

Until I was finally able to say to myself, definitively, that what I had been building and carrying and suffering with up to that moment was now irrevocably done; that this part of the journey was over.

Right at that moment, precisely as I said this to myself, there was a soft knock at the door.

I got up and floated over to answer and sure enough, it was Rinpoche.

He looked me in the eye, held up his hand and gracefully gestured with his index finger to follow him.

He walked me over to his room and lay on the bed, then stretched his legs out and wiggled his toes. It was time for me to massage his feet. And that is what I did. Rinpoche lay there reading his book and I massaged his feet.

I did so in a state of amazement and incredulity; suddenly awake to the ways of the world, to the ways of this amazing teacher and the teaching itself.

Tears poured down my cheeks. I felt I had finally arrived, finally become a student; that I was now ready to learn from this great and patient and absolutely fearless man, about freedom.

The whole dialogue with Namgyal Rinpoche was entirely different after that day.

To my relief, my internal grinding ended; to my surprise, so did Rinpoche's grinding of me. I had discovered something fundamental about serving another and it marked the beginning of a little ritual that I performed diligently for the next 25 years of our relationship.

At the start of each day, when I first set eyes on Rinpoche, my teacher, I would perform three prostrations. I would put my face onto the ground, as a way of reminding myself who I was and what my place was in the world; as a statement of the love and respect in my heart for this wonderful, compassionate teacher.

If reason and thought are kept in balance and used at the right time and place, there is nothing wrong with showing aggressive or angry emotions, or mixing them with other possible thoughts to get a reaction.

Jesus demonstrated this by kicking the money lenders out of the Temple.

Sometimes overly passive, non-violent people discover, that the very thing which would allow them to counteract an action directed towards them, is now gone because they subdued it in themselves.

Namgyal Rinpoche, Dharma Centre of Canada, 1980s.

Let it Shine! (Winnipeg, 1980s, Kinmount, 1990s) *Anna Woods*

I first met Namgyal Rinpoche at the railway station in Winnipeg. He was on a one hour layover traveling with students. A friend of mine had invited me along. As Rinpoche came off the train and into the station I appraised him, was introduced and we sat on a bench and chatted.

I remember enjoying the conversation, a nice, older man I thought, but I couldn't appreciate the odd behavior of the students, bowing, prostrating — what was this? But I liked him. Little did I realize what was happening during that polite conversation.

Somehow Rinpoche recognized something in me and although I didn't study with him until ten years later, from then on whenever I was in crisis, no matter where I was in the world, a student of Rinpoche's would enter my life and give a teaching from him.

Sometimes, only years later would I realize that it was from him. It was always there and I felt completely connected and fully supported by him.

Once, at the beginning of a retreat Rinpoche announced that the retreat was in silence — SILENCE! He said anyone caught talking would be asked to leave, adding that it was for the benefit of the retreatants.

I was working as usual in the kitchen and had my old Volvo station wagon to transport other staff and students to Tseringma house for the teaching. Running a little late, having finished prep in the kitchen, I hopped in the wagon with three other students.

A spontaneous joy arose in us and soon we were all singing *This Little Light of Mine,* sometimes in four part harmony. The little green Volvo was rocking!

Suddenly, turning the corner to the drive we stopped and stared at one another with humour and horror as we realized we'd broken silence.

We quietly filed into Tseringma House and found cushions amongst the packed bodies of students.

Terry pulled up with Rinpoche in the Volkswagen with its bobbing flower. Rinpoche strode forward and seemed to be dancing a jig.

The four of us looked at one another in utter surprise as the door opened and he sang, "This little light of mine, I'm gonna let it shine!"

With a grin he sat and donning his robe began teaching.

The Instructed Teacher (Florida, 1980s) *Matt Wright*

Once while Rinpoche and Terry were visiting us in South Florida, we decided to take a drive to the Everglades. Once there, and after a good humored 'short walk' (which wasn't) to a viewing spot where a variety of birds and creatures were displaying, we galloped back to the car with a squadron of aggressive summer mosquitoes hot at our heels and heads. All but Terry, who displayed his Canadian toughness by taking his time!

We then drove to the visitor centre where Rinpoche said he would wait for us in the car while we collected information from the park rangers. Before leaving the car, Terry briefly showed Rinpoche, who did not drive, how to operate the controls of the air-conditioner and affirmed that it would soon kick-in when he turned the key.

Upon our return we noticed Rinpoche sitting there streaming with perspiration and we asked, "What happened?"

He calmly answered, "I'm waiting for the 'kick-in.'" The ignition key had been turned to start the fan running, but not far enough to start the engine — so no air-conditioner. Even in the heat and having been given incomplete instructions, Rinpoche remained calm and cool in spirit if not in body. From time to time over the years when Terry and I are together and working on a machine or even cooking up a dinner in the kitchen one of us will say "I'm waiting for the kick-in," and we will smile at the memory.

Bridgeview (Kinmount, 1990s) *Carina Bomers*

We were standing on the bridge in Kinmount and looking at a house in the distance that was completely burned down in a fire the night before.

One of our Dharma friends had lost everything in that house and Rinpoche quietly said, "See how it can all go up in flames so fast at any time. It's best you get to work on your meditation. Those results do not disappear in any fire and last from lifetime to lifetime."

Actually there is no distinction between mind and matter. Study one and find the other. Awaken to God being aware of his own creation.

Namgyal Rinpoche, Toronto, 1971

The Book Mudra (New Zealand, 1987, 1988) *Alan Wilkie*

I once joined a yoga class for men that Rinpoche gave, expecting demonstrations of asanas or instructions on pranayama, but during the class there were none. It was a discourse during which Rinpoche suggested six books to read. None of the books were physically present, yet as he talked about them he seemed to 'place' each book in a kind of hierarchy, with slight changes in his posture. He began at the top with *Calm and Clear*, then 'placed' the *Six Yogas of Naropa* to the right, about his shoulder area, then *Kum Nye Relaxation* to his left, in a triangular formation. Then he added *Yoga and Health*, on a lower level in the centre, forming a diamond shape (or up-pointing triangle above a down-pointing triangle.) Then next to that, to his right he placed *The Serpent Power* and then to his left *Light on Yoga*, formed another triangle.

After the course I did hatha yoga in the mornings (using *Yoga and Health* as my main reference.) And in the evening, I often did drawing. I continued with yoga for a year until the next course in 1988, when Rinpoche suggested that anyone doing yoga tone it down and simply do a few exercises, forwards and back and side to side. Later, he gave some pointers on Mahamudra and asked us to put on paper which of three objects — an arrowhead, a lead ball and a feather — was clearest to us.

My initial response to this suggestion was a kind of shrug, my head swinging from one side to the other, while internally I pictured a ping-pong ball. I was aware he was looking at me, frowning in the distance and the ball slowed to become a white globe on the right, a white globe on the left and a planetary globe in the centre, a little higher than the other two.

It soon became apparent that this suggestion was actually more like an imperative that we each had to present him our piece of paper, as a kind of meditation report. When my turn came and I entered the hall, he definitely looked down to his left, then to his right, and I noticed two books, *The Song of Awakening* on his left and *Eliminating the Darkness of Ignorance* on his right. This raised a big question for me and I began to observe Rinpoche's body signs much more closely. In hindsight, reflecting on these book scenes, they appear like beads on a rosary, linking numerous recollections of Rinpoche, though arranged geometrically with 'Calm and Clear' at the apex or crown.

The Buddha pointed out the dharma of a ploughed field and beings attained awakening right then and there.

Namgyal Rinpoche, Dharma Centre of Canada, 2003.

The Wheat Sheaf Tavern (Kinmount, 1988-89)
Derek Rasmussen

The Kinmount Seminary and Academy was a three-year course initiated by Rinpoche at the Dharma Centre (1985-87 and 1988-1990.) Intended to train teachers, the program included science, world religions, art, music, Buddha dharma, public speaking, psychology, yoga and other subjects.

We focused on Namgyal Rinpoche as principal teacher but we learned much from Sonam Senge, Chorpel Dolma, Karma Chime, Tarchin Hearn, Cecilie Kwiat and others who taught courses.

I attended the Second Academy and was fairly new to the Teaching at that point, so I often didn't understand what Rinpoche was getting at with his analogies or stories. I relied on the senior teachers as a sort of translating corps and although I never said this out loud, I often felt like I was saying to them, "Excuse me; I don't speak 'Enlightenment,' could you translate what Rinpoche just said?" And they would. Here is an example:

At the end of the first year of the Second Academy we the students were tasked with designing the curricula for the second and third years. So we selected what we thought would be the best things to study, then started inviting the teachers and organizing a timetable — this was a great experience. The final stage was submitting the curricula to Rinpoche for approval and this is where things took an unexpected turn.

A few of the students had worked diligently on a third year curriculum that was heavy on alternative medicine: reflexology, shiatsu and other Eastern body therapies. One evening we were invited to Rinpoche's house after dinner to present the third year curriculum to him.

Rinpoche was sitting at the long dining table. While some of us tried to present him a flowery detailed description of the third year and its goals, he impatiently cut us off saying, "Yes, yes, just give me the piece of paper."

Our entire year's planning was on that sheet of paper. We handed it to him. He read it — and he flung it onto the floor. He shouted, "Why are you doing all these Asian therapies? Shiatsu and so on is all well and good on your own time, but this Academy is supposed to be about compassion — in the West! — about learning ways to help regular people — here in the West!"

"Doing all these exotic therapies is an indulgence. You're too esoteric, the lot of you. You're too removed. You don't have a clue about the suffering of ordinary people. How is any of this going to help the guys in the Wheat Sheaf Tavern?! Take this away!"

We high-tailed it out of there, dove into the car and drove back to the Dharma Centre. All the way back I was thinking, 'Why is he talking about the Wheat Sheaf Tavern? Where did he get that from?'

Back at the Centre, I went Tara cabin, to ask Senge. This was one of those, "Can you translate it for me?" moments.

Senge explained that when Rinpoche returned to Canada from the East in the mid-1960s, he went to work in a Toronto print shop. While there he got involved in trying to organize a union and he even occasionally went out for a beer (!) with his co-workers at the Wheat Sheaf Tavern on King Street.

When one of his students offered to support him, he left the print shop and went back to teaching Dharma full-time, but the Wheat Sheaf experience reverberated on. It was one of the benchmarks Rinpoche used to illustrate how the Dharma has to be able to reach all the people in society, not just the folks interested in esoteric Eastern things.

After talking with Senge, my next stop was Tarchin's cabin. After I told him what had happened, Tarchin replied by asking, "Do you know what the first book was that I ever studied with Rinpoche?"

"Umm, no?"

"It was *Character Analysis* by Wilhelm Reich. Sonam, Mark and I studied it in Toronto with Rinpoche — just the four of us. It was a pivotal book for understanding how people armour themselves, how the muscles of the body rigidify in response to trauma or neurosis. But, you know, I don't think Rinpoche has taught from that book since."

A couple of days later I had to go over to Rinpoche's house on an errand. I thought I could slip in and out, but Rinpoche was there. "Ye-e-ess," he said, in that drawn out way, "How's the curriculum going? Have you found anything worthwhile to put into it yet?"

I blurted out, "Well, we were thinking about maybe studying *Character Analysis*, sir."

"Hmm. Well, that's a very good idea. The whole of Reich's work is captured in that book. How to read the neurotic clinging in a being by just observing how they hold themselves, how they walk, talk, or breathe." A pause — "Carry on."

"Yes sir."

Rinpoche taught from *Character Analysis* the following year. (I never mentioned to anyone that it was Tarchin's suggestion.)

Opal (New Zealand, 1989) *Alan Wilkie*

When in India with Namgyal Rinpoche in 1972, I came across a travelling trader who set up shop on a patch of ground simply by unfolding a cloth containing his gems and laying it on the ground before him.

I spied an interesting stone, greenish yellow, which I purchased. It was a peridot, I later learned. I offered it to Rinpoche as *Dana* after an empowerment he gave in a retreat in 1973 near Rotorua, New Zealand.

Recently, I reflected on the Chakric Clearing Course Rinpoche gave in 1989. We departed Auckland, travelled north through the Maori heartland, shifting camp daily as Rinpoche discoursed on one of the chakras.

We returned to Auckland, ten days later, for Rinpoche's flight onwards. Meandering around the airport, we crossed paths. He ambled up beside me on my left. Extending his right arm he showed me a piece of jewelry a student made.

In his palm, there appeared to be a large moonstone on a black diamond-shaped pad of velvet. As he tilted his hand slightly, in the shift of light I realized it was actually an opal hemisphere.

This embodies Rinpoche's skill as a quiet magician — a gift to me.

I have no idea of the worth of that stone — nor does it matter. He didn't give it to me to possess — to add to my stash of wealth, like Scrooge McDuck, swimming around in my treasure vault, or as baksheesh, or alms for a starving beggar — who'd pawn it quick for another shot of meth.

Nope, he just showed me this simple beautiful thing — and walked on.

Jesus said, "The light of the body is the eye: if therefore thine eye be single, thy whole body shall be full of light."

If electrons in the magnetic field are in harmony, light is produced.

Most humans are unaware they have an electromagnetic field. Many aboriginal people feel changes in the magnetic field around them.

Namgyal Rinpoche, Dharma Centre of Canada, 1998.

Viriya is when will power comes into play, you have allied yourself with the unfolding of the universe. The previously blocked energy is released and allowed to function in the true discovery of your being and the world around you. A free being, the Arahat, has destroyed the go no-where energies, the writhing snakes that had chained his being. With the release of the neurotically dammed energies all that has been tied up in the struggle is freed to manifest in the wholesome. When the negative conditioning is slayed it is no longer the negative will power that is at work, but a natural flow of awakening. Those that have the eyes to see, let them see. If only you used your eyes. How much do you actually see, hear, and feel on the way to the grocery store? Most likely you will be thinking of this class or perhaps what you are going to buy. It is probably very rare that you are truly aware of the walking — you are either in the past or in the future and therefore miss the moment.

The Path of Victory, Discourses on the Paramita, Kinmount, Bodhi Publishing, 4th Printing, 2002, p. 48. Used with permission from Bodhi Publishing.

The Latter Years 1990-2003

In the last years of his life Rinpoche continued to travel and teach around the world in spite of health issues. Once in the late 1990s, while inviting students to join him on a scuba diving trip around several Indonesian islands, he explained: "What I am about is helping people break out of their stagnation so the natural processes of unfolding and evolution can continue. The teachings and practices of many traditions can be useful to support this but when I invite people to step out of their familiar settings to begin to function in new cultures and places, such as sending them ashore at the port of Dakar in Senegal to buy spices in the crowded market, they move more quickly out of habitual patterns to deal with the unfamiliar environment."

"In recent years I observed that when I take students into environments where humans don't normally go and where our ancestors would not have survived such as onto to a polar glacier or beneath a tropical sea swimming along a coral reef with sea turtles and sharks, people drop their trances very quickly in order to adapt and survive."

Rinpoche taught using many classical traditions and his own innovations. He was a master at creating context and inviting experience that supported students' opening of awareness and realization.

Incarnations (The Yukon, February, 1991) *Rab Wilkie*

Rinpoche's last visit to the Namgyal House in the Yukon prepared us well ahead of time for his passing. It was almost spring when he arrived at the Redwood House which had served us well for many years.

Much work had gone into that house. The oldest room had been a tent that had been encased in cabin walls one winter, almost a century ago — the headquarters of the Commissioner of the Territory, circa 1905. It was subsequently enlarged and decades later had been transported from the Yukon River valley to high land above Whitehorse, where it now stood.

The shrine room, the original one-room cabin, had been blessed by visiting Tibetan lamas, including the Karmapa in 1977. It had character. When the inside walls were replaced with new knotty pine, strips of tattered canvas were revealed, still clinging to the joists. Of the two small windows only the one facing west admitted much light, so during winter retreats it was a draughty dark womb. We didn't mind. It was cozy compared with -30° C outside. But after an empowerment one evening, Rinpoche voiced his opinion as he came out of the shrine room: "You should install larger windows."

The following morning, sitting in the living room in front of the very large window, students spread all round; he looked at us and shook his head slowly. "You should see yourselves, your eyes. What is it about this place at this time of year? Before spring everyone has this glazed look. Surely it's not too much meditation."

Someone suggested lack of sunlight and too much coffee. He nodded, "Aha," and compared us to wired-up teddy bears coming out of hibernation. He advised more daylight activities, outside, and proclaimed the advantage of larger windows. "Open up your heart and let the sun shine in!"

That night he gave another empowerment and afterwards asked us to gather in the living room. Times were changing, he said, and he was adapting. No more Guru up here, disciples down there. Everyone has to work together to build the group-mind and so we were to join him in meditation. He would share his meditation and guide us. He described the brilliant bluish white OM in the Brow chakra, and in the Throat, a red flower — floating in a clear pool of water in the midst of a Persian garden — in the courtyard of a beautiful palace. The flower was linked under the water by a green tendril to another red flower like the first one. "We are related," he said, "in love to other people — perhaps to one other special person. AHH!"

Then a third flower, linked in a similar way with the first pair. And so the flowers multiplied until the surface of the whole pool was covered with red flowers. "Yes — now to the Heart Chakra, a blue flower; of infinite depth and space — HOOM!"

Afterward, during a tea-break, Rinpoche intimated this might be his last Yukon visit, so we had better get on with the Work — and working together. "The Namgyal Guru doesn't incarnate often, you know."

Someone asked, "How often?"

"Ahh," he responded, "It varies, depending on the times," and took a sip of tea before standing up to walk around the room. In the middle of the room he stopped, his right arm gesturing upward and around as if to encompass the cosmos and myriad worlds.

"Yes, but just on average, about how often?" another person asked.

"It's not often that one Namgyal incarnation is immediately succeeded by the next," he cautioned. "Many years can pass — many decades, even many centuries."

"Okay, but over a few thousand years, ABOUT how often?"

"Well, mayyy-be every century, or three centuries." he replied. "Let's say on average — over the last Age or so — about once in 250 years."

Silence. Finally another student asked, "Depending on the times, you said, Sir — so what are the times like now?"

"Uh-hmm," he replied.

Rinpoche left early the next morning. Several of us joined him and Terry at the airport restaurant for breakfast before departure. As we sat there, all crowded into a booth, I was feeling a little peeved that none of Rinpoche's books had become best sellers. It was even rare to find them on public library bookshelves. How to broach this subject? With furrowed brow, during a pause in the lively chat, I finally ventured some words. "You know, Sir, I've been thinking — about your books."

"You have, have you?" he said archly. "Well, as a matter of fact, last summer we did begin some negotiations, with a European company — actually, the publisher of Kahlil Gibran. Yes? I've always wanted to have a book something like *The Prophet*, something accessible to the many. Poetic yet pithy; you understand?"

In order to explore we need a vehicle. The Vision sees Religion, Science and Art as vehicles, that is, as different ways to explore the same thing. These disciplines are not ends in themselves but avenues running alongside one another. Although our curiosity may be aroused by one avenue of exploration, we must maintain a non-selective curiosity, not clinging to any one part, but seeking to embrace the whole. We must be in a state of choiceless awareness: nonexclusive so that we may be all-inclusive. The Vision sees Man as being open to all possibilities, to all views or theories, to the vast amount of knowledge, and yet cling to none. We must not even cling to a Vision — that would be to misunderstand its nature.

The Vision and Other Essays, Bhikkhu Ananda Bodhi, Toronto, 1971; p. 9. Used with permission from Bodhi Publishing.

The Layered Gift (Kinmount, 1990s) *Lisa Cowen*

Rinpoche often gave Dharma talks in the living room of his house on Reid Street in Kinmount. He would sit on his couch or armchair and students would squeeze in, sitting on the chairs and carpet. We lived locally and rarely missed any opportunity to visit Rinpoche's house. My mother and I were at one such talk when I was nine or ten years old. I was sitting on the floor, positioned carefully so I could see him between the heads and shoulders of the people in front of me.

I was always intent on listening to Rinpoche in the classes. Even as a very young girl I considered myself to be a student like all the rest of the people there. Never playing with toys, fidgeting or drawing, I listened in what I considered to be a very adult way. So it came as quite a surprise when Rinpoche paused in class and addressed me, "Would you like a doll?"

When I realized he was talking to me, I was embarrassed and even taken aback. Why would I want a doll at a dharma class when I was listening like everyone else? So naturally I said something like, "Uh, no, I'm okay, thanks." People chuckled quietly. He insisted and sent Terry to fetch it through the door that led to Rinpoche's room and closet. All the interesting stuff seemed to come from there in those days — exotic fabrics, essential oil collections, rare gemstones.

When the doll emerged it instantly changed my concept of what was going on. It was an exquisitely crafted large Russian doll and not a toy at all. I took it apart with Rinpoche on the spot. The most special thing about the doll was its many nesting layers, smaller and smaller. The tiniest one was an unpainted doll-shaped piece of wood the size of a grain of rice. It was truly a beautiful, rare and painstakingly crafted item, and as it turned out later, a cleverly crafted time capsule of Dharma teaching.

Around that time I also received a yidam from Rinpoche — White Tara. In an interview I reported to him that during a meditation the room had filled with falling multicolored flowers as White Tara stood up from her traditional pose and moved towards me. Rinpoche instructed me in that interview to practice my yidam every day, but regrettably so far it has been one of my least developed practices.

Years later at 21, when I heard Rinpoche died, I experienced a life-changing few hours where a diamond blue-white light radiated above my head, and everything in my being turned irreversibly towards 'doing the work' and unpacking all the teaching I had passively received in the years when my teacher was living. I saved my money and went to New Zealand for a 3-month solo retreat at Wangapeka.

Among the countless inner adventures and confidence-building practices using what I had internalized from my teacher, there was a moment when I pulled out a White Tara Sadhana to touch on that untapped relationship with my yidam practice. This was a Sadhana I hadn't used much, if ever. The Sadhana described a visualization in which one builds around the self-arising yidam one layer after another of different colors of light, covered with shells of flowers.

Suddenly I got it — the visualization was building a subtle body much like a Russian doll! The gift from Rinpoche was a concrete object that carried a teaching on one of the subtle inner practices he had assigned to me for my life. Alone on a hilltop half way across the planet, deep in the solitude of retreat, I felt that he was truly with me and continuing to teach me in the present. I laughed, did a little dance, shed some tears and set to thinking of all the other gifts he had given me and what they might mean.

When I think about it now, what better way to teach a child who will grow up to be a practitioner than through gifts of symbolic objects? Later in life when I realized a meaning of the object, the teacher was instantly right there with me. I am so grateful to have been treated throughout my youth as a true student by Rinpoche and to have received such treasures to unpack throughout my life. If I ever see him again, I will be sure to give him something beautiful.

We are only individuals in the sense of our being unique manifestations of the dharmas. But we are not separate and distinct from one another on the spiritual plane. And it is to this plane that we must return. When our ego defenses that make us see ourselves as separate and distinct are no longer necessary, they can be dropped and the flow of communications on all levels between many beings will produce an Overmind, as it were. Human minds will meet for quite a distinct breakthrough in the evolution of consciousness. Many beings are beginning to emerge but they may still be in isolation from each other for the most part. The quantum leap means that the vibrations sent out from like consciousnesses will draw us together on a scale hitherto unknown in order to collectively leap out of our darkness and conceptual hypnosis into a new space, both inner and outer.

The Vision and Other Essays, Bhikkhu Ananda Bodhi, Kinmount, Dharma Centre of Canada, 1971; p. 13. Used with permission from Bodhi Publishing

Good Morning in Polish (Dharma Centre of Canada, 1993)
David Berry

During the 'Trance and Transcendence' course I asked a woman how she was doing on the retreat. She told me she felt isolated because many things were coming up for her relating to events and experiences in her childhood at a time when her only language was Polish. No one else on the retreat could speak Polish with her so there was no one for her to share her experiences with.

During the few minutes we chatted we had a good connection and I told her how much I enjoyed a trip to Poland many years before.

On the old coin phone behind the kitchen at the Main House I called a Polish-speaking friend to learn how to say "good morning."

My friend told me good morning in Polish was *Dzień dobry*. I practiced it on the phone to get the accent right and be sure to remember it for the next morning.

The following day in class, we rose to our feet as Rinpoche's car pulled up. He came through the main door of the temple, looked around and said in a clear loud voice, "*Dzień dobry!*"

I was amazed and remained silent because I knew who the greeting was for. No one answered and he repeated, "*Dzień dobry!*" and again there was no response.

The assembled students looked around but no one responded. It seemed none of them understood what he was saying or why he was saying it. A third time Rinpoche called out, "*Dzień dobry!*" as both he and I looked around the room for the Polish woman.

"*Dzień dobry,*" I responded. "Good morning, Sir."

"I see we have some sleepy heads here today, someone is still in bed. Good morning everyone!"

"Good morning, Sir," the class responded.

After class I walked back out the gravel road and there on the steps of the teahouse was a student telling the Polish woman what Rinpoche had covered in the morning session.

"*Dzień dobry!*" I called out.

"That's what Rinpoche said!" the student exclaimed. "I did not remember the words. He used."

"*Dzień dobry!*" said the Polish woman with a smile. My message had more impact and effect of inclusion since it was coming from Rinpoche.

I Know You (Galiano Island, British Columbia, circa 1992)
Gerry Kopelow (Lama Gyurme Dorje)

I arrived at my first retreat with Ven. Namgyal Rinpoche in a rather desperate state. Having been admitted into his circle, I was determined not to waste time and I quickly earned a reputation for asking about issues that others tended to avoid.

After delivering a discourse one morning, Rinpoche offered to take questions from the group and I put up my hand.

"What is it?" he asked.

"Sir, I am struggling with boredom when I try to meditate."

On hearing this, my fellow retreatants gasped — apparently this was a goofy question.

Rinpoche grinned, settled back in his big chair pointing a finger at me and began his response, his intonation dramatic, even Shakespearean.

"I know you," he boomed. "You are the Pasha." (He took his time over the word "Paaaasha.")

"Yes, the Paaaasha, surrounded by exquisite food, piles of jewels, beautiful dancing girls and music and gorgeous works of art. And yet, and yet — it is not enough. You are just so tired of all this beauty, all this wealth — tired, tired, tired."

"Pity the poor Pasha. He has so much, but it is not enough."

After this he paused for moment, still grinning, and then dismissed me with a wave of his hand, "Go talk to Jeff."

After class, I sought out Jeff Olsen (Lama Lodro) and I put the same question to him. He responded: "You have made all this effort to be here. Just quit resisting."

At that the logjam was broken and I started to make some progress.

Food tasted better, music sounded better and I was no longer bored in meditation or in life.

Buddha said, "I, too, use concepts but I am not fooled thereby."
This is the inner talk; I wouldn't mind if it were to a purpose.

Namgyal Rinpoche, Dharma Centre of Canada, 1998.

Ikebana (Dharma Centre of Canada, summer 1993)
Elizabeth Berry

I first met Rinpoche at a two-week retreat he named 'Trance and Transcendence.' Being new to this school, and not a regular practitioner of Tibetan Buddhism, I wondered what I needed to do to get the maximum benefit from the experience and how to incorporate it into my daily life.

Each day before he gave a talk, I walked the woods and fields around the Centre gathering flowers and other objects of beauty to make a composition to put next to his chair. I had studied flower arrangement for several years, and the Japanese form, Ikebana, in particular, so working with the local materials was a true pleasure for me.

No one told Rinpoche who was placing the flowers on the side table.

One day during his talk Rinpoche looked at my arrangement and said, "This isn't Ikebana."

Then he looked again and said, "Yes, it could be Ikebana. Ikebana is a complete spiritual path, the practice of which can lead to enlightenment." I knew he was talking to me and nearly fell out of my chair.

A few days later, I had an interview with him during which I asked for a practice. I realized that many people who practice Tibetan Buddhism do 100,000 prostrations, mantras and complicated visualizations. I honestly wasn't attracted to doing any of these things, but had such great admiration for Rinpoche; I was willing to follow his advice.

He advised me to learn an ancient Theravada Buddhist practice of making flower mandalas. I learned the practice and have since shared it with others.

Upon learning of Namgyal Rinpoche's death, I dedicated a flower mandala to him and experienced his presence very strongly as I was working with it. The message he conveyed to me is that this sacred energy would always be available to me through flowers.

Many techniques involve visualizations. I would like to change that to "imaginations." The neural network mind takes innumerable factors into consideration not just the visual. The deepest work makes use of all the senses.

Namgyal Rinpoche, Trance and Transcendence, Dharma Centre of Canada, 1993.

The Intuitive Gift (Kinmount, 1996) *Sharon Davison*

It was a wonderful summer day and Rinpoche was offering 21 days of Tara empowerments and teachings at Tseringma House. Unlike the others in attendance, I was new to the process of sitting and waiting for the car to arrive. It had only been a few short days since I first came into contact with the teacher.

One experience had told me that something was up, even though I had no idea what it was — and I intended to follow through on that feeling. It isn't often one finds they have stumbled onto the scent of 'truth' and if you got the scent you sure didn't let it go.

Towards the end of the class I had the thought, "I wonder how he feels about women and if enlightenment is possible for them." It seemed to me there was some belief in Buddhism that it is not possible for a woman to awaken, that she needs to be reborn as a man. As a woman, I didn't want to believe that was the case so I was curious what the teacher might think about this topic central to my own aspiration.

I had also heard a few comments, in the short time I had been around, to indicate that Rinpoche had some interesting thoughts and things to say about women. But being terrified of speaking up, I had no way for my question to be answered.

As Rinpoche rose to leave and I scrambled to rise, I heard him say, "You know, it's all there in the body of a woman and enlightenment is possible in a single lifetime." My head snapped around. I could not believe what I was hearing. How could he have known what I was thinking?

The question you must ask is to what extent are you supported by kusala karma, wholesome activity? To what extent are you in harmony with the motion of the universe, Buddha-karma? Are your activities wholesome, do they bring you peace and understanding? This is the essence of the Teaching . . . Enlightenment is interest, be realistic, be ordinary. Discover that all the Factors of Enlightenment, all the Paramita, are in your life right now. The sooner you realize that you are perfecting what is already present, the quicker the realization of the complete going beyond, the Sammasambuddho.

The Path of Victory, Discourses on the Paramita, Kinmount, Bodhi Publishing, 4th Printing, 2002, p. 1, 2. Used with permission from Bodhi Publishing.

Stones (Kinmount, 1995) *Sarah Berry*

I was a squirmy twelve year-old, sitting in a room full of quiet meditators. Some days on retreat at the Dharma Centre, I wanted to be somewhere else, like eating popsicles with my friends at our community pool, but I made the best of the place, taking walks and working in the kitchen. I collected rocks and practiced drawing.

After attending courses for several days with various teachers, I finally found myself one morning at the feet of a teacher about whom I'd heard endless wonderful things — Namgyal Rinpoche. He was animated and made me feel comfortable.

Several evenings later, the class was invited to his home to watch a video of his scuba trip and to look at precious and semi-precious stones. I am an artist and had taken courses in jewelry making, and already had a pretty good eye for identifying stones, or so I thought. I was blown away by Rinpoche's collection.

There were stones I thought were only found in fiery reds which he had in shimmering cool blues. There were other stones I'd only seen tumbled and polished, which Rinpoche handed me in their rough natural states. He called me to sit right next to him at the foot of his sofa and took care to show me many wonderful stones in his collection, and mentioned that he had a special string of prayer beads he wanted to show me. After tea and the amazing scuba video, we left under a sky of stars as sparkly as some of Rinpoche's stones.

The next morning during a break in his teaching, he called me up to his seat and pulled from his bag the prayer beads he had mentioned the night before. They were very nice, and a feeling came over me as I thought, "Wow, he really wanted me to see these. He remembered to bring this in to show me."

It was special, at age twelve in a room full of older people, to feel that somebody who was so important would remember that.

As simple as it may seem, I still feel grateful.

Promote a relationship of respect between beings - that's the first thing. Every being teaches but we teach in different ways.

Namgyal Rinpoche, Toronto, 1971.

A Last Meow (Retreat Center Halscheid, Germany, June 2002)
Anna and Stephan Hollnack

When our long-term feline companion Maureena was aged 16 it became obvious her life-force would not last very much longer. She got faint and fainter and during these days we offered her the best attention we could. Water and nutritious mash carefully maneuvered into her mouth she would accept gratefully.

We had to decide what to do since a retreat with Rinpoche was about to start which we really didn't want to miss. Finally we agreed on taking Maureena with us. She was greeted by the group with great compassion and concern.

At the first morning's meeting we asked Rinpoche's permission to have the cat with us during the teaching. This was granted readily and thus she was in his presence for a good while.

When the talk came to a close and Rinpoche was getting up from his seat, Maureena suddenly exclaimed a heart-rending meow — her first articulation in a couple of days and the last of her life, wisely used to call upon the radiance.

Rinpoche at once attended her. Bowing down and uttering a few simple words, he touched her head gently.

We then took Maureena to our room where, within the next half hour, she passed away peacefully.

Marananussati, or Mindfulness of Death, is the practice of bringing the mind back to reflect again and again on the theme of death. Normally this word death, or Mara, does not appear alone in Buddhist texts. It is usually Jati-mara, or life-death, and is seen as a temporary ending to a temporary phenomenon, it's not considered permanent. So Marananussati is really a meditation which should preserve and increase energy and ultimately produce compassion.

The Song of Awakening, A Guide to Liberation Through Marananussati, Mindfulness of Death, Boise, Idaho, The Open Path Publishing, 1979. p. 4. Used with permission from Bodhi Publishing.

Start A Group (Vancouver, Winnipeg, late 1990s)
Gerry Kopelow (Lama Gyurme Dorje)

I attended a retreat in Vancouver where Rinpoche was teaching The Six Paramis (perfections.) The final talk was about Dana (generosity.) During his discourse he discussed signs of accomplishment along the Path. A good indicator of progress, he said, was the spontaneous arising of the thought during an exchange with another person. "What can I do for this being?" rather than, "What can this being do for me?"

As Rinpoche spoke, it occurred to me that I was starting to think that way.

Immediately after class I had to catch a plane back to Winnipeg. Before I left I wanted to thank Rinpoche for his teaching and to say goodbye. I was unable to do this, however, because as I approached him he looked up at me and said, "Start a group in Winnipeg and we will come."

I was struck speechless at the thought of such an undertaking, but I did in fact return home and start a Dharma group, which, to my delight, continues to thrive to this day. I took the 'we' in Rinpoche's initial instruction to be the royal 'we,' and thereafter I repeatedly reminded him of his promise to come to Winnipeg to teach.

Several years later he did come, and Winnipeg was one of the last places Rinpoche taught in North America before his passing. While they were in Winnipeg, I chauffeured Rinpoche and Terry back and forth between the retreat centre and the hotel and, after the teaching was finished, I drove them to the airport for the journey back to Kinmount.

Just before he entered the security gate, Rinpoche turned to me and said, "Well done."

These were the last words he ever spoke to me, and I treasure them greatly.

Buddha taught motion. Move it! Is the Vajra Yogini deity in a Thangka painting sitting? — No.

Standing? — No.

Lying down? — No.

What is she doing? DANCING! Meditate on dancing in the mandala.

Namgyal Rinpoche, Dharma Centre of Canada, 2001.

Le Gourou Faramineux (Ayers Rock, Australia, 1990s)
Jangchub Reid

Le Grand Maître Namgyal Rinpoche is at once a fantastical guru and also a very human being. I deliberately use the present tense because he lives on, so vividly.

I use the word 'fantastical' in the sense of:

> visionary,
>
> amazing, astonishing,
>
> astounding,
>
> fabulous, fantastic,
>
> incredible,
>
> marvelous, miraculous,
>
> phenomenal,
>
> prodigious, stupendous,
>
> capricious,
>
> changeable, remarkable,
>
> unbelievable,
>
> wondrous, excellent,
>
> divine,
>
> glorious, sensational,
>
> splendid,
>
> superb, terrific,
>
> wonderful.

A vibrant mythology has built up around his exploits with students; stories so extreme as to challenge belief; and yet that's what he did — constantly challenge our beliefs about everything.

Marked by his extravagant individuality he is the excellent, superlative teacher who invites us still, to give up our fantasies and enter into the light of the real — in this present moment.

Every Dharma discourse with the Rinpoche was an empowerment.

Nevertheless, in the naiveté of youth, I once asked, "Rinpoche, sir, would you please give the Wongkur of White Tara?"

"I never give Wongkur!" was the short, sharp, thunderous response; and following in a softer tone, "The Deity gives the Wongkur."

"I have no name. I'm Sunyata, (emptiness — the spacious openness of interbeing) plus whatever you or anyone else wants to project."

For me, this extraordinary declamation, recorded on tape, reveals the freedom of the Rinpoche and simultaneously exposes the myriad fantasies we have of him.

However, it was in the quiet moments when he was most ordinary, not doing anything spectacular, that the most profound transmission of what it means to be fully human, occurred.

One early morning we were walking along in the quiet dusty desert streets of Ayers Rock, Australia, attending to the light of the sun. Just after the glorious sunrise Rinpoche asked, "Well Reid, will the sun rise tomorrow?"

For a few seconds the mind went into hologramic superhyperdrive considering the many possible answers to this simple question.

Then, equally rapidly a profound spacious tranquility opened and I replied simply, "Yes, Sir."

After a few more dusty steps he responded, "Fair enough." and so we continued down the road in silence.

> Fain?
>
> No Name! Excellent no name
>
> Presenting a present to
>
> Your mind; a light show
>
> of uncontrived eccentricity.
>
> "I am light, plus -
>
> Who are you?"
>
> Jangchub Reid,
>
> La pleine lune, janvier, 2009.

An Englishman's Sword (Germany, 1990s) *Brian McLeod*

The Buddha devised a very compact description of our struggles, reducing our ignorance to three primary forms: greed, hatred and delusion. Rinpoche used this teaching of the Buddha frequently and would sometimes allocate a student's personality to one category or another.

He always made it clear that being a Greed Type, Hate Type or Dull Type, as he called them, wasn't a life sentence so much as an indication of the work you needed to do, transforming the Three Fires to generosity, love and clarity.

He was not shy about extending this description to broad cultural groups. My friend Hugo told me about a class that took place after an initiation for Manjusri, an archetypal representation of discriminating wisdom in the Tibetan tradition. The Tibetan system has a wide range of these archetypes, each aimed at a different affirmative attribute, like loving-kindness, healing, compassion and so on.

Working with the visualizations and sound-forms of these meditations is intended to help you expand beyond what you imagine to be your own limitations by letting go into a wider range of positive possibilities.

Manjusri is always portrayed as holding a flaming sword in one hand, with a Dharma text perched on a lotus that he holds in his other hand. So, after a Manjusri initiation in Wuppertal, Germany, one student from England asked, "Sir, what is one supposed to do with the sword?" as part of the visualization work he was doing.

Rinpoche paused, looked at him closely, and said, "Well, a Frenchman would pick up the sword and feel the smooth sensuous steel, caress the hilt and run his finger along the blade."

"A German would snatch up the sword, wave it over his head and bring it down violently, yelling 'YAH!'"

"And an Englishman — well an Englishman would look perplexed and say, 'What do I do with this thing?'"

What's the difference between a rabbit and a hare? The rabbit digs a burrow and the hare lives on the surface on a shallow scrape. Don't be like the hare and remain on the surface in superficial inquiry. I don't mind you chasing rabbits — they go deep

Namgyal Rinpoche, Dharma Centre of Canada, 2001.

Dream Yoga (Dharma Centre of Canada, 1990s) *Gerry Kopelow*

On several occasions I experienced Rinpoche's teaching while in the dream state. One night after a retreat at the Dharma Centre, I dreamt that I was standing next to Rinpoche on the surface of a world that was covered knee-deep in excrement. This awful realm was populated by many terrifically unhappy beings that were listlessly crawling around through the foulness on their hands and knees.

Rinpoche was naked except for a loincloth. His body was black. His hair was an electrified halo.

He charged purposefully through the muck, energetically kicking and shouting at the benighted inhabitants: "Get up! Get up! Get a move on! You need to get out of here!"

Rinpoche's fury was at once irresistible and very sobering to witness. I was excited and amazed.

Just before I awoke, Rinpoche turned to me and said in a gentle voice: "You have to do what you can for them."

A few months later I visited Lama Sonam Gyatso in Toronto. I told him about my dream. He pulled a piece of paper from his filing cabinet.

Grinning, he showed me a dog-eared copy of an old black and white photograph of a Tibetan painting that depicted a dark-skinned, wrathful yogi holding a thighbone trumpet and a skull-cup, and surrounded by dancing Dakinis.

"Is this what you saw?"

Sonam explained that this was a very rare image of Namgyal Guru, discovered in a market stall in India by a student travelling with the Teacher many years ago — just before Rinpoche received his Tibetan name Namgyal from His Holiness the Sixteenth Karmapa.

During the early life, dreams tend to be karmic. Until age 30 or so, Freudian dreams predominate.

Jungian dreams come later. Jungian dreams are archetypal, raising questions about an evolutionary purpose.

Namgyal Rinpoche, Toronto, 1971.

Damascus (1990s) *Brian McLeod*

I was thinking about Rinpoche at 2:30 this morning — my plane was late into Ottawa and I got to the hotel after 2 am. Not able to sleep right away, I watched a great TV show about architecture around the world. One segment focused on Damascus, a place I've wanted to visit for a long time, and still haven't. The only time I recall ever seeing Rinpoche display envy was when I told him I was planning a trip to Syria. He looked genuinely surprised, a little hurt, and said, "Why haven't you asked me along?"

Syria must be one of about three countries in the world he HADN'T visited, and he clearly didn't like the thought of me getting there without him, or at least getting there first. These days, the more I myself teach, the more I see what a sweet, wonderful, adventurous, odd, remarkable, forgivable human being he was.

Vision (October 2009) *Karen Russell*

Hand woven a net lays dry on the bow

Dwindling darkness launches a fisherman on the water

Reflections swirl on the ripples left by the guiding boat

His net is thrust in space capturing the first rays of light

Dropping into its reflection in a velvet of moving waters

It sinks into the slow current

In the darkness below we struggle and resist

To the sweeping motion

Its knots brush our edges

Scooping us up

Light enters the darkness of our soul

Gently he gathers us

Inviting us into an unchartered boat in daylight Bathing us in an

ever moving mind

The fisherman lays down his net of love

For us to see the source of reflection so bright in day and night

Your Potential (Dharma Centre of Canada, 1990s)
Gerry Kopelow (Lama Gyurme Dorje)

During a retreat at the Dharma Centre, Rinpoche got into a psychotherapeutic mode. One morning he instructed us to compress the repetitive messages we had each received from parents and teachers into a couple of compact phrases then share them with the group.

"I'm a pretty, pretty girl. I'll always get along," one woman said.

"I'm a tough little boy, I don't have to cry," said someone else.

A third person related what they had received, "I will always be awkward and clumsy."

All the revelations were heartfelt and poignant.

And so it went around the room, until it was my turn. As it happened, I was seated on the floor directly in front of Rinpoche.

I dutifully offered up my recollection of my own childhood conditioning: "I am very intelligent, but will never reach my full potential."

Rinpoche elected to comment on this. In a loud voice he pronounced, "Just so! Your parents and your teachers were absolutely right!"

This elicited gasps from the group and I felt a wave of panic begin to arise — But before I plunged totally into self-pity, Rinpoche leaned over and whispered directly into my ear: "Because your potential is infinite!"

Just a very quick gesture and a very quick whisper, so quick I don't think anyone else noticed. But I certainly did, and in an instant was relieved of many years' of unpleasant baggage.

After class I was approached by a woman who was on retreat with Rinpoche for the first time. She described herself as a 'new-age therapist.'

"It must have been horrible to have been abused like that in such a public way," she told me, and then she offered to help me recover from the shock.

She was very puzzled when I declined.

Sometimes it only takes a word.

Namgyal Rinpoche, numerous places, 1966-2003.

Knife and Fork Wongkur (New Zealand, 1990s) *David Pooch*

Rinpoche was teaching at the Wangapeka Retreat Centre. The group had rented a farmhouse for him and it was my job to drive him and his attendant, Terry, back and forth.

On this particular day I had received a phone message to find another student, Jangchub and take him to the farmhouse for dinner.

Terry prepared a superb roast lamb dinner and afterwards on the way home, I was in a blissful mood, telling Jangchub how much I enjoyed the meal.

Jangchub replied that yes, the food was excellent and so was the Wongkur.

"Wongkur?" I asked. There was no Wongkur — just the dinner.

"Oh yes, there was." replied Jangchub. "Rinpoche conducted Wongkur during dinner. I could tell by his gestures with the knife and fork."

I fell silent and wondered; truly, this man had gone beyond all of us.

A Secret Teaching (Winnipeg, 2000)
Gerry Kopelow (Lama Gyurme Dorje)

In 1999 my Dharma group assisted Rinpoche's first teacher, Sayadaw U Thila Wunta, in the construction of a 21-foot pagoda at the St. Norbert's Arts and Cultural Centre on the outskirts of Winnipeg.

The pagoda project was a big success with lots of enthusiastic support from various ethnic Buddhist communities. During the process, I developed a warm relationship with Bhikkhu Vinita, an English-speaking monk that the Sayadaw had brought with him from Burma.

Several months after the completion of the project, I received a phone call from Rangoon. It was Bhikkhu Vinita on the line with an invitation to come to the Sayadaw's monastery for several weeks of instruction in what he described as "Secret Teachings of Anapanasati."

This was the very practice that Rinpoche had me doing for a decade or so, and I found the invitation to travel to Asia intriguing. I was tempted to drop everything and go, but thought it prudent to ask Rinpoche first.

So I emailed Terry and described the invitation and requested Rinpoche's opinion on the matter.

About ten days later I received another phone call. "Rinpoche would like to speak with you," Terry told me.

A moment later, Rinpoche's mellifluous voice intoned gravely, "Master Gerry, I understand you have been offered a secret teaching?"

"Yes Sir," I replied.

He continued, with a serious intonation, "You have a wife do you not?"

"Yes Sir, I do."

"Well, you will have to take her along won't you?"

"And you know it's very rough out there in the jungle, very primitive. She won't like it there. She won't like it there at all."

"Perhaps not, Sir." I responded, a bit deflated.

He continued, somewhat more cheerfully. "You have been doing good work out there in Winnipeg, and you know, I think you should stay there and accumulate further merit."

"What do you think?"

I was a bit disappointed, but I trusted Rinpoche always and accepted his judgment.

Then a surprise:

"You know, I could give you a secret teaching if you like."

This I could not resist. "Yes, yes Sir, I would welcome any teaching you would care to give me!"

Rinpoche paused dramatically, and then, in a conspiratorial whisper, imparted the secret teaching: "Keep breathing!"

This was the only time I spoke to Rinpoche on the telephone.

There is silence when willing ceases. This is meditation.

The seeker ceases. This is meditation.

Namgyal Rinpoche, Dharma Centre of Canada, 1967.

As If by Magic (England, 2000) *Sally Muir*

My first retreat with Rinpoche was at The Orchard centre in Herefordshire. He was teaching on the Heart Sutra. I had recently returned from a camel safari in the Sahara Desert and was very keen to find a way to go back to do retreat there because, for me, the desert was so incredibly expansive and informing.

At the morning talk, he was explaining that we needed to find a quiet place in nature to do our contemplation and meditation, like in a forest, or a field, or by a lake. He then paused for a few moments, looked into the distance and said, "Or in the desert."

The message for me was clear, to find a place of peace that is relevant and use it to unfold. It doesn't have to be the same place others would choose, just use what resonates with you.

On another occasion we were doing star gazing practice at Maitreya House, across from The Orchard. The sky was covered by roiling clouds, as the weather can be very feisty up there in Lower Maescoed. However, as soon as Rinpoche gave us instructions for the practice, the sky suddenly cleared and the stars were completely visible and utterly amazing. It remained clear for the three nights we did the practice then, reverted to its normal cloudiness and unpredictable pattern.

I believe Rinpoche had the power to create conditions to help us all, and I have found that when my intention is truly focused, the conditions needed for my practice also seem to magically appear like this.

In Sanskrit Tantra means loom — where threads are stretched and intertwined. It also means principle or doctrine.

Everything inner and outer is threaded together and connected — as declared in string theory or symbolised by the string placed around your neck after a wongkur empowerment ceremony.

The threads can cross like the spiral of DNA or the symbol of the staff with the two serpents which can be seen as channels or pillars. If the threads are knotted or tangled the inner psychic body is not radiant. You can't experience the radiance on the inner or the outer unless and until you become radiant.

Namgyal Rinpoche, Dharma Centre of Canada, 2001.

Namgyal Rinpoche at the North Pole (1980s)
Photo by Terry Hagan

Shit Disturber (The High Arctic and Antarctica, 2001)
Rosalie Fedoruk

I first met Namgyal Rinpoche in August 2001 on a journey to the Magnetic North Pole on a Russian ship — the Kapitan Khlebnikov.

Usually I spent summers on retreat with my teacher, Sogyal Rinpoche, but the previous year my husband Nicholas died and the thought of our international friends talking to me about Nicholas was unbearable.

When I heard about a trip to the Arctic with Namgyal Rinpoche, I thought, "Perfect, I can travel with a teacher and be in a place where almost no one knows me." So I bought my ticket and told my dharma friends that I was headed to the North Pole.

We flew to the Arctic. Gazing down at white icy landscapes, I was awe-struck at the vastness of the distances with no sign of human habitation as we flew hour after hour. Deep inside me something shifted.

We flew from the airport at Resolute out to the Kapitan Khlebnikov by helicopter. I encountered Namgyal Rinpoche for the first time on the ship and for me he was like the vast empty white landscape that I had flown over to arrive there.

On the ship only four of us were traveling with Namgyal Rinpoche and we ate most of our meals together. At the table he would give informal teachings or delight us with stories which were also teachings. We were in the midst of ninety passengers so we addressed him as 'Sir' rather than Rinpoche.

I treasured the opportunity to hang out with him informally and I asked him lots of questions, many that I had wondered about for a long time. Others in our group suggested I not ask so many questions.

One told me just to 'be there' attentively and Rinpoche would answer my questions without being asked. Another said "Just shut up and listen!" The value of deeper focused listening did not register with me at the time and I kept on asking questions.

We climbed mountains, hiked over ice and gravel beaches at the foot of high granite cliffs. We saw polar bears swimming miles from shore, a herd of musk ox near us that turned and galloped high onto a ridge, inquisitive but cautious Arctic foxes and multitudes of birds.

We stopped at the century old graves of members of the Franklin Expedition. Occasionally Namgyal Rinpoche would point out details we had not noticed. He commented in various ways on the vastness of the universe we are part of and on how small our individual dramas are.

As the trip ended, I felt satisfied with the experience in the company of such a Teacher, thinking that would be the only time such an opportunity would occur in my life.

Then the final morning, a representative of the expedition company came to our breakfast table with an interesting offer. A large group had cancelled their reservations for a trip to South Georgia and Antarctica and she asked if we would like to go for half price.

Just like that, Namgyal Rinpoche, who had been to Antarctica several times before, said he would go. The word spread among his students around the world and three months later twenty of us set out on another Russian vessel across the wild Southern Ocean.

The sights, sounds and smells ashore in South Georgia amid two hundred thousand nesting penguins, colonies of barking fur seals or clans of sea elephants with alpha males weighing over a ton are memories that will be with me for the rest of my life.

Climbing to the rim of a volcano to look down at the caldera of sea water with pools on the beaches warm enough to bathe in was an other-worldly feeling and a reminder of the ever present glorious beauty and diversity available when we let our attention expand beyond our conditioned limited states of mind.

Among the other passengers on the ship was a very intelligent English woman who was accomplished in many fields of endeavor and was a friend of the Queen. She noticed we students all treated Rinpoche with great respect and wanted to know who he was. She asked many of us and each person told her she should ask him directly.

There was a magical moment with Rinpoche, Terry and the English woman on the inflatable Zodiac as we sped towards shore from the ship with the spray flying all around us.

She kept asking Rinpoche endless questions until he looked at her and said "YOU ARE A SHIT DISTURBER."

And then he looked at me and said, "YOU TOO."

Being a constant questioner like my friend the English woman, I took Rinpoche's "YOU TOO" to heart.

During the voyage to the Arctic I didn't get how annoying and limiting my questions were until I had the opportunity to watch someone else doing my questioning number and Rinpoche called us both on it.

Three months earlier when I was grieving the death of my husband, Rinpoche had given me space to be. This time he called me on my constant questions but there was lightness and humor in his tone and I found the Canadian expression 'Shit Disturber' amusing.

I am still a Shit Disturber, but when I become quiet and present to what is happening around me, my world expands, becoming richer, deeper and more spacious.

Contemplating the meaning of Shit Disturber, I came to look at what I thought was mischievous playfulness in another light. I began to understand the value of being aware and letting things and people be. I began to learn to give other people the space that Namgyal Rinpoche gave me.

One of my pet peeves is when a student comes to class with a notebook and many, many questions — such as a dream from years ago — then says, "Oh I just thought of another one!" All bull and a waste of time!

So I say, "You can ask one question and only one, in one report — and be sure to hone it. But you can ask another question the next time you report. All those questions are nothing more than a defense.

Namgyal Rinpoche, Teaching Dharma, Dharma Centre of Canada, 2003.

Your Money or Your Life? (Teaching Dharma, Dharma Centre of Canada, 2003) *David Berry*

Namgyal Rinpoche performed his last ordination of students at the end of the *Teaching Dharma Course* at the Dharma Centre of Canada six weeks before he died.

In requesting ordination at that time after years of hanging back, I made a deeper commitment to awakening and to sharing the teachings with others. I had a feeling that this might be the last opportunity in this life to take this step with Namgyal Rinpoche.

Rinpoche conducted the ordination on September 11th, 2003, gave the *Mahakala* Wongkur on the 13th and the Namgyal lineage Wongkur on the 14th. When I went forward that morning for the lineage blessing, I presented the hem of my unfinished robe to him and handed him a fine-point marker pen to place sacred marks on the robe. He held up the cloth, moved the point of the pen toward it then stopped and said, "I need something hard to back up the cloth while I write."

I patted my pockets for something solid. "I have my check book," I offered.

"Your check book? Will you write some big numbers in there for me?"

"Yes sir, if you would like, to the extent I can."

A Lama standing nearby pulled a book from his shoulder bag and held it out to Rinpoche who looked at the book then turned to me. "What'll it be, *The Life of Milarepa* or your check book?" Milarepa was one of the founders of Buddhism in Tibet — a hermit yogi who lived in caves and subsisted on nettles and other wild plants giving his skin a green hue.

"*The Life of Milarepa*, Sir — nettles it is!" I replied. I have wrestled with the practice of applying that choice ever since.

Rinpoche made the marks on the hem of the robe that symbolize: the Buddha or the enlightenment principle; the Dharma referring to the teachings or underlying principals of the Universe; and the Sangha — the spiritual community or community of all living evolving beings.

Stagnancy is the delayed lama.

Namgyal Rinpoche, Dharma Centre of Canada, 1993.

Last Encounter with a Great Mind (England, October, 2003)
Mala Sikka

Rinpoche's last teaching in Britain was on *Dzogchen* (Clear Consciousness) and the Three Points That Strike to the Vital Essence: recognition, confidence and application or putting it into practice.

After the class he was mingling and chatting with people as he often did. When he began putting on his coat before heading out into the chilly wind and rain, he had some difficulty getting his arm in the second sleeve.

Immediately I wanted to help him but let my uncertainty get the better of me and I didn't move. I thought, "No, no, no, I can't possibly touch the Lama. He's a monk and you know — you don't touch him."

He looked at me with that twinkle in his eye and I immediately got the message, "Oh-oh, I got that wrong — do not hesitate!"

So I took the coat and he offered his arm, but made it hard for me to put his coat on. He began goofing around making it even more difficult, but finally he allowed me to help him.

He gave me a smile and I realized it was very simple.

His last teaching for me was just, "Do not hesitate. Any time it comes into the mind to help, go forth with confidence. Don't stop yourself."

No words were spoken — just a look in his eye, a little twinkle and the message came through to act on my intuition. The episode of putting on the coat was his way of silently teaching the Three Points That Strike to the Vital Essence: recognition, confidence and application or putting it into practice. In retrospect it is amazing to me that he transmitted the teaching so eloquently in silence just by goofing around with his coat.

As he got in the car I frowned.

He looked at me and said, "Oh, we have a little tikka in front of Mala Sikka."

I did not have a *tikka* mark representing the Divine Eye of wisdom painted on my forehead, as is the custom of Hindus in India where my parents are from.

Instead, I had frown lines, trying too hard to fathom the depth of what had just happened. His last comment to me transformed my perplexed frown into a blessing.

That was the last time I ever saw him.

Summer Seeds of Learning (Ottawa, 2001-2003) *Trudy Gold*

During three summer visits Rinpoche taught in Wakefield, Quebec while staying in Ottawa. The drive up to Wakefield was 30 to 45 minutes and usually Rinpoche taught once a day for five or six days. I learned a lot as his driver and those moments influenced many of the steps I've subsequently taken on the path. This is a teensy taste of what was learned:

✧ Driving slowly isn't a bad thing — slow can be a fascinating and profound state of mind.

✧ Speeding like a race car driver will only get you in trouble, one way or another.

✧ If you leave a flower in the car, be prepared to answer the question about what kind of flower it is.

✧ Tea plantations in Darjeeling, India are worth the trip and, somewhere in Darjeeling is a restaurant that serves excellent tea and provides an awesome view of the Himalayan foothills.

✧ When you ask someone to pray for you, a friend or member of your family — follow up afterward. Tell your lama, friends, or the people you asked, that the person has recovered, died, or is feeling better thanks.

✧ Realized beings, if they're hanging out on the planet, are as human as you are and every human being is happy to have their work acknowledged. It's so easy to say "Yes Sir — that was a fantastic class."

✧ Dharma is way bigger than what gets taught in class. It really is in every moment.

Poetry (Dharma Centre of Canada, 2003) *David Berry*

The class had just begun. Rinpoche looked at us and said, "According to some, poetry is the highest function of the human brain and math is the lowest. You're all cases of arrested development."

"Try writing a poem. I wrote one last night."

> *"A stillness, pond*
>
> *shattering rain,*
>
> *bubbles."*

"You may write it down, oh scribe."

"I'm already on it, sire." I said.

"I thought you would be. Is the rain shattering the stillness or is the pond shattering the rain? There is no shattering — still, bubbles."

Appearing, Disappearing (Oslo, Norway, 1996) *Ailo Gaup*

I was born in the northernmost part of Norway, the area of the Sami people. At the age of seven, I was moved to southern Norway, where I grew up. I now live outside of Oslo, where I teach Shamanism as a world heritage, based on Sami traditions.

Once in the last decade of the last century a Norwegian friend, Erik Jensen, invited me to attend a teaching by a Rinpoche, with whom he was studying.

I joined the audience in the meeting hall, waiting for the teacher to appear. The teacher's attendant came in first and nodded to us as he placed some things next to the empty chair in front of us in the room.

The Rinpoche entered, walked across the room and sat down in the chair as his attendant helped him adjust the red robe around his shoulders.

Namgyal Rinpoche started to talk about meditation but within a few moments, there in front of my eyes, I experienced the Rinpoche disappearing from view. I was sitting with my eyes open and was in a clear state of mind, I tell you. But instead of a person in a chair, a shining bright light opened up.

There was no longer an ordinary person in flesh and blood in front of me — just this extraordinary flash of light floating in the room. I could see nothing else in that moment.

Changes in subtle energy patterns and colors were not new to me as a shamanic practitioner and teacher but I had never come across anything like this before.

After a while the light resolved back into Namgyal Rinpoche seated in the chair speaking to us, as ordinary yet extraordinary as only he could be.

When leaving the hall that first evening, I suddenly came upon Namgyal Rinpoche on the stairs. Rinpoche turned and said the first words he ever said to me:

"Where were you when the dragon swallowed the black pearl?"

I was speechless.

Sometime later I got an invitation to teach workshops on shamanism at the Dharma Centre of Canada. All in all I visited the Centre seven times to teach and to study with Rinpoche.

Never did I feel as seen or as known as when in his presence, that first evening and in many other interactions over the years. From that first meeting and forward I considered Rinpoche to be my teacher, both in Buddhism and in Shamanism, universal as his approach was.

When I got the news of his death, I felt a great loss, like a hole opened in my life.

But then, when remembering how the light appeared when the Rinpoche disappeared, the light starts shining, as when I, for the first time, was in his presence . . .

If you want liberation in this life, there is no area that you do not watch. Watch the breathing, watch the posture, watch the flow of energy, watch the texture of the mind, watch the response to objects. This path leads to purification, illumination, clarity and the interpenetration of all dharmas.

The Breath of Awakening, A Guide To Liberation Through Anapanasati Mindfulness of Breathing, Kinmount, Bodhi Publishing, 1992, p. 60. Used with permission from Bodhi Publishing.

Close Encounter (Winnipeg, 2003) *Donna Youngdahl*

Rinpoche came to Winnipeg to give a closed retreat in the spring of 2003.

I very much wanted to meet him, but my baby had just been born a few weeks before and I was still recovering from the difficult birth. Attending the retreat was not physically possible for me.

Then in October, before I could meet him in person, Rinpoche passed away.

Although I did not meet him, I feel close to and inspired by Namgyal Rinpoche through his students, his written teachings and through a number of vivid and powerful dreams.

Several times I have had dreams of him in which he has given me short teachings and I awaken with blissful energy coursing through my body.

I only come here in the morning to give you problems; not answers. It's eminently satisfying to solve a problem.

Namgyal Rinpoche, Dharma Centre of Canada, 1998.

Teachings

Namgyal Rinpoche gave formal teachings in temples and church meeting halls, on the decks of ships and in open gardens and fields in many countries around the world. He also taught through example and through his comments, gentle nudges and sometimes an intense intervention could startle a student into awareness at any time. As had been related in this book, many of his transmissions were unspoken.

From the 1960s until his death in 2003, he taught courses based on Buddhist and Judeo-Christian traditions, Western Mysteries and many other spiritual, philosophical, scientific and psychological paths.

Whatever the declared topic, he would often intuitively add an aside to support the awakening and the development of compassion of the beings in the room. When he paused and said, "By the way —" students perked up and paid attention. Students sometimes took notes in the classes and several sets of notes have since been edited and published as the books and booklets listed in Appendix 2.

Traditionally, discourses heard from a teacher were passed on orally by introducing them with "Thus have I heard." As mentioned in the Preface, this is an acknowledgement of both subjectivity and of not being the source or author of the teaching. In this section recollections from a sampling of classes as heard by the students submitting the account are offered to give a sense of the variety of experiences students had when they received a teaching from Namgyal Rinpoche.

. . . admit your anger, frustration, and desire, and transmute it. Know what you really want and go for it . . . with determination! That, in essence, is the path.

The Womb, Karma, and Transcendence, A *Journey towards Liberation*, Kinmount, Bodhi Publishing, 1996, p. 213, Used with permission from Bodhi Publishing.

The Black Shirt Talk (Bridges to Transcendence, The Dharma Centre of Canada, July 3, 1996) *as heard by David Berry*

The class sat in silent meditation. We rose to our feet as one at the sound of the Volkswagen on gravel as it approached the Temple from the Main House. The car stopped at the top of the drive and the Venerable Karma Tenzin Dorje Namgyal Rinpoche came up the wooden stairs.

A student opened the screen door for him and he stepped in, slipped off his sandals and walked to his chair at the front of the room. A mug of hot tea and a flowering plant waited on the table beside him.

He began with the opening dedication three times, "*Namo tassa Bhagavato Arahato Samma Sambuddhassa.*" (Homage to the Blessed One, the Purified One, the Fully Enlightened One.)

He took a sip of tea and we settled back down on our cushions. Rinpoche then began his discourse.

"The trouble with youse! — You see I start with verbal abuse. Westerners want to start with exotic inner planes in meditation and those planes are there and are magnificent but inevitably there are imbalances to be dealt with first."

"You live in cities but the ancients lived in forests, in Nature. You whirl about in motorcars as in *Wind in the Willows* and eat fast foods and hear sounds not of nature but of machines and heavy metal. I'm not sure you have built within you a sufficient bridge to the outer."

"You are not the Native people. In general, men were hunters and women were gatherers. Now we neither hunt nor gather. We don't pay attention to our environment nor to our surroundings."

"We attempt to do work on the inner without a balancing revelation of the outer. In ancient times people hiked from place to place for nine months and only settled in during winter. In Tibet, people travelled vast miles on foot, trading, gathering salt and making pilgrimages. Even today, the average Guatemalan Indian approach to Dharma is very different, more introverted and pushing into sensational functions. But they work all day in the fields. Most people should not attempt to push hard in the inner until they do work on the outer."

"As some classical Buddhist teachings begin, 'Having gone to the forest or the foot of a tree —they established mindfulness of the breathing in front.' Start with outer mandalas, building with the hands, using flowers, or minerals. On their alms rounds in Burma and Sri Lanka the monks still use everything they find — a piece of plastic, embryo of a dog — to enrich each little moment."

"Those of you who are desirous of revelations on the inner plane should do more work with outer phenomena and experience. There are spiritual books that mention clouds within us. It would be better to learn types of real clouds: cirrus, stratus, cumulus and the great cumulonimbus that releases the thunderbolt!"

"Eyes are designed to look out, to see the patterns. If I could have my way with you, I'd order you to take a safari or go immediately to the Antarctic."

"Oh no! Not scuba!" you say. You have the wish-fulfilling jewel. If the proper motivation is there, all will be granted unto you. Have faith. The Grand Canyon will open the canyons within. The Antarctic, Arctic and Amazon provide a mosaic of enlightenment through adventure. I'm not a Luddite — your work-places are fine, even work with computers is better if done with a sense of the outer patterns."

"Do you realize you have a distorted view of sexuality and the body? Have you even watched an animal mate or seen how mating pervades the universe from the birth of kittens to the eggs of a moth? You need a deeper changing view of all activity and patterns."

"I'm getting nasty now — you're a klutz. A French lady travelling in Africa ordered two fried eggs every day for breakfast. Americans order bacon and eggs and steak when in China. You live by rote, rote, rote and you wonder why your meditation is so gray. You can practice different kinds of meditation such as Totality, Mind Only, or Sunyata or emptiness. You can also dare to have something different to eat in the morning. What is your mind feeding on?"

"Even nuns in Bhutan haven't had so many Wongkurs or empowerments as you have like the Green Tara we will give this week. They would give their eye teeth for this and you PICK your teeth with it."

"AUM AH HO: Welcome everyone to the feast, the festival. I wonder if in giving these lessons I am casting pearls before swine to trample underfoot."

"Jehovah prepared a great banquet before Paul. Delicious food like Thai food would be for you. '*Bitte esst, süsse Kinder*' — Please eat, sweet children. 'No, it's not kosher.' '*Bitte esst doch, liebe Kinder, esst!*' — Please eat it, dear children, eat! Again there was resistance. It's doing a number, the way we divide it up — I do this but not that. I eat this but not that. 'What God has called to be clean, call ye not unclean' and Paul ate."

"Like the monks on the alms round take what is given in life. Don't say, 'I don't look at fungus, I don't explore those smells, I don't eat *that* food.' Experience! Were it not for unclean things, life could not exist. Food is poop and poop is food for something else. The human stomach is strong;

we can eat many things. But cats, for example, are picky eaters. So you are losing your humanity as the food allergies show up. I mean that literally. Humans eat eggs, milk, meat; we have a versatile stomach."

"I know some of you have allergies. Don't infer that I am suggesting you suddenly begin to eat food that makes you ill. You can address allergies on a higher level and seek to transcend them. The first step is calming down about them."

"As you go to more restricted diets you limit your experience. Remember, one third of the humans in Ireland died when the potato crop failed. The natural instinct of humans is for variety. Variety is the mosaic feed to enlightenment."

"We say, 'As above, so below; as without, so within.' The ancient Greeks also said, 'Look within.' They had already searched the without. They would lie in a trough with showers at the seven chakras, (a symbolic baptism) and participated in sports at the gymnasium for health of the mind and body."

"In the Greek Mysteries candidates wore white robes and climbed a spiral staircase. They stopped at a cliff and were lifted to the Elysian Fields above, fields filled with flowers. They were lifted by a great red double-helix cord to that symbol of a higher plane."

"The spiral was used again: as an aspirant ascended, on the spiral they would pass niches or grottos. The hood covering their head would be winked up for just an instant so they would see figures of the archetypes or a vignette of a teaching."

"This is just like Tibetans who flash the card at you with an image of the deity during a *Wongkur*. With the hood lifted, the tableau appears just for an instant and the image goes to the depth awareness. The spiral staircase is the secret staircase. Yes, DNA is life on Earth. It is not helpful to say, 'I read the book.' You need real experiences."

"The other side of the portal looks outside. How can you experience the inner without the experience of Nature? Having received the gift of the senses, use them."

"Your whole day is spent on business, working for salaries and interpersonal affairs. Your eyes face forward. *You spend your life ignoring ignorance!* Eighty percent of human life is discursive fantasy. Not only is life but a dream, you make it a dream as you merrily row your boat, oblivious to the world around you. A giant computer filling a room would not be equal to your brain. With that great inheritance, what data are you running through YOUR brain? Bacon and eggs, bacon and eggs, kibble and bits?"

"You are in Sunday school where you see a little Tibetan picture of self-arising yoga and front-arising yoga. You really think enlightened beings need to come to you in Tibetan form or some other specific form?"

"I've got news for you: you don't even get the news. N — E — W — S"

"North!"   "East!"   "West!"   "South!"

The NEWS is experience in all directions."

"You are nit-picking nitwits. Pay attention to details. You look for the wind in the inner space and haven't even seen the wind in the tree. Go to a mountain and feel the wind. Don't you dare put an umbrella over me! I want to feel the rain, little warm drops or big splats. That's how the teaching is delivered by the way, in drops or splats."

"To get pure within, take pure food in so you can purify. Your problem is retention. You try to hold onto memories rather than obtain new experience."

"My beef with Dharma practitioners is that you neither hunt nor gather. You turn Dharma into a group of sickies who say, 'Heal me, heal me.' This is a Dharma Centre not a Drama Centre!"

"Jesus said, 'Arise. Take up your bed and walk!' Get up and do what humans are supposed to do. Your behavior disgusts me. For progress on the path we have to work, to struggle."

"Stop this number of, 'It's all an illusion, you know.' The only thing that is an illusion is you!"

"You say, 'My mother did this, my father did that.'"

"ARISE! TAKE UP YOUR BED AND WALK!"

"Look at Stephen Hawking in his wheelchair. Look at the power there is through all those handicaps to keep probing the universe. Give up the view that the life of Dharma is the life of therapy. Stop this defeated thing of alcohol."

"YES, I KNOW YOU ARE STILL DRINKING!"

"This is a conceit. This is the last place you should be. Remember the Fifth Precept about training yourself to avoid liquor and drugs that cloud the mind. Get out of all this! Society is full of drugs."

"TAKE UP THY BED AND WALK!"

"You say, 'We're abused, we're victims.'"

"TOUGH!"

"There are only two choices: Victim of life or Victor of life. We are hurled from womb to tomb. You can lie down to wait or you can get on with it! That's life — you have to get engaged."

"If you don't change your diet, you will end up with food like our friends from Norway here in class. Recipe: put fish in water, put fire under; if you are feeling wild, add salt. If you are feeling really wild, add pepper. On one course eight students had seven different diets. That is self-indulgence; it would never happen in a monastery. Awakening is not healing sickness or therapy. Within this fathom-long body there is a universe arising."

"If you are in the Dharma, you are not dependent on praise or criticism; not going from doctor to doctor. This is not an act of desperation — it is an act of silliness. It is ignoring experience. How silly to run from pillar to post! If what I am saying is offensive, forgive but don't forget. Use it! The minutes are going by; everything you find on the path even a pebble is an advance. Get a big appetite. All things live by nutriment. All things, all experiences sustain your life. If you reduce the diet of humans, the species will go extinct."

"I'm tired of teaching today. However, I must have hope. The seed of the flower can grow through concrete. Watch for the dreadful 'Thump!' The thunderbolt annihilates the rock. You're not worthy to be addressed and given an exercise. I should not come here. I should leave the dead to bury the dead. Jesus said the barren fig tree is cursed."

"So much energy goes into the maintenance of the false self. If you can hear me — just go out and start looking at the patterns. Look at Nature, look at the patterns."

Rinpoche gave a closing blessing: *"Idam te punna kamman asawakaya wayham hotu."* (By the merit of this strengthening activity, may there be cessation of all defilements.)

He looked down and said, "It must be the black shirt I wore today!"

I rose, applauded and shouted, "BRAVO!"

Rinpoche held up his arms and bent down as if he were ducking tomatoes, walked to the front door of the temple, slipped on his sandals and left.

The enlightenment process is going on within you in spite of your feeble attempts to thwart it.

Namgyal Rinpoche, Dharma Centre of Canada, 1993.

To get an idea of the depth meaning of Mahamudra, look at the seed syllables which compose the word itself. Ma is mother — Ha is Laughter, bliss, happiness. Mu means vanishing and Dra is foundation, stability. Mudra is movement; things in movement are already on their way to another form. Maha means great. So Mahamudra is mothering the joyful disappearance into the ground of being . . .

HA-HA, HA-HA, HO! THE GREAT UNFOLDING!

. . . a being progressing, not ecstatically, but simply knowing that suffering has vanished. There is the continuous, on-going, non-clinging sponsoring of good; more understanding going to greatness. This is the correct unfolding of the flower. Mahamudra is the Great Sign which is no sign. This realization is signless because the being is not clinging.

The Song of Awakening, A Guide to Liberation Through Marananussati, Mindfulness of Death, Boise, Idaho, The Open Path Publishing, 1979. p. 67. Used with permission from Bodhi Publishing.

✧

Preparatory Practices for Mahamudra (Rumtek and Kinmount, 1968) *as heard by Cecilie Kwiat*

In 1968, Namgyal Rinpoche led a group of students on his first visit to Rumtek Monastery, the seat of His Holiness the 16th Karmapa. We were given copies of a booklet translated from the Tibetan by the Englishwoman, Sister Palmo, one of Karmapa's assistants. The text was entitled *The Mahamudra Meditation which Clears Away Ignorance and Delusion.*

Shortly after our return, Rinpoche used the text as the basis for a teaching. For me, a good way to share the warmth, humour and compassion of this exceptional teacher is to offer my interpretation of his introductory words to that teaching:

Rinpoche gave the opening dedication and began: "Today I am going to talk about the preparatory practices for *Mahamudra*. Remember the two things central to the successful practice of meditation: calm and clarity.

When they are both present you will discover, as the Buddha said, the teaching is beautiful in the beginning, in the middle and in the ending."

"You may first notice that calm is increasing. Slowly the unwholesome mind-states recede — as you no longer hold on to them. Dull states of mind are banished more quickly because the goal of the teaching is the banishment of *Avidya*, of not-seeing, so that it's opposite, clear perception, can be present."

"Another sign of progress is a clarity or acuteness of sensing. Your hearing gets a little sharper and if you are deaf, you at least hear the deafness. The senses begin to be used to the full extent of one's capability."

"This clearing of all the senses — of hearing, seeing, tasting, touching, smelling — is a minor sign of clearing the ignorance that blocks the *panchadvara*, the five sense doors."

"The sixth door is called *manodvara*, the mind door. So at the very beginning of the path know that this practice will lead to alleviation of suffering. In your meditation check to see if the mind is calm and clear; that it is joyous. A calm and clear mind leads to joy — if not in an ecstatic sense, at least in the sense of illumination or clarity. And in the final analysis, the goal of the path is just calm clarity."

"Don't think of this state as a great WOW experience. All the wows are subject to loss and so they can actually cause disturbance of the practice. With a calm, clear mind it is possible to view all dharmas without distinction, without clinging to one experience or feeling adversity toward another. Calm clarity is present in enlightenment, although enlightenment is also a breakthrough into *other* dimensions of calmness and clarity. You should bear in mind that the beginning, the middle and the end of the path are one."

"Don't think what you are doing in your daily life — or the state in which you do it — is unrelated to the path. The extent to which you have developed calm is the extent to which you have developed *Samatha* or concentration, and the extent to which you have developed *Vipassana* or insight is the extent to which you have practiced the path."

"The *Abhidhamma* teaches that every moment of consciousness has concentration. There is never a time your consciousness is without concentration — you are always concentrating on something. This may astound you, but it is the nature of consciousness that, having arisen, a focus is always there."

"But in practical terms, concentration is not conducive to enlightenment unless it is accompanied by love and other wholesome states. If you are indulging in very weird, negative fantasies, concentration is present but it will not be conducive to your awakening. It is not *Samma Samadhi*; it will not lead into perfection."

"One of the differences between the Hinayana and Mahayana paths is that Hinayana can emphasize crushing out desire while Mahayana assumes that when the practitioner realizes there is concentration in every conscious moment that realisation can be brought into the centre of one's negative fantasies."

"By directly coming awake in these mind-states, you transform them. So instead of talking of crushing, you incorporate that energy by turning the negative into the path. This is really seizing the concentration that is within every conscious moment — and using it with awareness."

"When your mind is calm or in any positive, wholesome state, you should know that love is present. In Pali it is called *Kusala-Kamma* — wholesome action. When you go outside on a nice day and you feel good, love is present. When you are concentrated in an ordinary way such as being absorbed in reading a book or listening to music, love is present."

"It is erroneous to think that you don't have love. Any time you are in a positive state or even in a neutral state you are experiencing love. If you feel calm clarity of mind while sewing a button on a shirt, that's love. It's not always some big overwhelming emotion — it is an all-embracing sense of ease in which you feel at one with whatever is happening."

"This state is the basis for developing right view. There are certain *Miccha Ditthi* or wrong views that have to be put down in order to abide in love. And they are wrong views you may have been living with all your life and continue to hold on to. In Buddhist writings when the word *Ditthi* appears alone, it indicates partial view; a half-baked view. When the Buddha used the term *Samma-Ditthi*, he was referring to a right view, a view centered on the transcendent."

"One could say that you are practicing the path wherever you are throughout the many moments of the day, but usually unconsciously rather than with knowing. It is erroneous to think you do not progress along the path simply by living each day. The very fact that you are *here* in this class doing this rather difficult thing means you are not involved in negative or self-destructive actions. This is the first advance, the most minor aspect of your progression."

"There are many wholesome things each of you do in life which work to develop the path. You might go to science museums, play football, visit art galleries — the explorations are far too numerous to list. These are all positive progressions and you know this yourself. This is a dogmatic statement!"

"But unfortunately if you get into having nothing to do, nothing but to wither on the vine, this is not positive. So for those beings there is this teaching, this involvement with other planes."

"Any effort you make automatically creates movement along the path. People often think that they aren't getting results because they don't see that each effort made is an application of will. Something *is* being developed. This is the second point or view."

"When you understand this you understand the importance of dropping negativity. Every time you allow negative views, you retard your being so it is essential to stop feeling negative about your progress. Any difficulties you may experience because of some failing actually advance you because with a little more awareness you see that you fail a bit less with each effort. It is the idea that you aren't accomplishing anything that is the great retarding force."

"A third view, which may surprise you, is that you experience more wholesome moments than unwholesome in a day. That's why we keep on living; why so few people commit suicide. You might be amazed if you analyzed how much of your day is actually spent in positive states. Just walking across a room in a neutral state of mind can cause you to inch a tiny bit further along the way in your development."

"Unless you are living in the midst of a war, unless there are bombs dropping all around you causing total paranoia, the average human being dwells a little on the credit side of possible mind states. Perhaps they move at a snail's pace towards the awakening, but by adding up all the moments of consciousness in the course of a day, positive moments *do* predominate."

"There is a will to live in beings. Why then do some people seem so difficult, so negative? It's because we emphasize the unwholesome in our minds due to its unusualness — its actual rarity. And really it is 'Miccha Ditthi', erroneous view, for you to give it much attention. Your concern just increases the intensity of the unwholesome. If you were traveling on a highway that was 9/10ths newly paved and smooth and 1/10th under construction, full of bumps and holes, which would you remember? 'What a terrible road!' you would say."

"And this is the fourth thing you should know: Not only do you have everything going for you because by simply *being you* — you are inching forward and you are also being prodded forward and rather skillfully, too!"

"Attention *is* drawn to the negative and thus you are more able to dissolve it rather than dwell in it. You have so many forces operating to dissolve the unwholesome blocks that the actually difficult thing to do is remain unenlightened!"

"Quite seriously, you may struggle if you must, but then surrender gracefully. By the time you have reached the point where you choose to listen to this teaching, there is a very intense underground force for awakening going on in your being."

"Even you coming into contact with this teaching indicates that discriminating wisdom is present now. This comes from the depth understanding of the life-force and not from that so-called conscious mind of daily busy-ness. It is the result of the overall field of consciousness, the summation of hundreds of billions of life moments. It is your true consciousness, carried with you everywhere you go. This awareness *knows* where it's at, and in that sense so should you."

"The fifth point is that moments of goodness are actually increasing at a fairly rapid rate. A vehicle sitting on top of a hill doesn't need much of a push to start rolling. The Buddha said you only need a week of *full* practice of awareness to attain the first level of path. Not visualization, my dear friends, often used to garner calm concentration, but the practice of awareness alone is enough."

"Even if one undertakes this practice for only one week, so long as it is fully developed, it is sufficient to bring one into an experience of the path. And when that arises, it will not be a drama! It is a calm and utter certitude which will never pass from your being again.

Sometimes this is referred to as the awakening of faith. You may think you have faith now, but when you experience *the* transcendental — not the transcendental touted in commercials that continually bombard North Americans, but the true one, a complete certitude of Dharma, complete understanding of non-ego awareness will come and the first three of ten fetters to true knowing will fall."

"One of these first three fetters is belief in rule and ritual, particularly blind belief in the rules of ritual. There is no set of laws that you obey to attain enlightenment other than meditation. Do you find this to be a paradox? Why then is there so much rule and ritual in daily practice? It is skill-in-means; it is empty, void, but useful for expanding a fixed view. Really, it is the least of a teacher's aids!"

"The remaining two fetters that drop with one's first experience of transcendence are belief in an inherent self and skeptical doubt. After this experience you are bestowed with complete trust and confidence in the Dharma."

"There are four levels of *Satori* or openings of transcendence into path realisation. This first stage of the path is called 'Stream Entry' or *Sotapanna* in the Theravadin teaching."

"With the second level, the 'Once Returning' or *Sakadagamin*, two types of clinging are diminished; sensual craving and ill-will or aggression. These two are cut in half at this point, and when the third level of 'Non-Returning' or *Anagamin* arises they are eradicated."

"Everything is in flow, in that now the being is no longer caught by worldly desires. After the experience of *Anagamin* five fetters remain but they are a little more subtle. They are: craving for existence in a subtle material form, craving for immaterial existence, conceit in one's path, restlessness and ignorance."

"They fall when the last level, *Arahat*, is reached. With this attainment, the being is in a state of energy with absolute clarity. *Avidya* or not-seeing is gone. Every moment of consciousness they see that they see; they concentrate that they concentrate; and are aware with awareness. They watch the watch forever. There is no clinging to highs, to form and formless levels of experience. Highs and lows don't mean any more to them than any other phenomena. They have no need to indulge in the suffering of seeking any experience."

"So, the ten fetters are transcended as the path unfolds. Perhaps a little of this traditional understanding will help you to get some idea of what is being taught here. In any case, you can see that with the development of calm and clarity you are approaching the full experience of transcendence. It is true that the levels of attainment can arise very dramatically, but that is usually due to reacting with self-grasping. Strangely enough, even though the belief in ego disappears at the first stage of the path, it isn't until the final stage that conceit fully disappears. This is a paradoxical statement I'll leave for you to consider."

Any phenomenon is on its way to somewhere else. There is, in this universe, no such thing as a moment of birth or a moment of death. There is just flux. Nowhere does the stream arrest itself long enough for an object to be discovered. There is flux — from tree to table to ash to fertilizer to earth to a thousand seeds. Limitation is increased by Tanha for security/identity reasons, but this limitation is illusion. You are asked to break through the illusion of birth-death duality. Nothing is born. Nothing dies. No permanent identity can be found. This is the practice of Mahamudra.

Body, Speech and Mind, a manual for human development, Kinmount, Bodhi Publishing, 2004, p. 28. Used with permission from Bodhi Publishing.

Question Period (Dharma Centre of Canada, August, 1993)
David Berry

Questioner to Namgyal Rinpoche: "Would you say that —"

NR: "Don't accuse me like that!"

Q: "But you don't know what I am going to ask!"

NR: "But I'm being set up. Even though you know I don't know what you are going to ask, you don't know what I *would say.*"

Q: "I don't know — that's why I am asking the question."

NR (turning away): "That's right. You don't."

Q: "Thank you."

If you think you don't have to give yourself permission consciously to indulge or not indulge in each action you do each day, then you're not friends with your own thoughts, cravings and emotions.

We can't control things we do not understand. When we don't understand ourselves, then we can't control ourselves and are instead controlled by our random thoughts, habits, cravings and emotions. Then we pay the price of time and life wasted: 'Dukkha' or suffering.

Namgyal Rinpoche, Dharma Centre of Canada, 1990's.

The Monkey and the Elephant (Dharma Centre of Canada, summer, 1996) *as heard by David Berry*

In the mid nineties, the Dharma Centre of Canada held a series of courses entitled 'Bridges to Transcendence' and I was invited to teach there for the first time.

I was nervous about this, having only been to the Dharma Centre when Namgyal Rinpoche was teaching. To say he set a high standard for what a teacher did would be a grievous understatement. I was very aware of my limitations in that domain.

The course was scheduled for the last week of July. To get back in touch with the feel of the place and to have a week of contemplation and inspiration, I participated in a teaching in early July to help me prepare to deliver the course on Nature a few weeks later.

During that week, Rinpoche finished a class by asking if there were any questions. A female student raised her hand and Rinpoche nodded to her.

"Yes?" he resonated with a deep tone.

"Sir, I have meditated and practiced for a long time and sometimes I feel I am making progress. Then I hit a wall and for a long period I feel stuck and don't seem to be getting anywhere. I even feel that I have slipped back. Then I get back into a practice and feel like I am making progress again and then I come right up against the same wall and seem to be stuck in the same place. Then I slip back and drop the practice. Then I begin to practice again and —"

A thunderous shout interrupted the thought loop, "YOU — will — NEVER — break — through — that — wall!"

Rinpoche was so loud that some of us jumped in our seat which is not easy when sitting cross-legged on the floor.

I looked over at the woman and his words had gone through her like a pin through a butterfly. She was pinned and vibrating — held in the moment, her eyes wide and staring — lower lip quivering — just as most of us would tend to be upon being impaled by such a spear of strong energy.

Rinpoche continued, "The Kingdom of Heaven must be taken by storm. The monkey expects to enter Heaven and it goes on about repetitive spiritual practices which without attention and awareness amount to mumbo jumbo. The monkey will never break through that wall. Meanwhile, the elephant continues slowly ascending in spirals."

"The monkey repeats prayers and mantras and comes to classes and reads books and tries to sit still and stare at the wall. And the monkey learns lots of facts and memorizes things and perhaps does calm down a little but feels it is not really making progress. And it isn't. And the elephant continues slowly ascending in spirals."

"The monkey can go on like this indefinitely until one day, the elephant breaks through the wall."

"Now they might take the monkey and put a crown on its head and call it a saint or a *Tulku*,"

He paused and looked around the room with a wide chimpanzee-like grin.

"Yet it is still a monkey — and the elephant continues slowly ascending in spirals."

I was dazzled and inspired by this vision of the superficial awareness in us seeking awakening, running around trying to get somewhere while the depth present in every being eventually bursts forth into the 'Kingdom' in its own time.

There was a sense of the inevitability of eventual awakening I had not recognized before. This was thrilling news! We could not hold back the ascending and awakening even if we tried!

What a relief! What a motivation to be attentive to a practice and practice compassion and awareness in daily life — to "get on with it" as Rinpoche said.

Three weeks later I was back at the Dharma Centre and teaching a course in the afternoons on Nature and Spirituality. Rinpoche continued with classes in the morning.

One day he mentioned the Heart Sutra as an example of a point he was making. "Form is emptiness; emptiness is form," he said, "emptiness is form going away."

Then he asked, "Are there any questions?"

Two thirds of the people in the room had just arrived at the Centre a few days before and had not participated in the previous classes. But the woman who three weeks before had asked about hitting the wall was still there and she raised her hand.

"Yes?" came his melodious deep voice.

"Sir, I have a question about elephant karma," a comment no doubt puzzling to most of the people in the room.

Up came the volume again, "Elephant karma?"

"ELEPHANT KARMA!"

"You don't have karma. Elephants don't have karma. You ARE karma."

"Karma means activity! There is no separation between form and energy. Admiral Nelson's purported last words were, 'It's kismet Harry.' But it is NOT fate. It is all simply energy fields moving."

Rinpoche placed his hand on the vase of flowers next to him, moved it a few inches farther away from him and then moved it back.

"If a block falls on you it is not just because of fate or the karma of previous action. At that moment you were an unaware being. The cart follows the hoof of the ox that is drawing it."

"Fate is this moment right now. Practice the grand surrender; blaming something on fate or predestination can be a victim's cop-out. You are predestined to exercise your will!"

"There is no death, there is departure and transformation. *Jati* is a word for victory or birth. *Marana* means death but it comes from the roots *Mara* or illusion and *na* or not. So death means 'no illusion.' *Jatimarana* means birth-death. I suggest you meditate on the causes of death."

"You are called to victory. The more treasure you give away, the more you have. The surrender I am talking about is not '*I* will surrender.' You are rendering it up every moment. YOU will never break through the iron wall."

I was writing notes as fast as I could to capture what was to me a thrilling teaching. When Rinpoche mentioned breaking through the wall, without a thought about holding back, I called out loud: "And THAT is where the elephant comes in!"

He looked at me. "Another one!" he said.

He smiled and repeated "Another one!"

I nodded and went back to my rapid scribbling. There was a long pause. I was happy to be catching up in the notes. I got up to writing the words: 'iron wall'."

"You!"

I had my head down and kept on writing, thinking another javelin was about to be hurled to impale a trance state.

"I am addressing YOU!"

I looked up.

"Yes, you. She can't hear me."

"That's clear sir."

"It's the Ten Bulls."

I thought a moment. "Yes sir, it is."

"Would you explain this to her outside of class so we can move on?"

"Yes sir, I will."

"Thank you. Now, are there any other questions?"

After class, as I thought about my assignment with the woman it struck me that he said 'the Ten Bulls' — the name by which I first encountered the Zen images and verses more often called 'the Ten Ox-Herding Pictures.'

The next day I wandered into the sun-lit library and crouched down next to the bottom shelf on Zen. There were two copies of the book of Zen stories I had read seventeen years before and not since.

I took a copy of the book and sat in a comfortable chair in the solarium among the vibrant plants next to the picture window where a hummingbird hovered at a feeder outside.

With Rinpoche's talk in mind, I rewrote descriptions of the ten images in a form I thought would be most helpful when I had a chance to share the images and the connection with the monkey and the elephant with the woman.

Then who do you suppose came into the room?

There at the serving table, pouring herself a cup of tea was the woman who had asked about hitting the wall. We were the only people there.

"You and I have some homework to do." I said.

"What homework is that?"

"Yesterday in class, Rinpoche asked me to share 'the Ten Ox Herding Pictures' with you."

"Oh yes, I remember he said something to you about that," she said.

"Are girls even or odd?" I asked.

"Girls are odd and boys are even." she said.

"That's what I thought too. You read 1,3,5,7 and 9, and I will read the even numbers."

And so we began to read while looking at the Ten Ox Herding Pictures:

1. I am desperate to find the lost ox. I wander in search but there is no trace of him anywhere.

2. I see the tracks of the ox on a forest path. The ox is real and is nearby. There is clear evidence of its existence right in front of me.

3. There, just ahead, I glimpse the ox as it disappears again into the trees.

4. I run to catch hold of the tail of the ox but have no reins or bridle so I struggle to control it.

5. Through discipline I learn to train the ox. It walks with me calmly.

6. I climb on the ox and ride it home while playing a melody on flute.

7. I become as one with the ox. It is my true self. My long illusory quest is over.

8. The separation of personal self and totality has been transcended. All merge in the space of the circle which represents emptiness.

9. All things are the way they are. They always have been and always will be the way they are at each moment. Self and things are left behind at the source of all existence — the place of "no thing."

10. I enter the busy market place and do ordinary things of the world. I share enlightenment with people on the street and with all living things. I do not cling to this life — I accept death as a natural change.

"I got it!" she exclaimed. "Our sense of personal identity and the stream of thought in our conscious mind is the monkey and our depth consciousness or fully realized nature is the elephant or ox."

"And that completes the homework," I said.

The Sword Blessing (Teaching Dharma, Dharma Centre of Canada, 2003) *David Berry*

At the end of his last teaching at the Dharma Centre, Rinpoche gave the already dispersing group a final word. "I'll give you the double-edged blessing: May what you wish for others, come true for you."

"Permission to transmit?" I called out.

"Give them something and right away they want to transmit it — yes, you may transmit that."

Is it important to help people in a corrupt society?

If you only help them conform to existing patterns, are you not maintaining the very causes that make for frustration, misery and destruction?

Namgyal Rinpoche, Toronto, 1967.

Missing the Tea Blessing (Dharma Centre of Canada, 1989)
Rob McConnell

We were studying the Buddhist teaching of Totality in a class in the temple at the Dharma Centre.

I asked an 'intellectual question' on the nature of the totality.

He roared, "SO YOU WANT TO KNOW ABOUT TOTALITY?"

"Yes sir," I trembled.

He picked up his warm cup of tea and threw its contents at me. I ducked.

"Why did you duck?"

"I don't know."

Discriminative wisdom cuts through ego referencing, the fantasy projections about the future and the past, helping you develop a naked awareness of the present. The more secure your being is the more you will be able to abide in the infinity of the moment. You can not be in the 'here and now', that's a cliché that comes from the infantile religious mind. Where is the here and now? A full experience of the moment, now that is different, for then there is the transcendence of time-space referencing; it is all time and all space, it is the Totality.

The Path of Victory, Discourses on the Paramita, Kinmount, Bodhi Publishing, 4th Printing, 2002, p. 48. Used with permission from Bodhi Publishing.

The word discipline comes from disciple, a follower of truth. People too often view discipline as a set of rules which must be rigidly followed. This is too harsh an interpretation. Discipline is not a set of rules or a technique. It is a yoga or a yoke, a binding. The deep meaning of discipline is union. It is a path to union to making oneself over into union. Discipline is harmonizing, following the truth, not a concept or an order from someone, but a training of oneself into harmony. It's making an effort but it's not "you must do this," but rather, "this must be done." The precepts taken by Buddhists are used as a mental training in compassion.

The Song of Awakening, A Guide to Liberation Through Marananussati, Mindfulness of Death, Boise, Idaho, The Open Path Publishing, 1979. p. 49. Used with permission from Bodhi Publishing.

Reflections and Appreciations

Demonstrating the Dharma *Tarchin Hearn*

During the many years I traveled and studied with Namgyal Rinpoche, he would often challenge me in extravagant and innovative ways. He challenged me physically, emotionally and intellectually. He challenged me conceptually. He challenged me in the areas of food, money and sex.

These challenges took many outer forms but all of them called me to re-evaluate who and what I thought I was. Sometimes they were direct verbal or physical confrontations. Sometimes they took the form of his propelling me into an activity that led to much learning and transformation through interaction with others. Although many of these exchanges could easily become the substance of fantastic and at times outrageous guru tales, on par with any Gurdjieff or Zen episode, in retrospect, all these anecdotes would be more about me than about the being I thought of as my teacher.

I'd like to relate a different type of situation, one that was very quiet and unspectacular yet, at the time, one that touched me to the core. From the very beginning these moments resonated within me something precious — something fundamentally sane and profoundly natural. These moments of being with Rinpoche, often with no one else around, could happen in a car, sitting in a hotel lobby, in his room or outside enjoying a magnificent vista — dwelling in silence, comfortably still, as Rinpoche gazed pensively at seemingly 'no thing' in particular, his glasses off, utterly relaxed and uncontrived and not being anything for anyone.

At these times, there seemed to be a huge space of presence — no conversation, nothing to be said, and I felt completely at ease and effortlessly attentive. There was something blessed about these moments — a demonstration of ordinariness, naturalness and spontaneous awakeness. Now, I recognize them as transmission; a wordless demonstration of heart dharma.

When I think of Rinpoche today, I feel those moments of contact. Everything else seems like decoration on a cake; a gathering and refining of myriad qualities of being so that this ever present always available mystery could self-reveal.

The Virtues of Silence (Japan, 2008) *Sensei Doug Duncan*

Unfortunately, I don't feel I can contribute to these Namgyal stories for the following reasons:

Some aspects of the teaching should remain oral and personal to the guru-student relationship. In my mind these are by far the most interesting stories.

Because the root conditioning is so stubborn, sometimes quite strenuous means must be applied to uproot them. These are also the most interesting stories.

Although we like to think the teaching is democratic, the democratic may not be the most adequate model. Beings are at different places at different times on the path so a teaching that might apply to one being may not be appropriate for another. (This may be the whole story with regard to the differences that distinguish Theravadin, Mahayana and Vajrayana teachings.)

When things become too public and are seen at a distance, they lose context and impact. The written word is one way in which this happens.

I hope that this list while not exhaustive is at least indicative of why I will remain silent for now.

Shining the Light (Burma, 2010) *Christine Wihak*

Since Namgyal Rinpoche died, I haven't made any similar connection with another teacher or Dharma community, although I've sought teaching from many.

This absence somewhat concerned me until last year when I went to Myanmar and visited the Sayadaw U Thila Wunta, who ordained Rinpoche as Ananda Bodhi in 1956. He was very, very frail and spending most of his time in bed. He happened to be awake at the time when I arrived at the monastery, bearing gifts from his students in southern California.

One of these gifts was an LED flashlight, very useful in the frequent power cuts in Yangon. The Sayadaw picked it up, turned it on and shone it inside his own mouth.

All his attendants were puzzled or amused but for me, it was a silent but eloquent answer to my unvoiced question —

Quel relief!

Transcendence (1978 – 2003) *Mark Arneson*

Of all the time I was involved with Rinpoche and his Teaching, the most significant thing to me was his way of communicating the Dharma.

Rinpoche was constantly breaking open the box of dry repetitive and routine meditation practice and bringing in the light of transformation and transcendence.

I met no one else like him who could bring Dharma to life so well, who opened up the universe and made meditation a total exploration of transformation and transcendence.

Here are examples from my notes: "You have to develop a firm sense of commitment to progress and flow. All illness is a type of paralysis, an obstacle to joyful flow and you flourishing."

"You are suffering from spiritual varicose veins, calcified layers of ignorance in the body that have silted up the system of the Divine body. Come to see the crystal lattice of Earth — *pathavi*. This is a necessary prelude to the experience of total awareness — *Mahamudra*."

Rinpoche spoke of a vision he experienced of a very dense black cloud containing all the knowledge and wisdom of the universe being revealed to him.

He also spoke of a vision with the croaking of frogs as the sound of Transcendence.

Meditation should be a harmonious flow, the purpose of which is to come to a state of going beyond. On the way there may be intense activity and involvement but there will be transcendence, a going beyond the attempts to do something. No more trying, there is just abiding in the natural state: non-action or effortless effort. THE meditation is no meditation, no formal practice. All practice will be abandoned. Although there is no practice there are formal practices. This is a paradox because . . . freely arising states which cannot be practiced . . . exist in your being and there are ways of allowing the seed to grow, to come to the surface. You can only practise the meditations on compassion and love if they already exist in your being.

Paleochora Discourses, Part I Exploring the Language of Liberation, Part II Healing, Faith and Karma, Kinmount, Bodhi Publishing, 2009, p. 62. Used with permission from Bodhi Publishing.

Crystal, Clarity (New Zealand and Australia) *Lama Chime Shore*

All events, interactions and changes happen around service — the gladly done practice. This was the central thread of experience throughout knowing my good teacher and friend Namgyal Rinpoche. He demonstrated that the Teachings can pass through very different people, places and times. I saw in him a willingness to engage and a love of beauty.

Rinpoche taught through much more than words. He showed us a beautiful gem displayed with more ordinary ones. I think a lot of friends drew an insight from that gesture — encouraged to love crystal in a land of poverty.

Awakening is one thing and Realisation another — together they are the human enlightenment project.

I love the feeling when a personal relationship is felt as part of a vast expression, a universal company.

I eventually understood a little about transmission and lineage network through the practice of service and the idea of *Mahamudra* lineage became clearer. We have built a *Khadampa* Stupa here at Coorain to celebrate this idea and to honour the ashes and memories of this original, kind friend.

Guru Mind (Dharma Centre of Canada, 1990s) *Gail Angevine*

One day after class, I approached Rinpoche to ask a question. Because so many people were crowded around, I stood closer to him than I normally would and spontaneously entered his energy field. There was a sudden and dramatic expansion in my consciousness and to my surprise, I found myself viewing a brilliant star in an infinitely expanding galaxy.

This was a brief but powerful moment of revelation — a direct seeing of Guru Mind — a jewel-like consciousness of inconceivable vastness and profundity, unimpeded and totally open, uncompromisingly awake, embracing the totality of creation in the one heart.

This is what he so skillfully and compassionately transmitted through his teaching and his presence — constantly reminding us that this is possible; constantly admonishing us to relinquish our clinging to our tight secure ego cocoon.

To wake up! To break the chains! To make the determination to join him in his glorious and unending dance with the universe.

Interview (excerpt from interview, October 2004 Victoria, BC)
Stuart Hertzog with John de Jardin

Stuart Hertzog: What was your first meeting with Rinpoche like?

John de Jardin: My first meeting with Rinpoche was at Kinmount during His Holiness the Karmapa's first visit to North America in the fall of 1974. I went to Ontario from Winnipeg with Khema Ananda and a few other people who related to him as a teacher. I had heard of Namgyal Rinpoche and wanted to meet him and this seemed a great opportunity as His Holiness would be there at the same time. Rinpoche was very gracious; he allowed the five of us to stay in a cabin on the property since we were students of Khema from out of town. I got to serve the Karmapa breakfast one morning!

My first sight of Rinpoche was as he stood outside regaling a group of students. He had just showed up on the property and I wandered over. He already seemed familiar to me. Of course, I had seen photographs of him and heard many stories, but right from that moment I had a feeling that "This is my Teacher." This strong conviction has never changed — I've never had doubts about it. Also something about Rinpoche's students made me realise immediately that this was the direction I wanted to take.

S.H.: What was it about his students that gave you this realisation?

J.deJ: A sense they had actually had a real experience — not just words in books; there was a lived dimension to what was happening. It was exciting — real transformation happening in people's lives — and these people had critical intelligence, something I was looking for. They weren't just slavishly following someone or something. This teaching spoke to me right from the start.

S.H.: Besides the recognition, what else about Rinpoche attracted you?

J.deJ: I believe there is an element of past lives. Who knows? But I felt a connection with him already and that was the single strongest underlying factor. And I believed, because of the effects in his students' lives that this guy was the 'genuine article.' The deeper I got into it and the more I got to know him, the more I felt this was the case. He didn't want publicity; he didn't seek to become a media star. He worked one-on-one. As you delve into what the teaching really is and the stories of the experiences of the ancient masters — Tilopa, Naropa, Marpa and Milarepa — you say: "Yes, that's how it works!" It's got to be teacher to student, one-on-one and close. Millions of people call themselves the Dalai Lama's students, but how many engage personally and directly with that Being? It's impossible. So this was something rare in the world — to actually have the opportunity to practice and to really be involved.

S.H.: When did you start studying with Rinpoche?

J.deJ: I went to the course in Norway in 1976. He got sick and had to leave for a while. We all travelled to meet him in Assisi and then Crete to do a *Mahamudra* retreat. At the beginning of that retreat he announced, "Is there anyone who wants to help out and do some service?"

I volunteered and went to the interview in a house on the hill above Chania. That interview was my first direct contact with him and I said, "Look, I really do want to help out."

He said: "Why? Why do you want to do service?"

"I want to be of use." That was a good answer, I thought, but Terry Hagan got the job.

After lunch, Rinpoche came up behind me and grabbed my trapezius muscle, almost lifted me off the ground. Ugh! Later he would give me a poke in the ribs, repeatedly, every time I got into his orbit. I was constantly flinching, protecting myself. I knew I had to let go, but it was hard to do.

S.H.: So your relationship with Rinpoche went through phases, as you've described.

J.deJ: Yes, though I think that depended mostly on my own mind state at any given time. But I want to turn to what he was teaching — leaving aside the direct personal relationship — what he presented to all students as a Teacher and what was unique about his teachings in relation to the outer world. It's hard to disassociate the way he taught publicly with from the personal teaching because my experience of him in class was a continuation of that. His teaching was based on who was in front of him. On many occasions there was an announced topic and he completely deviated from it due to circumstances and what was coming up. He answered questions in the minds of those present. If there is one thing that characterizes his teaching it's his ability to use everything as a vehicle — anything and everything. For beings like me, who are somewhat obsessive and like everything orderly — who want to be given an A-B-C-D of just what you need to get enlightened — it could be very frustrating!

In his teaching is that the onus is always thrown back on the student. "Figure it out, get on with it, I'm not going to spoon feed you. You've got to make effort, investigate and do it for yourself." He was simply an embodiment of the vastness and constantly changing nature of the awakened mind — so he would never stay with any A-B-C-D. Rinpoche was always on to new horizons. From the point of view of an individual student needing to penetrate the fundamentals of Dharma, it was left up to you to get that on your own because he was always going further.

If you tried to stay with his latest thing — with whatever Rinpoche happened to be into — it would be difficult because you'd always be looking at something new, never staying with one thing long enough to thoroughly understand it. It was left to the individual student to be responsible for that, to take something and penetrate it in depth.

S.H.: Yes, so with that note of open and therefore questionable eclecticism about the way Namgyal Rinpoche has transmitted, what is his legacy? Do you see his students who are teaching now as his legacy? Is that what he's leaving to the next generation? He's gone physically, so what's left?

J.deJ: I believe there are a number of genuinely realized students of his who are going to take things further. Their realisation is on track and will deepen, and they will do some good work.

S.H.: So what part has Rinpoche played?

J.deJ: It's too soon to make an historical judgment. In a hundred years I guess we'll know. My sense is that probably his role has been crucial. I'm so grateful that Namgyal Rinpoche was my Teacher — SO grateful. He was able to cut through to the heart of things as if it was just obvious and normal and sensible. That's missing with some other people and Teachings. They're infatuated with the exotic, the 'wow!' and that's deluded. People get caught up in the form and it's beautiful — a different culture and all — but we don't need to become Tibetan or Japanese.

What's important is true realization, the genuine article, Mind itself. It's tough — a slippery bar of soap and hard to grasp. I went to Plum Village and did a retreat with Thich Nhat Hanh, a wonderful guy, but again, there are thousands of people trying to relate to that Being as their Teacher, and very few really have a personal relationship with him. He is somebody you could recommend without hesitation to anyone. You know they'll be helped to some degree, but they won't get what some lucky beings were able to experience with Namgyal Rinpoche, which is: "Here you go, here's the mirror, kiddo — held right in front of you. You want it, you got it." That's a very rare thing in this world, and why I think his impact is going to be important to the development of the Teaching. There are a lot of people who will be around for a while who had some very good teaching from him and have a clarity and a perspective that is rare and will bear fruit in time.

S.H.: Yes, there are a lot of people — as I get into this research I'm finding more and more.

J.deJ: Amazing numbers of people. The last thing I want to say is that I think his death has had a cathartic effect on many, many beings who, like me, are feeling "Let's really get on with it now. Time is passing, Rinpoche is gone, and it's entirely up to me what I do with the rest of my life here."

In Honour of the Great Lama Namgyal:
Namo Guru Manjughosaya-Namgyal! *Lama Mark Webber*

This morning when I woke up, I especially felt the great blessings of Dharma riches and jewels that were literally pumped into my veins by that great teacher, Namgyal Rinpoche. In fact, this discovery is a beautiful mystery — that nothing really got pumped in. However, much was revealed and it is available to all — like peeling back layers of gauze. It brings mist to my eyes to consider how deeply shaped and influenced I am by his vast mind, ideals and principles. Like a bright kernel in my heart and a stupa above my head, I am so often speechless with joy when he comes to mind.

He was a big guy in so many ways! Rinpoche was a great father to me, always encouraging my talents, not letting me slip into what was easy. One day in Norway, when I was 20, during a walk, Rinpoche asked me, "What do want to be?" I replied, "Like you, a meditation master!" He said "That is fine, but being a meditation master is not enough!" For a week, once a day we would go for a walk and he would ask me the same question every day — what did I want to be? And I would reply, "If not a meditation master, then — a such and such." Every walk I would offer something of my history, another becoming that I could see myself taking on like a costume: the 'meditation master,' the 'doctor,' the 'acupuncturist,' the 'chemist,' the 'biologist,' and so forth. And every day he would say, "That is okay, good." Then he would talk about the occupation's merits and say, "But try again, what else?"

At the end of the week, he turned to me and said, "Mark, become nothing!" My god! What a momentous instruction! Like a nail driven through a wall, I really heard it — an instruction I have tried to attain and keep very close to my heart.

He was remarkable. A few words of his, here and there, of pith and essence, support and un-support, testing and re-testing could shift your being deeply. He raised the Banner of question and determination, challenge and enquiry, love and wrath, compassion and bright clarity throughout my being. Rinpoche was great — constantly challenging everything you were holding on to. He always taught and demonstrated the essence of non-clinging awareness, one moment with fierce determination, the next moment with love and humility, the next with pride and mystery, then with abandon and humour. He could display all the Emotions of the Dance with blazing, awake splendour. Above all he kept raising the Banner of Victory for all who had the eyes to see.

Namgyal Rinpoche had the highest of ideals and some quirky notions, some of which I don't even agree with to this day, but that does not matter a drop. What was important was he did not miss a moment of awareness of Dharma, probing to the very heart of the matter. If you did well, there was always more. If there were profound experiences, then there were more discoveries to be unearthed! And so too, he never stopped questing and discovering; that was so beautiful to witness. I enjoyed watching the joy in his voice and face when he unearthed another gem of realization, another way to teach liberation, a new sparkle of the natural state.

My teacher loved to teach, as he said to me before he died, "That is my duty." His teaching of Dharma was wondrous and magnificent. A melodious voice of such depth, luminosity and power — always striving to bring about an 'edible' experience, a living presence of that which he spoke of through his remarkable speech, whether it was classic Buddha-dharma, meditation states or technique, Sufi dancing, Dzogchen, rose gardening, the Christian mystical life, animals encountered, stars and galaxies, scientific discoveries or a universal vision of Liberation.

Outside of a Dharma class or Empowerment he rarely would allow those with him to use any Dharma jargon, Pali or Sanskrit words. Thus every activity, including the most seemingly mundane, such as watching a grade C movie, eating a meal from a can of spaghetti, shopping for gems, watching birds or talking politics, was an enriching tapestry of natural vivid awakeness. He was so compassionate, so awake and so utterly human: an exemplar of the teaching of the 'Two in One.'

No phenomena and no Dharmas were ever stale to his mind. He had the most wondrous ability to cut away all chaff and penetrate to the essence. He drove right to the heart of liberation and understood in a continuous stream, the unity of the Path and the Fruit and the factors for Enlightenment. He kept raising the Banner of Victory, often fearlessly, showing the investigative mind unified with mindfulness and awareness. He was a great explorer. He blessed everything in his path — sometimes by dissolving everything in his wake! Yes, he was fearless, he understood that liberation is not about institution building but both building and dissolving — he really practised and manifested non-clinging. That could frighten the boots off many and bring anger to some! He lived the ancient tradition of the Bhikkhu, the wanderer, the accomplished Yogi; in search for truth and to declare freedom, always more discoveries to be made.

Rinpoche did not make it easy for some of us to meditate, but that made us even stronger. He always pointed to awareness, not to the meditation, even while teaching the most arcane points of technique. He was a tracker and a hunter of detail to bring out the majesty of God. Rinpoche was a big collector too! He loved to collect things so as to better gain understanding and share the amazing splendour of nature and the crafts of all beings. He displayed and discussed the joy of life and the wonders of all that is: detail, detail, detail. He brought forth a universe of gifts for all manner of people and creatures to experience, but above all he pointed to — from the moment I met him — the vast Guru Mind, Buddha Nature. It was like always being in a vast mandala of Awareness. The Wongkur was unbroken and unshakable.

I remember the first time I met him. In the early 1970s Chorpel Dolma (Ms. Raff,) my first Dharma teacher invited Rinpoche to bless the Sāvaka House in Toronto, where she was the teacher and I lived for a time. I was vacuuming and tidying up the teaching space when a tall man entered. There was instant recognition, a smile and a warm hello. "Oh, you, hello there," as if we had known each other for many years. But what really struck me was the feel of his mind in my experience — like water merging with water it was like tasting a clear bright crystal field. There was no doubt in my mind that this being was highly awake and I wished to study and learn from him as much as possible. I had been waiting a whole year!

Rinpoche was very human in his quirks and ways, yet, with the combination of extraordinary awakeness, knowledge and wisdom, he was an astonishing presence. He lived an awake vivid life without stories and rarely referred to his past. Liberation flowed naturally in his cells. This was a palpable experience for many of us and was not something he had to think about. One day, after a class in Nelson, British Columbia, as we were climbing the stairs in my house, he turned back to me, paused, a light shone in his eyes, and he told me how much he enjoyed teaching from his direct experience and not having to read, rely on ancient texts or the writings of other teachers.

His legacy will live on not because of anything 'particular' at all — no institution, no religious dogma and no scientific theory — but like a perfume or essential oil, so gossamer and utterly refined — a legacy and dedication to vast exploration with consummate awakeness and compassion; to the joy of knowledge and sensing; to discovery; to visiting all places and worlds; to challenging every idea and tradition; to non-sectarianism; to fierce or gentle compassion based on realization; to contemplative mind and continuum of awareness — these are some of the main notes of the oil that lubricates this precious thread.

Like the Venerable Namgyal Rinpoche, any attempt to organize, define, ritualize or structure it, will of course deaden this spirit and his precious lineage.

I rarely ever think about what I have learnt from Namgyal Rinpoche or stories about him. Now that I am prompted to do so, a few joyous simple words sprang up, and a handful of stories offered. Via this precious transmission I have grown to love blowing the conch shell of Dharma and discovery, for as many beings as possible, in the midst of confusion and misery, joy and laughter.

May all beings awaken quickly!

True Love *Abrah Arneson*

At the first class I attended, Rinpoche toyed with ideas about time and space travel. He told us of a journey he made to the sun — fury and heat beyond comprehension. In our minds, he painted prehistoric landscapes, before humans walked the planet. He quoted Shakyamuni Buddha, "In this fathom-long body — subject as it is to illness, old age and death — I show you the coming into being and passing away of the universe." At that moment, my life changed. Rinpoche gave voice to possibilities that drew me from my slumber. Perhaps my life was about more than I had imagined. During the second class I attended, Rinpoche led rebirthing exercises to rhythms of Gregorian chants — an experience terrifying beyond reason, yet there remained the possibility of something greater.

The journey with Rinpoche had begun, one wonder after another: wild orchids, a sea of jellyfish, diamonds in seven different colours, the scent of an antelope, mystic visions, whale blubber — his mind never stopped exploring. His interest was vast. Each moment in Rinpoche's presence revealed another facet of this immense universe. And he imbued each moment with exquisite love and care. He cherished passionately each intricately woven detail of life. He spoke of finding an animal dead in a hole, the claw marks of its desperation engraved on the dirt walls. He shuddered as he told of discovering drowned kittens in a barrel and trembled describing aborted human fetuses in garbage pails. During these times, his beautiful, vast love would become terrible, like an earthquake. Confronting the desecration of that which he held most sacred, the magnificence and vulnerability of life sent him into a passionate fury. Nothing could stop Rinpoche's love.

He was a great storyteller. He would begin with a casual wave of his hand and a slight nod of his head. As the story unfolded, he would draw out each word, weaving a net in which to catch his unsuspecting audience. His eyes would grow wide. He would pause — expectation catching the breath of his listeners. Then the punch line and ensuing howls of laughter, or perhaps an unsettling feeling in the gut, announcing it is time to wake up. Such was the story he told of a man who went shopping for toys for his children: he left the children in the house alone. When he returned the house was on fire, and the children inside. The father called to the children, "Come out, the house is on fire!" But the children were too busy with their games to heed his cries. Frantic, he cried out, "I have toys for you, children!" But the children locked the doors, believing they already had the best toys.

A pause; he caught our eyes as the image of a house on fire exploded in our brains, and quietly, almost a whisper, he said, "And the toys are real."

Thinking of My Lama (August 2004, Mana Retreat, New Zealand) *Tarchin Hearn*

Thinking of my lama.
Those days of summer 2003
You graced the world with profound pith.
The ultimate perfection resting, just as it is.
You poured out your treasure vase a cornucopia of jewels,
    myriad eclectic ways of fathoming dharma
    through the means of body, speech and mind.
Great traditions of empowerment you scattered
    far and wide sowing seeds in the living earth of beings' minds.
You opened your worldly treasury, weavings and jewels
    and perfumes and music and food and telescopes, using these
    wonders to feed the marvelling minds of flowering bodhicitta.
You continuously pointed to material
    to embodiment and showed the way of
    love through celebrating the detail.
Sitting now in New Zealand, a remembrance,
    of all of us
    with you
 The Great Empowerment of Mahamaya
Sun streaming in the windows
Row on row of red robes
Moist eyes
Blessed Recognition
This poem has no end.
A golden dandelion flower bloomed in our midst
 gradually becoming seed
And the summer winds of Kinmount
    gently blew through the hall and
    the entire seed head floated out and up and over
Catching thermals and crosswinds and down drafts
Drifting on jet stream and planting flowers
    of laughing golden radiance
Not lineage but multiage
A vast blessing for the world
In all the realms of experience
    may I never be separate from my lama.
Bodhisattva stages flourish at every level of being.
May I use with joy and abandon all the teaching that arises.
May the love and clear seeing —
    the wondrous blessing of the Victorious Ones
Flower everywhere for everyone.

An Appreciation *Mark Eisenberg*

The Rinpoche was the most remarkable teacher and friend one could be blessed with. It was a constant treat and challenge to be in the presence of such an engaging, brilliant, compassionate and joyful powerhouse of a human being. Whether it was the thunder of the master shaking the roots of one's being or the great pleasure of sharing a fine meal, an inspiring symphony, the change of autumn leaves, or a good joke, life with Rinpoche was a feast of cosmic proportions.

His approach to life was so simple, so real, and so completely inspiring in its breadth and generosity. He lived at the epicenter of every moment. His was the dance of the dagger-wielding warrior, the inquisitive scientist, the wise and wondrous Guru, and the child at play in the fields of the Lord. Along with the dagger came a gentle outstretched hand and an unbelievably honest voice which constantly beckoned and cajoled: "Over here! This way! Breathe slowly. Listen carefully. Sense fully. Study assiduously. Tread gently. And surrender completely."

I cared so deeply for Namgyal Rinpoche, and in many small ways would try to give in return some of the great kindness he showered upon me. It was an honour and a joy to run errands for him, (endless); to run and try to keep pace with him, (impossible); to shop until you drop with him, (expensive); and to share the treasures of this beautiful and fragile planet with him (expansive.)

I loved making the Teacher laugh, whether through cleverness or stupidity. I loved drinking in the endless wisdom. I loved diving into frigid waters and swimming to sit on an iceberg. I loved the stream of fascinating friends and seekers who made their way through his life. I loved the shy, quiet, thoughtful, idiosyncratic and forceful fatherly ways of the teacher who would chastise for not receiving a Father's Day card, who would whip up a salad that would knock your socks off, who would lament the difficulty of helping people live more consciously and the reality of sometimes being misunderstood.

Sir — Forgive our slow understanding. May the multitudes of people you inspired awaken speedily for the sake of all beings everywhere. We humbly thank you. God Speed Sir.

Everything involved in any process is constantly changing — always moving in all directions — changeless change or changing changelessness. Nothing can be said about it.

Namgyal Rinpoche, Toronto, 1971.

Karma is dependent on two things: previous actions and present supporting circumstances. Given that you are in a precious human incarnation I have no doubt you have all the potential capacities for enlightenment. I will do all in my power to relate it to your understanding.

Namgyal Rinpoche, Dharma Centre of Canada, 1968.

Appendix 1: The Global Community of Namgyal Centres and Teachers *(Partial list, Spring, 2012)*

Canada East

DHARMA CENTRE of CANADA, Retreat Centre, (Kinmount, ON)
adminoffice@dharmacentre.org, www.dharmacentre.org 705.488.2704

BODHI PUBLISHING, (P.O. Box 144, Kinmount, ON K0M 2A0)
bodhip@halhinet.on.ca, www.bodhipublishing.org
Dharma Teacher, President and Editor: Karma Chime Wongmo

HANIEL HOUSE (Peterborough, ON)
hanielhouse@sympatico.ca, www.pansophic.info
Contact: Dennis Delorme

PETERBOROUGH DHARMA GROUP & OM NAMGYAL HOME
(Peterborough, ON) ptbodg@gmail.com;
Sharon Davison (Lama Tashi Namgyal), sharonedavison@gmail.com
Rab Wilkie (Karma Lungrig Nyima), rab@astrocyclics.com
Jack Connelly, jleeconnelly@gmail.com

SARVAYANA (Peterborough, ON)
sarvayana@sympatico.ca Contact: Lama Sherab (Paul Curtis)

TORONTO NAMGYAL CENTRE (Toronto, ON)
info@torontonamgyalcentre.ca http://www.torontonamgyalcentre.ca
 Spiritual Director: Lama Sonam Gyatso

TORONTO SANGHA, (Toronto, ON)
Contact: Lisa Cowen lisamichellecowen@hotmail.com

JIM McNAMARA ((Toronto, ON)
jim@livinginstitute.org

SAKYA-NAMGYAL CENTRE, Sakya Thubten Namgyal Ling, (Uxbridge,
ON) wesley@sakyanamgyal.com, www.namgyal.ca
Sakya Shasanadhara: Wesley & Angelica Knapp

CRYSTAL STAFF (Ottawa, ON)
info@crystalstaff.org, www.crystalstaff.org

MORIN HEIGHTS DHARMA HOUSE (Morin Heights, QC)
Contact: Jane Marenghi; janemarenghi@hotmail.com
Teacher: Derek Rasmussen; dharma_eh@yahoo.ca

TERRY HAGAN AND MALA SIKKA (Kinmount, ON)
http://www.malasikka.net/ (In long-term retreat 2012-2014)

MONTREAL OPEN MEDITATION GROUP
mettamtl@gmail.com Teacher: Derek Rasmussen

KIM SAWYER, (Toronto, ON,)
ksawyer@assyst.ca

CHARLENE JONES (Stouffville - Markham, ON)
Charlenej@rogers.com

ROB McCONNELL & KAREN RUSSELL (Zephyr, ON)
robmcco@xplornet.com, sukha@xplornet.com

TRYG SCHONNING, (Ottawa, ON)
Trydana@magma.ca

STEVEN & CHERYL GELLMAN, (Ottawa, ON)
s.gellman@sympatico.ca

MELODIE MASSEY (Port Hope, ON)
melodie@eagle.ca

HEATHER RIGBY, (Claremont, ON)
triplegem@look.ca

Canada - Central

DHARMA CENTRE of WINNIPEG (Winnipeg, MB)
gkphoto@yahoo.com, www.dharmawpg.com
Teacher: Lama Gyurme Dorje (Gerry Kopelow)

RIVER AND BRIDGE MEDITATION & STUDY GROUP (Winnipeg, MB)
http://riverandbridge.wordpress.com/ riverandbridge@gmail.com
Teacher: Brian McLeod

NOVAYANA SOCIETY (Edmonton, AB) www.novayana.org, don.madkenzie@shaw.ca Teacher: Cecilie Kwiat, ckwiat@shaw.ca

DHARMA IN MOTION (Calgary, AB,)
www.dharmainmotion.com, http://clearskycalgary.org/
Evangelos Diavolitsis, evangelosd@gmail.com

Canada West

YUKON DHARMA SOCIETY (Whitehorse, YK)
2 Redwood Street, Whitehorse, Yukon Y1A 4B3 Canada
Teacher Lama Lodro (Jeff Olson) Contact: tigger@polarcom.com
yukon.dharma@yknet.ca

CRYSTAL MOUNTAIN – A Society for Eastern & Western Studies
(Galiano Island and Vancouver, BC) www.crystalmountain.org,
crystalmountainsociety@yahoo.ca Teacher: Lama Mark
Webber www.markwebber.org lamawebber@yahoo.ca

SUNSHINE COAST RETREAT HOUSE (Roberts Creek, BC)
www.retreathouse.bc.ca
Teachers: Bonni Ross and Matthew Eades retreathouse@dccnet.com

CLEAR SKY MEDITATION & STUDY CENTRE (Cranbrook, BC)
contact@clearskycenter.org, www.clearskycenter.org
Founding Teacher: Acariya Doug Duncan Sensei

ATI MARGA (Alert Bay, BC)
atimarga@cablerocket.com, www.atimarga.org
Teacher: Sonam Senge sonam.senge@hotmail.com

MUDITA BC, (Vancouver, BC)
www.muditabc.com info@muditabc.com
Teacher: John de Jardin www.walkingshadow.net
Contact: Lynn Hauka, lhauka@shaw.ca

DHARMA FELLOWSHIP (Denman Island, BC)
http://www.dharmafellowship.org, info@dharmafellowship.org
Teacher: Lama Rodney Devenish

GAIL ANGEVINE, (Gibsons, BC)
gailangevine@yahoo.ca

ABRAH ARNESON, (Red Deer, AB)
abrah@shaw.ca

USA East

FAIRHAVEN LANTERN CENTER, (Fairhaven, MD)
http://www.fairhavenlantern.com, awakening@fairhavenlantern.com
Teachers: David Berry, Elizabeth Berry (Ikebana)

USA West

THE OPEN PATH, (Boise ID,) A Center for Eastern and Western Studies
Contact: Steven Stubbs, Chairman theopenpath@clearwire.net

SAN FRANCISCO MEDITATION (San Francisco CA, USA)
www.sanfranmeditation.org Teacher: Acariya Doug Duncan Sensei
Contact: Greg Molkentin, greg@gregmolkentin.com

Central and South America

XO KI'IN RETREAT CENTER (Sian Ka'an, Yucatan, Mexico)
http://annawoods.com/WordPress/
Contact: Anna Woods: xokiin@yahoo.com

NOVAYANA*BRASIL,* Dharma Pure & Simple
http://www.novayana.com/
Teacher: Jangchub Reid

Europe

CRYSTAL GROUP (UK) www.crystalgroup.org.uk/index.htm
Chair: Sally Muir, sallymuir@manushi.com

THE ORCHARD (Lower Maescoed, HEREFORD HR2oHP UK)
www.soniamoriceau.org, http://www.touchingstillness.co.uk/
Teachers: Ad Brugman, ad.brugman@zen.co.uk,
Sonia Moriceau sonia@soniamoriceau.org

LONDON MEDITATION (London UK)
http://www.londonmeditation.org, londonmeditation@yahoo.com
Teachers: Acariya Doug Duncan Sensei, Sally Muir
sallymuir@manushi.com

CORNWALL BUDDHISTS:
http://cornwallbuddhists.org/crystal.shtml

DHARMAGRUPPE (Germany)
www.dharmagruppe.de info@dharmagruppe.de
Contact: Ludger Muller ludger@dharmagruppe.de

AILO GAUP (Oslo, Norway)
http://www.sjaman.com, ailo@sjaman.com

Pacific

WANGAPEKA STUDY & RETREAT CENTRE (Wakefield, New Zealand)
retreatcentre@wangapeka.org, www.wangapeka.org
Teacher: Tarchin Hearn, tarchin.mary@clear.net.nz

QUEENSTOWN DHARMA HOUSE (Queenstown, New Zealand)
Contact: Alan Macalister qtndharmahouse@yahoo.com
Teacher: Lama Mark Webber, lamawebber@yahoo.ca,
www.markwebber.org

AUCKLAND SPHERE GROUP (Auckland, New Zealand)
www.aucklandsphere.org Teachers: Lama Mark Webber, Tarchin Hearn,
Leander Kane, Bonni Ross, Chime Shore.

ORGYEN HERMITAGE. (Kaitkati, New Zealand)
www.greendharmatreasury.org
Teacher: Tarchin Hearn, tarchin@greendharmatreasury.org

ORIGINS CENTRE (Balingup WA, Australia)
origins@iinet.net.au, http://origins.mysouthwest.com.au
Teacher: Lama Chime Shore, Manager: Robyne Garnham

COORAIN HOUSE (Perth WA, Australia)
coorain@sctelco.net.au Contact: Anne Clark, anneclark@space.net.au

DHARMA JAPAN (Kyoto & Tokyo, Japan)
www.dharma-japan.org
Founding Teacher: Achariya Doug Duncan Sensei
Resident Teachers: Paul Jaffe, Linda Yamashita (Kyoto)
John Munroe (Tokyo) Yumedono (Kyoto)
Temple Manager: Nicole Porter: contact@dharma-japan.org

"If you are involved in building up an awareness of life, an awareness of the foundation, reading books is only a way of escaping from that work. Any book, no matter how profound, is escape literature if you are attempting to develop right hemisphere activities. The only value of books is to get you to do the work. They are like the proverbial finger pointing at the moon. Occasionally they can be wholesomely used for escape, for relaxation. This teaching is trying to bring you to enlightenment by getting you to watch what is occurring. In fact, all the books you read may very well make you fall asleep, although you won't necessarily know that you're dimming your awareness by reading them. They are just dreams if they talk about something that is not here and now for you."

Body, Speech and Mind, a manual for human development, Kinmount, Bodhi Publishing, 2004, p. 214-215. Used with permission from Bodhi Publishing.

Appendix 2: Bibliography

What Namgyal Rinpoche taught was direct and spontaneous experience, beyond words, but he often began with a book. He would quote 2000-year-old Buddhist and Christian scriptures, weaving ancient wisdom into his talks as easily as the latest theories in astrophysics, gleaned from the paperback on his coffee table, perhaps about 'black holes' and the first one discovered, Cygnus X-1, at the nearby Dunlop Observatory.

All books were fair and eclectic game — if they aroused keen interest and awakened minds to wonder and investigation. After an interview with the teacher, a student might be turning titles over in mind, "I have to find a copy of *The Jewel Ornament of Liberation* and a sci-fantasy novel by Terry Pratchett?!" Or, a student might mention to Rinpoche that he'd been blown away by a book on alchemy and the following Monday a series of classes would begin. "Here's what Titus Burkhardt has to say on this subject, Chapter One . . ."

The following bibliography is a list of books made from transcriptions of discourses by Namgyal Rinpoche. This list is just the tip of a 'book berg.' There were many books that Rinpoche recommended to his students over the years on a vast range of subjects. Some of them are mentioned in the stories contained within this book.

You may Order Tales of Awakening at
https://www.createspace.com/3850183

Bibliography I

The Teachings of Namgyal Rinpoche from Bodhi Publishing
P.O. Box 144, Kinmount, ON K0M 2A0.
bodhip@halhinet.on.ca, www.bodhipublishing.org

Books

The Vision and Other Essays, Bhikkhu Ananda Bodhi, Transcribed by Margaret Aboud, Kinmount, Ontario, Dharma Centre of Canada, 1971; Property of Bodhi Publishing.

An Introduction to Meditation, Edited by Stuart Hertzog, Toronto, Ontario, Pegasus Press, 1976.

The Song of Awakening, A Guide to Liberation Through Marananussati, Mindfulness of Death, Edited by Karma Chime Wongmo, Boise, Idaho, The Open Path Publishing, 1979. Property of Bodhi Publishing.

Unfolding Through Art, Edited by Karma Chime Wongmo, Boise, Idaho, The Open Path Publishing, 1982. Property of Bodhi Publishing.

The Dome of Heaven: Speculations Upon An Awakening Universe, Toronto. Ontario, Namgyal House, 1983. Property of Bodhi Publishing.

The Breath of Awakening, A Guide to Liberation Through Anapanasati, Mindfulness of Breathing, Edited by Karma Chime Wongmo, Kinmount, Ontario, Bodhi Publishing, 1992.

The Womb, Karma and Transcendence, A Journey towards Liberation, Edited by Karma Chime Wongmo, Kinmount, Ontario, Bodhi Publishing, 1996.

A Body of Truth, Empowering through Active Imagination and Creative Visualization, Edited by Rab Wilkie, Leslie Hamson and Karma Chime Wongmo, Kinmount, Ontario, Bodhi Publishing, 1997.

The Womb of Form, Pith Instructions in The Six Yogas of Naropa, Edited by Christopher Stevens, Second Edition, Kinmount, Ontario, Bodhi Publishing, 1998. Property of Bodhi Publishing.

Glimmerings of the Mystical Life, Compiled by Margaret Morris, Kinmount, Ontario, Bodhi Publishing, Second Edition, 2002.

The Path of Victory, Discourses on the Paramita, Edited by Sonam Senge, Fourth Printing, Kinmount, Ontario, Bodhi Publishing, 2002.

Body, Speech & Mind, a manual for human development, Edited by Cecilie Kwiat, Kinmount, Ontario, Bodhi Publishing, Second Edition, 2004.

Suchness, the Diamond State of Realisation, Teachings on the Diamond Sutra, Edited by Karma Chime Wongmo, Kinmount, Ontario, Bodhi Publishing, 2006.

Right Livelihood and Other Foundations of Enlightenment, Edited by Karma Chime Wongmo, Kinmount, Ontario, Bodhi Publishing, 2008.

Paleochora Discourses Part I, Exploring the Language of Liberation, Part II, Healing, Faith and Karma, Revised Edition, Kinmount, Ontario, Bodhi Publishing, 2009.

Booklets (Booklets may be out of print and some publication details are unknown)

Holistic Clearing Meditation; An Anti-paralytic Meditation for Human

Liberation, Kinmount, Ontario, Bodhi Publishing, Revised 1989.

The Meditation on Peace, Edited by Karma Chime Wongmo, Kinmount, Ontario, Bodhi Publishing, 1986.

Event Horizon (magazine), Boise, Idaho, The Open Path Publishing, 1980.

Approaching Death, Edited by Cecilie Jones (Kwiat), Crystal Group UK.

Meditation On Love; talks, Hamburg-Peru 1974.

Scarthwaite Discourses; talks at Penrith, UK 1974.

The Pamukkale Series, Edited by Cecilie Jones (Kwiat) Turkey 1975.

Foundations of the Path; Course at Assisi, Italy 1975; Toronto Namgyal Society Sakya-Namgyal 1980.

Healing the Seven Senses, Edited by Christine Vicary; Banon, France 1985.

Dumo Heat, Edited by Christopher Stevens, Crystal Staff, Ottawa 1980.

Morality & Higher Ethics, Precepts & Practices; Edited by Wesley Knapp Sakya-Namgyal 1990.

The Dome of Heaven: Awakening; Edited by Cecilie Jones (Kwiat) 1980; Kinmount Ontario, Bodhi Publishing 2004.

What is Wongkur? With H.H. Sakya Trizen; Edited by Wesley Knapp, Sakya-Namgyal 1993.

The Brahma Viharas, Edited by Wesley Knapp, Sakya-Namgyal 1974.

Dharma Notes, summer 1976; The Power Of The Group Mind, Star Group Meditation; Toronto Publishing Workshop.

World Peace Meditation, Sakya-Namgyal.
Event Horizon (magazine), Open Path, Boise 1980.

Bibliography II: Partial List of Publications by Namgyal groups & students of Namgyal Rinpoche

Hearn, Tarchin

Meditative First Aid, Wangapeka NZ, 1990

Natural Awakening: The Way Of The Heart, Wangapeka NZ, 1995.

Walking in Wisdom, Wangapeka NZ, 2003

Marcher en Sagesse, (French Translation of *Walking in Wisdom*) Francoise Autin,

Growth & Unfolding: Our Human Birthright, Wangapeka NZ 2004.

Breathing: The Natural Way to Meditate Wangapeka NZ 2005; Wangapeka NZ, 2008

Daily Puja, Wangapeka NZ, 2007

Something Beautiful for the World, a shakuhachi sandana, Wangapeka NZ 2008

Sphere Group

Dhatu Pon Zon: Gathering of the Precious Elements; biography of Sayadaw U Thila Wunta; Sphere Group NZ 1983.

Senge, Sonam

Altruism: Contemplations for the Scientific Age, Open Path, Boise, 1986.

Webber, Lama Mark

Union of Loving-Kindness & Emptiness, self-published, www.markwebber.org, 2006

Why Meditate?; A Heartsong of Vast Release, Bodhi Publishing, Kinmount, 2000

Web Publications, Downloadable Files and Resources

Bodhi Publishing, Kinmount, Ontario. Books and downloads of MP3 audio discourses: http://www.bodhipublishing.org

Sakya Namgyal, Uxbridge, Ontario. CD's, booklets and downloads. http://www.sakyanamgyal.com

Namgyal Rinpoche in the Rio Negra,
Amazon region, Brazil, 1999. Photo by Susan Rejall

Alright, now get on with it!